WINDOWS™

MAGAZINE

ACCESS™

FROM THE GROUND UP

S0-EKZ-931

Other Prima Computer Books

Available Now

Advanced PageMaker 4.0 for Windows
Desktop Publishing Sourcebook: Fonts and Clip Art (IBM-PC)
Desktop Publishing Sourcebook: Fonts and Clip Art (Macintosh)
DESQview: Everything You Need to Know
DOS 5: Everything You Need to Know
Excel 4 for Windows: Everything You Need to Know
Excel 4 for Windows: The Visual Learning Guide
Harvard Graphics for Windows: The Art of Presentation
LotusWorks 3: Everything You Need to Know
Microsoft Works for Windows By Example
NetWare 3.x: A Do-It-Yourself Guide
Novell NetWare Lite: Simplified Network Solutions
PageMaker 4.0 for Windows: Your Complete Guide
PageMaker 4.2 for the Mac: Everything You Need to Know
WINDOWS Magazine Presents: The Power of Windows and DOS Together
Quattro Pro 4: Everything You Need to Know
Smalltalk Programming for Windows (with 3½" disk)
SuperPaint 3: Everything You Need to Know
Windows 3.1: The Visual Learning Guide
Word for Windows 2: The Visual Learning Guide
Word for Windows 2 Desktop Publishing By Example
WordPerfect 5.1 for Windows By Example
WordPerfect 5.1 for Windows Desktop Publishing By Example

Upcoming Books

DOS x: Everything You Need to Know
WINDOWS Magazine Presents: Encyclopedia for Windows
Freelance Graphics for Windows: The Art of Presentation
PageMaker x for Windows: Everything You Need to Know
Quattro Pro for Window: Everything You Need to Know
QuickTime: Making Movies with Your Macintosh
Superbase Revealed

How to Order:

Individual orders and quantity discounts are available from the publisher, Prima Publishing, P.O. Box 1260BK, Rocklin, CA 95677-1260; telephone (916) 786-0426; fax (916) 786-0488. If you are seeking a discount, include information on your letterhead concerning the intended use of the books and the number of books you wish to purchase.

WINDOWS™

MAGAZINE

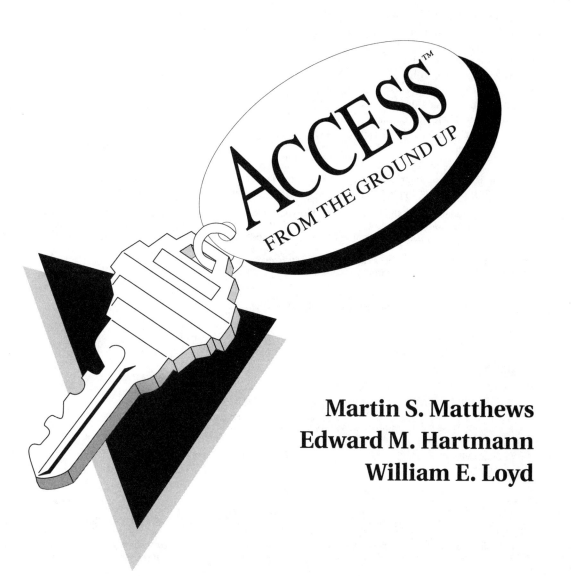

ACCESS™

FROM THE GROUND UP

Martin S. Matthews
Edward M. Hartmann
William E. Loyd

Prima Publishing
P.O. Box 1260BK
Rocklin, CA 95677-1260
(916) 786-0426

Prima Computer Books is an imprint of Prima Publishing, Rocklin, California 95677

Managing Editor: Roger Stewart
Project Editor: Stefan Grünwedel
Production Editor: Laurie Stewart
Copyeditor: Harriet O'Neal
Technical Reviewer: John Cronan
Production: Sybil Ihrig, VersaTech Associates
Proofreader: Fran Lesser
Indexer: VersaTech Associates
Book Designer: Emil Ihrig, VersaTech Associates
Cover Designer: Kirschner-Caroff Design

Microsoft Access is a trademark of Microsoft Corporation. If you have problems installing or running the software, notify the software manufacturer. Prima Publishing cannot provide software support.

Windows is a trademark of Microsoft Corporation and is used by CMP Publications, Inc., under license from the owner. *WINDOWS Magazine* is an independent publication not affiliated with Microsoft Corporation. Microsoft Corporation is not responsible in any way for the editorial policy or other contents of this publication.

Prima Publishing and the authors have attempted throughout this book to distinguish proprietary trademarks from descriptive terms by following the capitalization style used by the manufacturer.

Library of Congress Cataloging-in-Publication Data

Matthews, Martin S.
    Access from the ground up / Martin S. Matthews, Edward M. Hartmann, William E. Loyd.
       p.   cm.
    Includes index.
    ISBN 1-55958-303-7 : $19.95
    1. Data base management. 2. Microsoft Access. I. Hartmann, Edward M.
II. Loyd, William E. III. Title.
QA 76.9.D3M3857 1993
005.75'65—dc20   92-45156
                                                                      CIP

Printed in the United States of America

93 94 95 96 RRD 10 9 8 7 6 5 4 3 2

Contents at a Glance

Contents

Acknowledgments

Behind most books there are many people without whom the book could not be completed or, at the very least, it would be sorely lacking in content, style, and quality. This book is no exception and has depended on a number of people. Among these are the following:

- ◆ Emil and Sybil Ihrig of VersaTech Associates in Escondido, California, are responsible for the excellent design and painstaking layout of every page in the book. This task demands not only considerable skill but also an unbelievable attention to detail.

- ◆ Stefan Grünwedel, Project Editor, and Harriet O'Neal, Copyeditor, had the very substantial task of turning computerese into readable English. While this includes punctuation and consistent word usage, it also—and more importantly—includes meaning and clarity. They did this with expertise and finesse that still allowed the authors to be the authors.

- ◆ John Cronan, Technical Reviewer, made sure the book was technically accurate and that all the instructions worked as advertised. He did this in very little time and with much attention to detail.

- ◆ Stephanie Seymour and Patricia Shepard deserve credit for providing much needed help on Chapters 4 and 6, respectively. Stephanie did her work in some very difficult circumstances and Patricia jumped in at a moment's notice and did her work in very little time.

All of these people have not only provided their skill and labor to this book, but they have also added some of themselves, and it is a much better book as a result.

Introduction

There is so much hype surrounding new computer products that it is hard to know when a new product is truly great. Microsoft Access is such a product. For the first time, a person, without programming, can easily and completely utilize a very powerful and fully relational database management system. Even more important is that this use is interactive with the Microsoft Windows graphical environment providing the means to communicate with Access. There are other powerful database programs, but you literally have to be a programmer to use them fully. There are also some other Windows database programs that are not difficult to use, but they lack the full relational power of Access. Only Access combines both the substantial relational database management capability with an interactive, graphical ease of use.

The purpose of *Access from the Ground Up* is to give you a quick means to fully utilize all that is Access—to create or import databases; to build reports, forms, and queries; and even to use macros to automate the use of the product. The book goes a major step further in that it not only shows you how to use Access, but it also explains how to build databases that effectively utilize the relational capability inherent in Access. With so much power so readily available, one can build cumbersome, inefficient database structures as easily as not. A major focus throughout the book, then, has been to demonstrate and explain effective relational database design and how to implement that in Access.

Who Should Read This Book

If you have recently purchased or are thinking of purchasing Microsoft Access, then *Access from the Ground Up* is for you. This book takes you from the shrink-wrapped Access package to a completed, sophisticated database with all the accoutrements and without any programming or anything like it. If you want to build a database of any substance, with multiple tables, forms, reports, and queries, and you want to do it fast and easily, then Access and this book are your ticket.

Access from the Ground Up does not assume that you have any knowledge of Windows, Access, or other database applications. At the same time, it is fast-paced and compartmentalized enough so that if you have Windows and database experience, you can easily get the Access knowledge without being overly burdened with things you already know.

How This Book Is Organized

Access from the Ground Up resembles the way a building is built—it starts by constructing a firm foundation, adds a strong skeletal structure, and finishes with the elements necessary to use the building fully. In this book, the foundation is laid in database design and in the Windows and Access environments. The skeletal structure is made up of how to build and use databases, tables, reports, and forms. The finishing elements necessary to use Access fully are queries, macros, and the ability to transfer information with other applications. Each of these sections—the foundation, the skeletal structure, and the finishing elements—contains three chapters.

The Foundation

In Chapter 1 you are introduced to a systematic method for designing databases. It provides step-by-step guidelines for their creation with many pointers to help you avoid the common errors.

Chapter 2 introduces you to Windows and walks you quickly through the common features and functions of Windows that are used by Access.

Chapter 3 looks at the Access environment and how to use it. The Access database window is reviewed and the menus are discussed, along with some of the associated dialog boxes. The six primary database objects (tables, reports, forms, queries, macros, and modules) are described, including their purpose, how Access treats them, and where in the book you can learn more about them. Finally, the extensive Access Help system is explored, including how to use it.

The Skeletal Structure

In Chapter 4 you are led through the creation of an Access database that you are encouraged to build on you own computer as you read the chapter. Included in this database are three tables: one for customers, one for suppliers, and one for the product sold (books in this case). In subsequent chapters, you will refine these tables and add reports, forms, queries, and macros and even some additional small tables. This database is discussed throughout the book.

In Chapter 5 you will see how to create, modify, and print both normal reports and mailing labels using the tables you built in Chapter 4.

Chapter 6 shows you how to create and modify forms based on the same tables and then how to add check boxes, command buttons, and drop-down list boxes that in some instances tie in a second table.

The Finishing Elements

Chapter 7 demonstrates how to build and use both select and action queries with single and multiple tables. Included are selecting and linking tables, identifying the fields to use, establishing the selection criteria, sorting, using calculated fields, grouping, and building a crosstab query.

Chapter 8 provides the techniques for transferring data to and from Access. Data to and from other databases, spreadsheets, and word-processing programs is covered.

In Chapter 9 you see how to automate your database with macros. Included are macros to show related items on another form, macros to find a record in a table, macros that create a custom set of menus, and macros that control your database.

Conventions Used in This Book

To make this book easier for you to use, several conventions have been consistently applied. These are as follows:

- ◆ Words in italics are being defined, need special emphasis, or are words used as themselves.

- ◆ Words or characters in boldface are to be typed by you on your keyboard.

- ◆ DOS commands that you are to enter are shown in all uppercase letters but you can type them in either lower- or uppercase.

- ◆ Individual keys on the keyboard are shown as miniature keycaps. For example, Enter or A.

- ◆ Keys that are to be used together are identified like this: Alt-F6. This means to press and hold Alt while pressing the F6 function key.

- ◆ Messages and other direct quotes from the screen are in a display font that looks like this:

  ```
  Save changes to table "Table1"?
  ```

Databases and Their Design

No matter what database management program you use, certain principles remain the same. In this chapter, you will explore the more important aspects of databases, and create a foundation of knowledge that you can use in the rest of the book. Database management programs are the most complex programs commonly used. Most people know enough about writing to produce acceptable letters with a word processor and know enough math to create a usable budget with a spreadsheet program. But many people commit some basic design errors when they set up a database. The errors are not always obvious, and often do not show up until the database has been in place for some time. In this chapter you will read about a systematic method for designing databases. It provides step-by-step guidelines that will help you avoid many common errors.

Database design is not a linear process; it is iterative. You create a database design, then go back and refine it based on what you have learned about the database. The second time through you learn more, so you go back and refine it again. As you learn more about the subtleties of the data, you refine the database more. It is important not to rush this. If you lock yourself into a design too early, you will have to live with the mistakes for a long time.

Everything in your database system will be built around the database structure. The programs, reports, data entry screens, and special calculations all depend on the database structure. If you have to drastically change the database structure late in the development process, you will have to redo a lot of work.

What Is a Database?

A *database* is a collection of data. This covers everything from a phone list to the Library of Congress. While this definition is accurate as far as it goes, it is too limited to help you build a useful computerized database or understand fully what the capabilities of a database are. For that purpose, define a database as a collection of data organized in a way that lets you extract any desired combination of related facts. The key word is *organized*. If you throw a bunch of names and addresses into a box, you have a collection of data, but it is not very useful. When you design a database, you must consider the eventual use of the data, so you must organize the database to provide for that use. For example, if you want to find people by their last names, you must place the last names in a field separate from the first names. You can then search on just that field.

The most fundamental level of database organization is called database *architecture*. Database architecture refers to how the database is structured. Historically, computerized databases have evolved through several major architectures: flat-file, hierarchical, network, and relational. The term *network* in this context refers to a particular database structure that was once commonly used in mainframe databases, and has nothing to do with local area networks. To avoid confusion, modern networkable databases are referred to as *multiuser* databases. Hierarchical and network databases are difficult to create and maintain, and provide job security for a lot of mainframe database specialists. They persist mainly because the cost of converting them is so high. Fortunately, you do not have to work with these database architectures.

A new type of database architecture, *object-oriented*, is starting to emerge. Object-oriented databases might be important in the future, but you can ignore them for now.

On desktop computers, the two major database architectures at present are *flat-file* and *relational*. A flat-file database lets you work with only one group of data at a time. A relational database lets you work with several related groups at once. A flat-file database lacks the flexibility you need to manage your data well. It is simpler to work with at first, but you have to exit from one group before viewing the data in a related group. You can produce reports on only one group at a time, which is extremely limiting. The database functions in spreadsheets, word processors, and "works" programs use flat-file databases. Some flat-file databases are "pseudo-relational," meaning they can do limited cross-referencing between groups. To develop powerful, flexible databases, you need to use a relational database. Access is a relational database, and the rest of this book will pertain only to relational databases.

Examining Relational Databases

A relational database is a collection of data that is organized into related *tables*. Each table is a uniform group of something of interest. It can be a group of customers, products, or transactions. Each table consists of a set of rows and columns that represent facts about the data stored in the table. Each *column* in a table contains the same kind of data for every entry in the table (for example, a last name). Each *row* contains a complete set of data for one entry in the table.

Database terminology is a little fuzzy since publishers have introduced their own terms. In this book you will see the following terms used:

- A *database* or *file* is a collection of related tables.
- A *table* is a collection of data about a single topic, such as a group of customers.

◆ A *row* or *record* is a complete set of data representing one entry in the table, such as a customer.

◆ A *column*, *field*, or *data element* is the smallest piece of data in a row. It contains the same type of data in every row, such as a customer's last name.

Simple Relational Example

Figure 1-1 shows a Customers table that contains data about the customers of a bookstore. Each row contains a complete set of data for one customer, and each column contains the same kind of data for all the rows of the table.

If all databases consisted of just a single table as simple as the Customers table, you would not need this book. But most databases are more complex than just a single table. Figure 1-2 shows all the tables a bookstore might have in its database. Each table in a multitable database represents one group of similar objects. Each row in a table contains a complete set of data for one object in the group. For example, each row in the Customers table is complete in that it contains the basic information you want to record about each customer. Data about each customer's orders, requests, or special interests belongs in other tables. Later you will see guidelines to help you determine where to place any given piece of data.

Figure 1-1

In this Customers table each row contains data about one customer.

CusID	Last Name	First Name	Company	Address1	Address2	City	ST	ZIP
1	Cummings	Richard	Horizon Manufactu	11415 W. 15th S.		Seattle	WA	98151
2	Potter	Sarah		1582 S Beacon		Edmonds	WA	98040
3	DeMuth	Donald	DeMuth Fabrics	4516 E. Pine		Seattle	WA	98113
4	Vanderbilt	Jeanette	Pacific NW Trading	Pacific Trade Cent(	4115 Western Ave	Seattle	WA	98151
5	Farquhar	Eric	Fashions Supreme	C/O Fashion Mart	2237 Fourth Ave. S	Seattle	WA	98112
6	Fakkema	Edwin	Evans and Fakkma	3497 Westend Ave		Lake City	WA	98206
7	Rondell	Mary		5517 Lighthouse D		Clinton	WA	98236
8	Eskenazi	Ralph		1956 Dalphin Lane		Langley	WA	98260
9	Stevens	Thomas	Blanchard Mem. H(	416 Ninth Avene		Bellevue	WA	98004
10	Anderson	John		53 Summitt Drive		Redmond	WA	98060
11	Dailey	Stephan	Minning Machinery	415 Dark Mountair		Black Diamond	WA	98627
12	Martinez	Susan		5654 Wispering Pir		Bow	WA	98435
13	Sato	Yas	Empire Graphics	32 Sentinal Avenue		Renton	WA	98334
14	Barton	Barbara	Western Antiques	735 Elliot Avenue		Seattle,	WA	98151
15	Gallagher	Linda		92 Vancouver Driv(		Bellingham	WA	98532
17	Devereaux	Shelly	NW Stone and Cor	6758 Hwy 553 E.		Kent	WA	98456

Figure 1-2

The bookstore's database is made up of several related tables that work together.

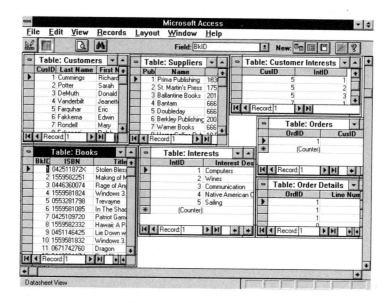

Defining Relationships

There are relationships within a table, and there are relationships between tables. Each table in a database is related to at least one other table in the same database in one of three ways as defined here:

♦ **One-to-one (1:1).**   For example, one person has only one social security number (ignoring fraud and errors).

♦ **One-to-many (1:M).**   For example, one order contains one or more books ordered.

♦ **Many-to-many (M:M).**   For example, one book can cover several topics, and each topic can be covered in several different books.

In these definitions *many* can be zero, one, or more than one.

There are three fundamental guidelines involving relationships (the reasons for these guidelines are explained in detail later in this chapter):

♦ Two tables with a direct link to each other should be related with a 1:M relationship. This 1:M relationship between the tables lets you store multiple entries in one table and relate them to a single entry in another table. For example, multiple rows in an orders table would hold the orders for one customer in a customer table. Figure 1-3 shows a 1:M relationship between a Customers table and an Orders table based on the customer ID number.

◆ Columns within a table should be related with a 1:1 relationship. Every row in a table is uniquely identified by a value known as the *primary key*. In a given row, the primary key value points to a single value for each of the other columns. This guarantees that when you look up a customer by a unique customer ID number, you will find one first name, one last name, and one address (see Figure 1-1). If you found more than one address, you would not know which one to use. You will see the importance of this guideline in the section on primary keys.

◆ M:M relationships must be handled in a special way. An example is relating customers and their interests in books. Most customers will have several interests, and most interests will be shared by several customers. You cannot directly link two tables in a M:M relationship. Instead you must make an intermediate table that acts as a bridge between the two other tables. You will see an example of this later.

Figure 1-3

The Customers table and the Orders table have a one-to-many (1:M) relationship based on the customer ID number.

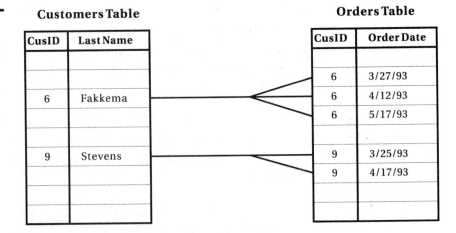

The process of refining a database structure, going from total chaos at one extreme to perfect organization at the other, is called *normalization*. If you follow the guidelines presented in this chapter, you will create a database with a high degree of normalization, and avoid most common database problems.

Designing a Database

The process of designing a database can be broken into several steps. Most of the remainder of this chapter explains these steps in detail. Here is a summary of them:

1. Brainstorm the data elements to include in the database.

2. Decide what groups (tables) to make from the data elements.

3. Assign a primary key for each table. The primary key contains a unique value in each row in the table.

4. If two tables have the same primary key, combine them into a single table.

5. If one or more data elements in a table can have multiple values for a single value of the primary key, move those data elements to a new table.

6. If two tables have a many-to-many (M:M) relationship, introduce a third table to act as a cross-reference between them.

7. If a table has no links to any other table in the database, either create a link or remove the table from the database.

8. Place a new data element in the table in which it has a one-to-one (1:1) relationship with the primary key. If necessary, create a new table.

Brainstorming the Database Design

When you first set out to build a database, the purpose of your database is probably a vague idea, such as "I want to keep track of all my customers." To start designing your database, list all the data elements you want to track. Do not worry about organizing these elements yet. If you see obvious clusters of elements, go ahead and group them together, but it is not critical at this stage. An outlining program may be useful. Some of the items you list will become columns, some will become tables, and some will become relationships. As you refine the design, you will work out the details. For now you are just brainstorming. You want to list all the data elements to include in the database, without regard to just where they fit. Listing the data elements is a separate step from organizing them. The list you develop now will likely be revised later, even if the list completely satisfies today's data requirements. Once you find out how useful your database is, you will want to use it for more functions than originally intended. If you design the database according to the guidelines presented here, you will be able to add to it without tearing apart the structure you already have. If you lock yourself into a design that fits only the current data needs, you will find it difficult to add to the database later.

Getting Input from Others

If you are designing a database for someone else, you might not be aware of all the data you need. In that case, use the following resources:

♦ Talk to the people who will use the database. Keep them involved throughout the design process. They are your best source of information, and if you have involved them, they will feel more committed to supporting the database.

♦ Look at existing reports, data collection forms, worksheets, computer files, and anything else in the current system. You want to see what data is used now, and how it is used.

Caution

Use these resources to find out what data you should track, but not how you should organize it.

One good reason to ignore an existing database design is that the person who designed the previous database did not necessarily know the proper way to organize a relational database.

As you consider what data elements to include, keep in mind the following questions:

- ◆ How will you want to sort the data appearing in reports?
- ◆ What calculations will you need to perform?
- ◆ What data will you need in order to find specific entries?

The answers to these questions will help you discover needed data elements that might not be obvious.

Grouping Data Elements

After you have a list of data elements, cluster them into related groups. Each group will become a table in the finished database. Do not be overly concerned about creating the one right structure at this point. Some of the groups will be obvious. For example, name, address, and phone number all fit into the Customers group (although you might call the group Clients or Contacts). Some data elements might not fit neatly into a particular group. Just keep track of them in a miscellaneous group for now. Later you will learn about a test to help you decide where to place these stray data elements.

Be sure that each data element is the smallest piece of data that's useful to you. For example, use First Name and Last Name rather than Name. In general, it is easier to combine two small data elements for reporting purposes than to split one large data element.

This is a good time to start a *data dictionary*. For each data element you have listed, record the following information:

- ◆ A short name for the data element
- ◆ A brief description
- ◆ The data type (for example, text, date, number, currency)
- ◆ The range of acceptable values (for example, you might want all credit limits to be in the range $1000 to $5000)

- ◆ The maximum number of characters (for text)

- ◆ The default value for new entries (for example, you might want to automatically assign new customers a credit limit of $2500, with the option to change this manually)

- ◆ Whether a value is required in every row (for example, you might require that each customer's entry must contain a last name)

If you do not have all the information right now, record what you can and fill in the missing pieces as you go along.

As you refine the database design, you will probably discover the need for tables that are not evident now. You will see examples of this shortly.

Adding Keys

Refine the database structure one table at a time. Each table contains two classes of data: the data you are interested in, and data the database needs to link this table to others. This latter class of data is known as a table's *keys*. Sometimes these two classes of data overlap, but often they do not. There are two major kinds of keys in a relational database: *primary keys* and *foreign keys*. A primary key in one table links to a foreign key in another table. The tables are the skeleton of the database, and the keys are the ligaments holding the skeleton together. When you create the physical database later, each primary key will become an *index*. An index is a tool that speeds up access to the data. You will learn more about indexes in later chapters.

Primary Keys

Every table should have a primary key. The primary key is a set of one or more data elements or columns that together have a unique value for each row in a table. In some tables the primary key consists of a single column. In other tables the primary key consists of several columns working as a unit. The only data that reliably distinguishes one row from another in a table is the primary key. All non-key columns in a table have a 1:1 relationship with the primary key for that table. For example, if you establish Customer ID Number as the primary key of the Customers table, then the 1:1 relationship guarantees that every customer ID number identifies a single name, home address, and credit limit. If you create a new table and try to save it without a primary key, Access will remind you that you need a primary key, and ask your permission to create one automatically.

Every table in the database must have a different primary key. If two tables have the same primary key (for example, Customer ID Number), you should merge those two tables into one. This is because each data element belongs in the table in which it has a 1:1 relationship with the primary key. If two different tables were to have the same primary key, a data element that belonged in one of the tables could just as well belong in the other table. Such ambiguity makes it difficult to manage a database.

Requirements of Primary Keys There are two absolute requirements of a primary key:

- Every row must have a value for the primary key. In database terminology, this means there can be no *null values* (a null value is a missing value). This assures that each row has a value that can link it to data in other tables.

- Each row in a table must have a *unique* value for the primary key—that is, you cannot duplicate primary key values. This guarantees that there are no duplicate rows in a table. When you look up a key value in the table, you want to find a single exact match.

Strong Recommendations for Primary Keys There are several strong recommendations regarding primary keys too. You can ignore these recommendations, but only if you are aware of the potential problems and are willing to work around them. The recommendations are as follows:

- Keep the keys as small as possible. Since keys link tables together, you want to repeat as little data as possible. For example, ID Number uses much less space than a combination of First Name + Last Name + Middle Initial.

◆ Use numeric keys. Integers (whole numbers) work best. Numbers require less storage space than text, and work more efficiently.

◆ Use abstract (meaningless) keys. Numbers assigned sequentially as new rows of data are entered have no meaning beyond indicating the order in which the rows were entered. If a key has some meaning (for example, a customer's initials plus a date code), you will be tempted to change the key if the meaning changes. You will drive yourself crazy if you do this. This leads to the next recommendation.

◆ Once you assign a key, leave it alone. If you alter keys, you risk destroying the links between the tables.

◆ Do not reuse keys. If an account closes, retire that account number. There are lots of new numbers to go around.

◆ Use keys that you assign and control. Better yet, let the computer automatically assign keys, and prohibit people from changing them. If you use numeric keys, simply assign the next highest number. Access has the counter data type that does this automatically. Take advantage of this feature. If you use non-numeric keys, you will have to create a procedure to calculate appropriate primary keys. Figure 1-4 shows a table structure in Access, using the counter data type as the primary key.

Most of the data you put in a database is useless as a primary key. Last names are not unique, nor are combinations of last names plus first names. If you include the street address and phone number, you might find two cousins with the same name living at the same address and sharing the same phone. Even if last name + first name + street address + phone number creates a unique combination, this is far too much information to duplicate in different tables just to link them together. Also, this kind of information is not stable over time. People regularly change their addresses and phone numbers, which would ruin the keys.

Social Security Numbers   Social security numbers seem to be likely candidates for a primary key. The government uses them.

Figure 1-4

Access provides
a counter data
type to make it
easy to include
an abstract
primary key in
a table
structure.

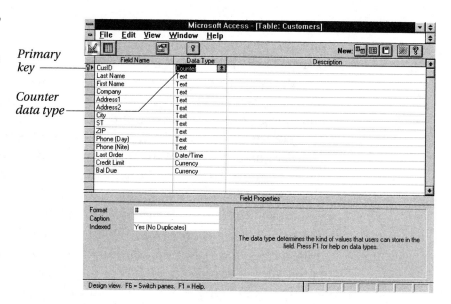

But there are two problems with social security numbers. First,
the data entry person cannot guarantee that any given social
security number is accurate. Mistakes and fraud result in people
using incorrect social security numbers. If you change a social
security number that has been used as a primary key, you will
destroy the link between at least two tables. The second problem
with social security numbers is that they are not always available
when you need them. Recall the requirement that a primary key
must always have a value. What if a new customer has lost his
wallet? If he does not know his social security number, and your
accounting system uses social security numbers as the primary
key, you cannot log that person into your database until he finds
his social security number. If you assign your own customer ID
numbers, you can enter the new customer into your database,
then fill in the missing social security number when he finds his
card.

Abstract Keys   People often object to using abstract primary
keys on the grounds that they cannot possibly remember every-
one's unique number. They argue that if they used initials, they
could figure out a person's key by asking her or his name. But you
do not have to memorize ID numbers. If you build a data entry

form, Access lets you display an alphabetical list of names and pick the proper name from that list. Besides, what if a customer changes her or his name? Either your association trick will fail, or you will need to find every occurrence of the old ID throughout the database and change it to the new one. This is a waste of time and energy. It is possible to build a database in which every person (company, product, etc.) has a unique ID number automatically assigned by the database management program. The users never have to work directly with these numbers. They use the alphabetical listings of the data, and the database management system uses the numeric primary keys to link the tables together.

Using Access to Create Primary Keys   All of the preceding requirements and recommendations regarding primary keys can be satisfied if you create an ID column in each table and make it a counter data type. Access automatically increments the keys in a counter data column, and assures that the keys are unique. The CusID column in Figure 1-1 shows an example of the counter data type.

Foreign Keys

In a properly designed database, a given key is a primary key in only one table. When that key appears in another table, to form the link between the tables, it is called a *foreign* key. The tables are linked together by combinations of the primary key in one table with a foreign key in a related table. A table can have several foreign keys as well as its own primary key. Some tables are made up only of foreign keys and their own primary key. These tables serve as cross-references between other tables.

A foreign key must correspond to the primary key in another table. For example, it makes no sense to have an orders table with a customer number column if no other table has customer number as its primary key. It is a good idea to give the foreign key the same field name as the corresponding primary key. This makes it easier to look at the table structures and figure out which columns are being used to link tables.

A foreign key can have duplicate values. In an orders table, the same customer number can show up several times. This indicates you have had repeat business from the customer.

You do not generate new foreign keys as you do primary keys. Since a foreign key in one table links to a primary key in another table, the only foreign keys allowed are primary keys that already exist in the related table. Access lets you define *validation rules* to enforce this requirement. This is important to protect the integrity of the database. If a table contains rows with foreign keys that do not correspond to any known primary keys, those rows are called *orphans.* You should either remove orphan rows or create a row with a primary key matching the foreign key of the orphan rows.

The relationship between two tables is based on the primary key in one table and the corresponding foreign key in the other table. The table with the primary key is called the *parent* table, and the table with the foreign key is called the *child* table. The relationship is called a *parent-child* relationship. It is a 1:M relationship, based on one primary key and many matching foreign keys.

When you first design the structure for a database, all you need to identify are the tables and the keys. If you properly identify the tables, primary keys, and foreign keys, you will have a framework for placing the data elements you are interested in. Some tables will not be obvious until you start to place the data elements. This is why you need to go through the design several times, refining it each time. You'll see an example of this later in this chapter.

Placing Data Elements

Data elements are the columns in a table. Once you have prepared the skeletal structure of the database, you can start placing the data elements. There is a simple guideline for placing data elements: A data element belongs in the table where it has a 1:1 relationship with the primary key. In some cases, the proper location of a data element is obvious; in other cases, it is not clear at all.

Building a Database

The example used in this book shows the design and development of a database for a small bookstore. Let's say you are the owner and you want to keep track of your customers, the books you sell, the book suppliers (publishers), and other information that might be important to your business. You realize that the database must be designed in a way that will let it grow as your needs expand. What follows is a step-by-step example of how to design such a database.

Listing the Data Elements

For the example, start with the following list of data elements:

```
Customer first name
Customer last name
Customer address
Customer city
Customer state
Customer zip code
Customer day phone number
Customer night phone number
Customer last order date
Customer credit limit
Customer balance due
Customer topics of interest
Book title
Book author
Book price
Book supplier name
```

You can probably think of other data elements for this list, but these are enough to illustrate the steps.

Grouping the Data Elements

What data groups do you have? It looks like there are two groups: Customers and Books. Remember, each group will become a table in the database.

Establishing a Primary Key for Each Group

What can you use as a primary key for each table? Use numbers: customer ID number and book ID number. Now assign the data elements to their respective tables. An asterisk in front of a data element name indicates the primary key.

```
Table: Customers
*  Customer ID number
   Customer first name
   Customer last name
   Customer address
   Customer city
   Customer state
   Customer zip code
   Customer day phone number
   Customer night phone number
   Customer last order date
   Customer credit limit
   Customer balance due
   Customer topics of interest

Table: Books
*  Book ID number
   Book title
   Book author
   Book price
   Book supplier name
```

It is a good idea to place the data element(s) making up the primary key of a table at the beginning of the table structure. This makes it easier to see the primary key when you look at the table structure.

Looking for Problems with the Design

There are some problems with this design. First, there is no connection between the tables. In real life you probably find that any one customer will buy several books, and several copies of any one book will be sold to different customers. Why not just record the customer ID number in the Books table, or the book ID number in the Customers table, or both? Because there is no way to do this without either repeating a lot of information, or violating the requirement that a data element should have a 1:1 relationship with the primary key of the table it is in. If you place a single Book ID Number column in the Customers table, how do you record the fact that a particular customer has bought more than one book? To do this you would have to duplicate the row for the customer data, with all values being the same except for Book ID Number. But then you would violate the requirement that only one row in the Customers table can have a given customer ID number. You run into exactly the same type of problem if you place a single Customer ID Number column in the Books table. So this approach will not work.

How about placing multiple Book ID Number columns in the Customers table? You could label them Book ID Number 1, Book ID Number 2, and so on. (Or you could place multiple Customer ID Number columns in the Books table.) But how many Book ID Number columns should you use? If you have a strict business rule that you drop a customer after she or he orders five books, you could impose a limit of five Book ID Number columns. In real life, there usually is not such a business rule. If you ever need to store data about more books than you have allowed for one customer, you will need to restructure the database.

Maybe you could make a single column called Book ID Numbers, and make it big enough to accommodate lots of books. This is just a variation of using multiple columns for repeating data. At some point you will have to make the column bigger, which means restructuring the database simply to store more book ID numbers.

Tip

If you ever need to restructure a database simply to add more of something that is already stored in the database, there is a flaw in your database design.

Remember that all the reports, data entry screens, and programs get built around the database structure. If you change the structure, you will have to alter at least some of these supporting objects. You might be able to change the table structure in a few minutes, but it could take you hours or days to change the related objects.

Several other problems result from having either a single wide column or several repeating columns to accommodate multiple book ID numbers. One is that you waste space on every customer who has bought fewer than the maximum number of books. With hard disk prices steadily dropping, this is not a major problem, but it is still a consideration. A second problem is that you cannot easily search the Customers table for a specific book. If you have separate book number columns, you have to search through all of them. If you have one multivalued Book ID Numbers column, you have to use inefficient search methods. The most serious problem is that you cannot effectively link the Customers table and the Books table with this structure.

Developing a Solution

It turns out there is a simple solution to all these problems: introduce a new table to cross-reference the Customers and Books tables. Here is the result (this shows only the significant columns):

```
Table: Customers
*  Customer ID number

Table: Customer Books
    Customer ID number
    Book ID number

Table: Books
*  Book ID number
```

The new table, Customer Books, contains only foreign keys that reference the two original tables. This structure lets you store as many combinations of Customer ID Number and Book ID Number as you need. You will never need to change this structure if one customer buys many books, or if many customers buy copies of the same book.

What is the primary key of the Customer Books table? Remember, a primary key must have a unique value for every row in the table. Customer ID Number by itself will not work because a customer can buy more than one book. Likewise, Book ID Number by itself will not work because one book can be bought by more than one customer. But the combination of Customer ID Number and Book ID Number is unique. If you happen to enter the same combination of Customer ID Number and Book ID Number more than once, you have added no new information to the table. You can remove all additional occurrences of the same Customer ID Number, Book ID Number combination, and lose no information.

If you identify the primary key of each table, the database structure (tables and keys) now looks like this:

```
Table: Customers
*  Customer ID number

Table: Customer Books
*  Customer ID number
*  Book ID number

Table: Books
*  Book ID number
```

Can you add more columns to the Customer Books table? Yes, if you come across some information that belongs there. You will see such an example later in this chapter.

Looking for Additional Problems

Look more closely at the Customers table. You might already have noticed something wrong with the structure.

One problem is with the column identified as Customer Topics of Interest. This column contains the names of topics in which the customer is interested. Placing topics in the Customers table creates a problem similar to the one you had when you considered placing a Book ID Numbers column in the Customers table. How many topics should you allow, and how much room will they need? If you allow room for five topics, what happens when someone comes along who is interested in six topics? You will have to change the database structure to accommodate more topics. You have already read about the problems changing the structure can cause.

Once again, the solution is to create another table. The new table should contain the key column(s) from the original table, and a single-valued version of the column (or group of columns) causing the problem in the original table. In this case the result looks like this:

```
Table: Customers
*  Customer ID number
   Customer first name
   Customer last name
   Customer address
   Customer city
   Customer state
   Customer zip code
   Customer day phone number
   Customer night phone number
   Customer last order date
   Customer credit limit
   Customer balance due

Table: Customer Interests
*  Customer ID number
*  Topics of interest
```

Note that the key in the Customer Interests table is made up of both columns. Neither column by itself will contain unique values, but the combination is unique. Again, other columns can be added to the Customer Interests table if they belong there.

The Customers table contains another potential problem. Do you want to store the date of just the last order, or do you want a historical record of all the orders placed by a customer? If the date of just the last order is sufficient, the structure is okay as it is. If you want a history of all orders, you need to make a separate table. This is a business decision. There is no right or wrong answer.

Creating Reference Tables

There is yet another problem that is going to catch up with you if you do not take care of it. Look again at the Customer Interests table:

```
Table: Customer Interests
*  Customer ID number
*  Topics of interest
```

How are you going to identify the interests? Look at just three interests: computers, science fiction, and organic gardening.

You could type the name of an interest each time you need it, but that would get tedious, and different people might type variations of the same interest. The problem gets worse as the interests' names get more complex. A more efficient way to handle this is to assign each interest a code, and enter the codes in the Customer Interests table. Here are some sample codes:

```
COM :  Computers
SF  :  Science fiction
OG  :  Organic gardening
```

The best solution is to assign a meaningless number to each interest, like this:

```
1  :  Computers
2  :  Science fiction
3  :  Organic gardening
```

The Customer Interests table now looks like this:

```
Table: Customer Interests
*  Customer ID number
*  Interest ID number
```

Where should you store the reference list that identifies each interest by number? The worst place to store such a list is on a piece of paper stuck in a desk drawer. If you lose the reference list, the interest numbers in the database become useless. Anytime you use reference codes or numbers, you should store their meanings in a table in the database. This might result in some tables with only a few rows of data, but do it anyway. This makes the database self-contained. In this example, create another table to store the interest descriptions and reference numbers:

```
Table: Interests
*  Interest ID number
   Interest description
```

For the same reasons, replace Book Supplier Name with Supplier ID Number in the Books table, and create a new table to reference the suppliers:

```
Table: Suppliers
*  Supplier ID number
   Supplier name
```

This would also be an appropriate place to record supplier addresses and similar information.

Reviewing the Database Design

Here is the current skeletal design of the database, showing tables, primary keys, and foreign keys:

```
Table: Customers
*  Customer ID number
```

```
Table: Customer Books
*  Customer ID number
*  Book ID number
```

```
Table: Books
*  Book ID number
   Supplier ID number
```

```
Table: Customer Interests
*  Customer ID number
*  Interest ID number
```

```
Table: Interests
*  Interest ID number
```

```
Table: Suppliers
*  Supplier ID number
```

Placing New Data Elements

A common difficulty is deciding where to place new data elements in the database structure. Here is a guideline to help you: For each new data element you want to add to the database, decide which table has a primary key that has a 1:1 relationship with the new data element. The data element belongs in that table. This analysis might also cause you to rethink the database design, as the following example shows.

Suppose you decide to keep track of book discounts. Where should they be recorded? Discounts could be determined by any of the following criteria:

- The book being discounted: there might be a sale on a particular book.

- The supplier: a particular supplier might discount all books for a special promotion.

- The customer: good customers might receive special prices on all books.

- The topic of interest: all science fiction books might go on sale.

- A combination of the customer and the supplier: a special customer might receive discounts on all books from a particular supplier.

- A combination of the customer, the book, and the date on which the customer purchased the book.

There are other possible combinations, but these will illustrate the point.

Each of these six possibilities results in a different placement of the discount. To decide where to place the discount, first determine which criterion controls the discount. There is nothing inherent in the data that makes one criterion better than the others. That is strictly a business decision. The bad news is that business decisions can change. If a new owner takes over the bookstore and changes the criterion, the placement of the discount will change. This will require a change to the structure of the database. You will probably also need to change some reports, data entry screens, and programs.

Once you know which criterion to use for the discount, determine which table has a primary key that matches that criterion. That is where to place the discount. Here are the options:

♦   The book being discounted: Books table

♦   The supplier: Suppliers table

♦   The customer: Customers table

♦   The topics of interest: Interests table

♦   A combination of the customer and the supplier: Since no table currently has a primary key made up of Customer ID Number + Supplier ID Number, you would have to create a new table with that key and place the discount in that table. The following table would work:

```
Table: Customer Supplier

*  Customer ID number
*  Supplier ID number
   Discount
```

♦   A combination of the customer, the book, and the date on which the customer purchased the book: This suggests a revision in the database structure. The database already contains a Customer Books table, which cross-references customers and the books they have purchased. This table could be expanded into two tables to keep track of orders. Two tables are required because one order can have more than one book. The tables have the following structures:

```
Table: Order Headers

*  Order ID number
   Customer ID number
   Order date
   Order amount
   Sales tax
   Total amount
```

```
Table: Order Details
* Order ID number
* Order line item number
  Book ID number
  List price
  Discount
  Selling price
  Quantity
```

These new tables would also provide a history of all orders placed by a customer, so you could remove the Last Order Date from the Customers table.

Writing Down the Final Design

Once you are satisfied with the database design, write it down in one place. Here is the "final" design for the example you have been following ("final" because you might make further refinements as you work more with the design):

```
Table: Customers
* Customer ID number
  First name
  Last name
  Address
  City
  State
  Zip code
  Day phone number
  Night phone number
  Credit limit
  Balance due

Table: Books
* Book ID number
  Book title
  Book main author
  Supplier ID number
  Book list price

Table: Customer Interests
* Customer ID number
* Interest ID number
```

```
Table: Interests

*  Interest ID number
   Interest description

Table: Suppliers

*  Supplier ID number
   Supplier name
   Address
   City
   State
   Zip code
   Main phone number
   Main contact person

Table: Order Headers

*  Order ID number
   Customer ID number
   Order Date
   Order amount
   Sales tax
   Total amount

Table: Order Details

*  Order ID number
*  Order line item number
   Book ID number
   List price
   Discount
   Selling price
   Quantity
```

Summary

This chapter has introduced you to the concept of databases and especially relational databases. Most important, the chapter has shown you how to design a relational database with these steps:

1. Brainstorm the data elements to include in the database.

2. Decide what groups (tables) to make from the data elements.

3. Assign a primary key for each table.

4. If two tables have the same primary key, combine them into a single table.

5. If one or more data elements in a table can have multiple values for a single value of the primary key, move those data elements to a new table.

6. If two tables have a many-to-many (M:M) relationship, introduce a third table to act as a cross-reference between them.

7. If a table has no links to any other table in the database, either create a link or remove the table from the database.

8. Place a new data element in the table in which it has a one-to-one (1:1) relationship with the primary key. If necessary, create a new table.

The next chapter will provide an overview of the Windows environment and its use. Since Access runs under Windows, this knowledge is fundamental to using Access.

The Windows Environment

To run Access, you must have Windows running on your computer. Access uses Windows to provide what you see on the screen, to support the use of the mouse, menus, and help system and to perform many peripheral functions such as printing. Windows is vital to the operation of Access. This chapter introduces you to Windows and walks you through the common features and functions of Windows used by Access. If you are already familiar with Windows and the mouse, just skim this chapter to make sure you are familiar with the terminology used in this book.

Windows is the *interface* between you, the user, and Access. Access communicates with you by presenting information on the screen using Windows and a standard Windows layout. You communicate with Access using Windows and standard Windows tools including the mouse, keyboard, and objects on the screen. The two main ingredients of this interface, then, are the Windows screen with its standard features, and the mouse with its standard functions.

After a brief introduction to Windows, the next two sections of this chapter cover the Windows screen and the mouse. This is followed by a discussion of how to get around Windows using the mouse, the keyboard, and various objects on the screen. Using the Windows File Manager, Control Panel, and Print Manager are then described and the chapter ends with a look at how to lay out your Windows screen. Even if you are familiar with Windows, quickly reading this chapter is worthwhile to make sure you are familiar with the Windows terminology used in the rest of the book.

What Is Windows?

Windows is called a *graphical user interface* or GUI. As you just read, Windows presents what you see on the screen and interprets what you type on the keyboard as well as the movements of your mouse. This is the *interface* between you and Access. It is a *graphical* interface because, unlike the pure character orientation of DOS, Windows provides many graphical objects on the screen to assist in the communication between you and the computer. Figure 2-1 shows a typical Access screen with many graphical elements.

Figure 2-1

In this Access screen you can see the many buttons and boxes that make Windows a graphical user interface (GUI).

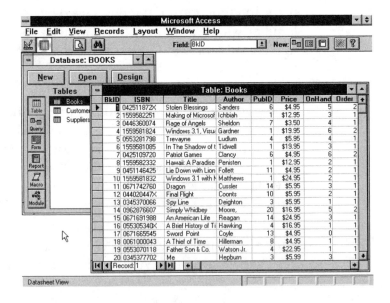

The Windows GUI makes communicating with your computer easier, faster, and more intuitive. You have a visual reference to remind you of a function (for example, the various buttons on the screen) and you have immediate visual feedback of many operations that you perform (for example, dragging a file on the screen to copy it from one directory to another). Of equal importance is the fact that this GUI is standard for all Windows applications such as Access, because all Windows applications use Windows to interface with the user. This means that if you learn how to use the various screen objects, mouse moves, and keyboard shortcuts in Access, you can use the majority of that knowledge with Excel, PageMaker, CorelDRAW!, Word for Windows, or any other Windows application. Your investment in learning how to use Windows is quickly returned.

In addition to its GUI, Windows provides two other important capabilities: loading more than one application at a time and easily transferring information between applications.

The ability to load and use multiple applications is called *multitasking*. The benefit of it is that if you need to repeatedly use more than one application during the same period of time, you can load them all and then easily switch among them. Without multitasking, you must repeatedly load and unload one application before loading the next application, taking a lot of added time. The collecting of sales information from sales people is an example of where multitasking is useful. In that situation, you want to enter new customers into a database application, collect sales data in a spreadsheet application, and type narrative in a word processing application. With Windows you can load all three applications and quickly go from one to the other without having to load and unload each many times.

Transferring information among Windows applications is just as easy and the applications do not have to be loaded at the same time. Windows uses a feature called the Clipboard to temporarily hold the information being transferred. To transfer information, you *copy* it to the Clipboard in the originating application, switch applications, and *paste* the information in the second application. For example, you can copy some information from Access (when you use the Copy command in Windows applications, the copy of the information is automatically placed on the Clipboard), switch to Word for Windows, and paste the information into a Word document (the Paste command in Windows applications automatically places a copy of the information from the Clipboard into the document you are currently using).

Also, Windows provides a number of mini-applications called *accessories* including Write for word processing, Paintbrush for drawing, Terminal for communications over phone lines, and Calculator. These accessories are all available to you at any time when you are using Access (see "Starting and Switching Among Applications" near the end of this chapter). One particularly useful accessory is the Character Map. It provides a list of all the characters in the font you are currently using as shown here:

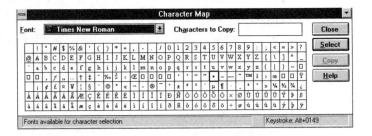

To use a character not on your keyboard, you load the Character Map, select the characters you want, copy them to the Clipboard, and then paste them into your document. You will see each of these steps demonstrated as this chapter progresses. First, though, look at the elements of the Windows screen.

The Windows Screen

The opening Windows screen shown in Figure 2-2 contains many elements that are common to most Windows screens. (Depending on how you installed Windows, the version you are using, and the items displayed, your opening screen may look different.) Figure 2-2 contains two windows, an *application window* entitled Program Manager, and a *document window* entitled Main. A *win-*

Figure 2-2

This opening Windows screen shows the elements that are common to most Windows screens.

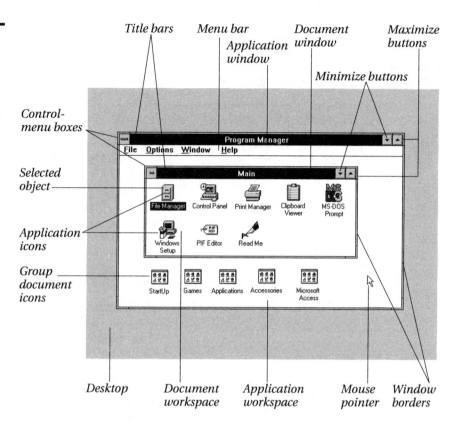

dow is any space enclosed with a *window border*—a double, segmented line around the space. You can tell the difference between an application window and a document window because the document window is always inside an application window and a document window does not have a menu bar. The other common window elements are described in Table 2-1.

The Windows screen is a very dynamic display that uses three features to indicate to you the objects on the screen that are currently active. First, you can tell which window is *active* (where you are currently working) because its title bar usually has a darker color with light letters and the window border is filled in. (Only one application window and one document window can be active at any instant). Second, some object on the screen is highlighted or *selected* (the File Manager icon is selected in

Window Elements	Description
Desktop	The space outside of all windows
Workspace	The space inside a window and not occupied by another object
Title bar	The top bar in each window that identifies the window
Menu bar	The bar immediately below the title bar that contains the names of the menus currently available
Control-menu box	The box on the left end of the title bar that opens the Control menu. This menu allows you to move, size, and close the window plus choose other functions that are unique to the window. You will read more about the Control menu later in this chapter.
Minimize and maximize buttons	The two buttons on the right end of the title bar. These buttons allow you to reduce the window to an icon (minimize) or enlarge it to fill the screen or the window that encloses it.
Icons	Small graphic images that represent a closed window. Application icons start the application when the icon is expanded to a full window. Document icons may start the application that created them or just expand into a window depending on the icon and the relationships that have been set for it.
Mouse pointer	Generally an arrow, but can be other shapes that show you where the mouse is currently pointing on the screen.

Figure 2-2). The selected object is used in many operations. For example, you must select something before you can copy it. The third indicator is the mouse pointer which, as you already know, shows you where the mouse is pointing. All three indicators work together with the more static screen elements to provide an effective form of communication between you and the computer.

The Mouse

The mouse gives you the means to move the mouse pointer on the screen and to identify objects there. As a result, the mouse is a very important tool with which you can communicate back to the computer. Windows allows you to do virtually everything with the keyboard, but the mouse is generally easier and more intuitive. While there will be some discussion of how the keyboard is used, this book assumes that you have a mouse and that you are using it in the instances where that use is appropriate.

When you move the mouse on your work surface, the mouse pointer moves in the same direction and by a proportionate amount on the screen. When you move the mouse so the mouse pointer is on top of an object (*pointing on* the object), you can press a mouse button to activate or *select* the object. If the object is a button, moving the mouse pointer to it and pressing a mouse button (*clicking on* the object) activates the button on the screen and that button's function is performed. For example, clicking on the maximize button maximizes the window. If the object is an icon, clicking on it selects it for some future action.

Mice come with one, two, and three buttons. The standard mouse has two buttons: left and right. The left mouse button is the one normally used and is referred to as *the* mouse button. If you are left handed or have some other reason, you can swap the left and right buttons in the Mouse section of the Windows Control Panel as you can see here:

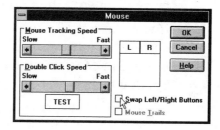

The Mouse control panel is demonstrated under "Using the Control Panel" later in this chapter.

The second mouse button, the one not frequently used, is called the *right* mouse button. If you have swapped buttons or have more or less than two, you will have to keep this in mind as you read. Many three-button mice have left and right buttons that perform the standard left and right button functions and, in addition, have a third button in the middle that performs the same function as holding down the left button; you will see why this is convenient in the next section.

Using the Mouse

If you have not done so already, turn on your computer and start Windows. When Windows has completed loading, use the following instructions to practice using the mouse: (It is assumed that your screen looks something like Figure 2-2, which is approximately how the screen looks immediately after installing Windows. If your screen does not look something like Figure 2-2 you can either try to translate these instructions to your screen or ask someone to restore your screen so it looks like Figure 2-2.)

1. Place your hand on the mouse with your fingers over the buttons and the cord leading away from you.

2. Move the mouse in any direction and watch the mouse pointer move on the screen.

   The mouse pointer will move in the same direction as you move the mouse: if you move the mouse to the right, the pointer will move to the right and if you move the mouse away from you, the pointer will move up on the screen.

   If you run out of room to move the mouse on your work surface, simply pick the mouse up, place it in the middle of the work surface, and continue to move it as you were. Try that next.

3. Move the mouse to the edge of your work surface, then pick it up, place it in the middle of the work surface, and continue to move it in the same direction as you originally were. Notice that the mouse pointer continues on the screen without any indication that you picked the mouse up.

4. Move the mouse until the mouse pointer is over (*pointing on*) a window border, not in one of the corners. Notice that the mouse pointer changes to a small double-headed arrow like the one shown at left.

    When the mouse pointer changes as you just saw, it is telling you that it is prepared for an alternate purpose, in this case to change the size of the window. If you press and hold down the mouse button (the left one) while moving the mouse, you will *drag* the window border in the direction you move the mouse. Try that.

5. Make sure the mouse pointer is still a double-headed arrow on a window border. Then, press and hold the mouse button and move the mouse in either of the two directions indicated by the double-headed arrow, as shown in Figure 2-3.

6. Move the mouse pointer to a corner of a window. The pointer becomes a double-headed arrow again, but now the pointer has a diagonal line instead of a horizontal or vertical line. The pointer is now telling you that you can drag the window on a diagonal and change two sides at once.

Figure 2-3

As you drag a window border, a frame appears that shows you what the new size will be.

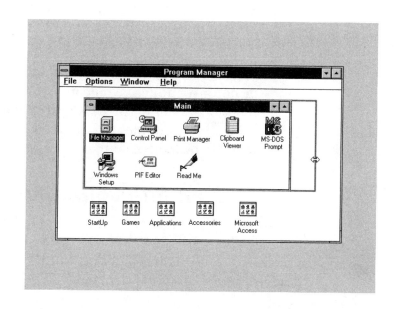

7. While still pointing on a window corner, press and hold the mouse button while moving the mouse. You can see that you are now dragging, and thereby changing the size of two of the window's sides.

8. Move the mouse until the pointer is on (*pointing on*) a program icon that is not highlighted. Press and release the mouse button (*click*) and note that the icon becomes selected.

9. Point on the Games icon. Press and hold the mouse button while moving the mouse to *drag* the Games icon around the Program Manager's workspace. Note that you cannot drag Games outside the Program Manager's window.

10. Drag the Games icon back to its original position.

11. Point on the minimize button (downward-pointing arrow in the upper-right corner) in the Main document window and click (this two-step process of pointing on an object and clicking is called *clicking on* the object). The Main document window will shrink to an icon in the bottom of the Program Manager's window as you can see in Figure 2-4.

12. Click twice in rapid succession (*double-click*) on the Main icon. It will again expand into an open window. You may need to practice a couple of times to get the double-click just right.

    If Windows' double-click rate is not right for you (too fast or not fast enough), you can adjust the rate by opening the Mouse section of the Control Panel (with the Main group open, double-click on the Control Panel icon and then on the Mouse icon).

Mouse Command Summary

As you have just seen, you can do a great deal with the mouse, and you will in this book. To make the terminology as concise as possible, the terms in Table 2-2 will be consistently used to describe the actions opposite them.

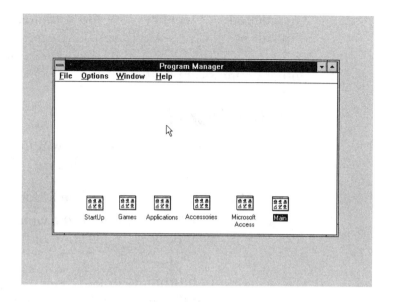

Practice using the mouse until you are comfortable with it. The
mouse is a very important part of the Windows GUI.

Using Windows

In the previous two sections on the Windows screen and the
mouse you were introduced to some of the ways you can use
Windows. Now look at how you can size, position, and determine

Table 2-2

Mouse
Terminology
Used in This
Book

Term	Action
Point on	Move the mouse so that the mouse pointer is on top of an object
Click	Press and release the mouse button
Click on	Point on an object and click
Double-click	Rapidly press and release the mouse button twice
Drag	Point on an object and press and hold the mouse button while moving the mouse
Select	Point on an object and click (same as "click on")

the contents of windows; use the menuing system; use the keyboard; start and switch applications; get help; and leave Windows. You will use all of these functions with Access and other Windows applications.

Sizing Windows

In addition to dragging on a window border, all windows have three buttons that affect window size. These are as follows:

- **Minimize button** Shrinks the window to an icon
- **Maximize button** Expands the window to fill the desktop if the window is an application or fill the workspace if the window is a document
- **Restore button** Returns a maximized window to its former size; the restore button only appears when the window is maximized

You have seen how the minimize button works. Now try the maximize and restore buttons with these steps:

1. Click on the maximize button (the upward pointing arrowhead in the upper right) of the Program Manager's window. The window expands to fill the desktop and the maximize button changes to the double arrowhead of the restore button.

2. Click on the maximize button of the Main group document window. The Main group window expands to fill the Program Manager's workspace as you can see in Figure 2-5. Note that the Main group's restore button and Control-menu box have moved into the Program Manager's menu bar.

3. Click on the Program Manager's restore button in the upper right. The Program Manager's application window returns to its original size, but the Main group document window remains maximized within the Program Manager's workspace.

4. Click on the Main group's restore button on the right of the Program Manager's menu bar. Your screen should return to its original layout resembling Figure 2-2.

5. Drag the lower-right corner of the Main group window, first out toward the lower right of the Program Manager's workspace and then back in toward the upper-right corner until the Main group window looks approximately like that shown in Figure 2-6.

A window can be as large as the desktop (screen) or the work-space that contains it and, in the latest version of Windows, as small as a small section of the title bar or, in earlier versions of Windows, about ½ inch by 1½ inches.

Positioning Windows

Windows, like icons, can be easily dragged around the screen by dragging on the window's title bar. Try that next:

1. Drag the Main group's window by dragging on its title bar until the window is in the lower-right corner of the Program Manager's workspace.

Figure 2-5

When the Main group document window is maximized, its title bar is absorbed by the application window.

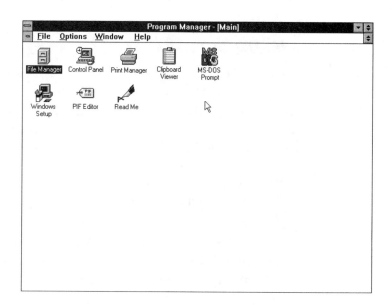

Figure 2-6

By dragging a
corner, you can
enlarge or
reduce a
window to any
size you want
within its
boundaries.

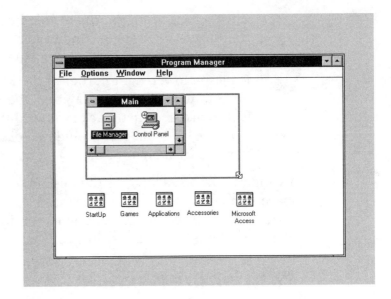

2.   Drag the Program Manager's window to the lower-right
      corner of the desktop. Your screen should look like Figure
      2-7.

3.   Drag both the Program Manager and the Main group win-
      dows back to approximately their original positions as
      shown in Figure 2-6.

Using Scroll Bars

A window can be very small, as you can see in Figures 2-6 and 2-
7. To see all of the window's contents when the window is smaller
than its contents, *scroll bars* are added on the right and bottom
sides of the window. Each scroll bar provides three ways to move
the contents of the window as follows (see Figure 2-8):

◆   **Scroll Arrows** There are four scroll arrows, one at each
    end of each scroll bar. Clicking on a scroll arrow moves
    the window's contents by a set amount such as one line or
    one column.

◆   **Scroll Box** Each scroll bar has a scroll box. The scroll box
    shows the relative position of what is currently shown in

the window to the overall window contents. For example, if the scroll box is at the top of the vertical scroll bar, you can see the top of the window's contents. You can drag the scroll box to move the window's contents. If you drag the scroll box a little bit, you will move the contents a little bit and if you drag the scroll box a lot you will move the contents a lot. The scroll box gives you the most precise control.

◆ **Scroll Bars** You can click on the scroll bar itself in areas other than the scroll arrows or scroll boxes and move the window's contents by a larger preset amount, often the height or width of the window.

The three ways to scroll give you three degrees of control: clicking on the scroll bar moves the contents by a larger fixed amount, dragging the scroll box moves the contents by a very precise variable amount, and clicking on the scroll arrows moves the contents by a smaller fixed amount. See this for yourself with the following steps:

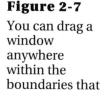

Figure 2-7

You can drag a window anywhere within the boundaries that confine it.

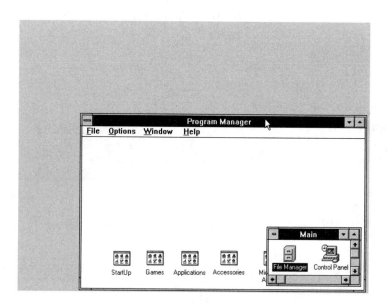

1. Click on the down scroll arrow and notice how the window's contents move up to display the items that were below the original items.

2. Click on the right scroll arrow. Now, the window's contents move to the left so you can see the items that were to the right.

   In general, when you click on a scroll arrow or scroll bar or drag the scroll box, the window's contents move in the opposite direction so you can see new items in the same direction as you click or drag.

3. Click on the horizontal scroll bar between the scroll box and the right scroll arrow. Notice how the window's contents move by a larger amount.

4. Drag the horizontal scroll box, first by a very little bit, then by a lot, and then drag it back and forth. Notice how very precisely you can move the window's contents in small to large amounts.

   Practice using the scroll bars until you are comfortable with their operation. You will use them often.

5. When you are done practicing with the scroll bars, drag the lower-right corner of the Main group window until it completely displays all the icons it contains, as shown in Figure 2-2.

Figure 2-8

Scroll bars provide scroll arrows, scroll boxes, and the scroll bars themselves to move the window's contents.

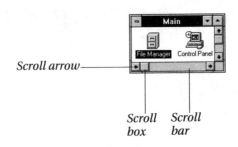

Using Menus and Dialog Boxes

A *menu* is a list of options. Most instructions that you give Windows or Windows applications are initiated by choosing an option from a menu. The menu bar lists the names of the menus that are available to you at any time. By clicking on a menu name (*selecting* a menu) you can open the menu and see the options it has available. For example, by clicking on the File menu name in the Program Manager's menu bar, the File menu will open as shown here:

Once a menu is open, you can click on an option to choose it. You can accomplish the same result by dragging the highlight bar (which is on New in the above illustration) to the option you want and releasing the mouse button. There are also keyboard techniques for using menus which you will see in the next section.

Options on a menu can directly carry out a command, like Open and Delete in the File menu, or they can open a *dialog box* to collect additional information, like New and Move. For example, if you click on New in the File menu, the following dialog box appears asking what type of new object you want:

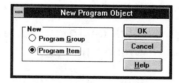

You can tell which menu options directly carry out commands and which open dialog boxes by the ellipsis (three dots) that follows the options that open dialog boxes.

You will sometimes see options that are dim or not as dark as the other options. The dim options are not currently available. For example, in the File menu illustrated on the previous page, the Move and Copy options are not available at the moment because nothing has been selected for moving or copying. Also, some options open other menus. These options have a right-pointing arrowhead on their right.

Look at two of the Program Manager's menus now with these instructions:

1. Click on File in the Program Manager's menu bar. The File menu opens as you saw above.

2. Click on New in the File menu. The New Program Object dialog box opens as you also saw.

3. Click on Cancel to close the dialog box and then click on the Window menu. It opens as shown here:

At the bottom of the Window menu there is a list of document windows that are available. Next to number 5, the Main group window, there is a check mark indicating that it is the currently active document window. Clicking on a different window makes that window the active one.

4. Click again on Window in the menu bar to close the Window menu.

Using menus with the mouse is very intuitive and easy to do. You will find yourself doing a lot of it as you get into Access.

Elements of a Dialog Box

The dialog box that you saw above was very simple—it allowed you to choose between two types of objects (Program Group and Program Item) with a pair of *option buttons*, and it gave you three *command buttons* to accept the selection of the object and close the dialog box: OK, Cancel to close the dialog box without selecting an object, and Help to get help. Besides options buttons and command buttons, there are several other elements used in dialog boxes. Figures 2-9 and 2-10 show some of these.

The common elements used in dialog boxes along with their functions are shown in Table 2-3.

Dialog boxes are the primary means of giving information to Windows and its applications. They are largely intuitive, but you need to be comfortable with them.

Using the Keyboard

In most instances, the keyboard needs to be thought of as an alternative to the mouse, not the other way around. You, of course, need to type text, and there are some keyboard shortcuts that are fast, but usually the mouse is a preferable device for choosing commands. With that established, it is still important for you to learn how to use the keyboard to do more than just type text.

Figure 2-9

Access' Open Database dialog box shows some of the elements used in dialog boxes.

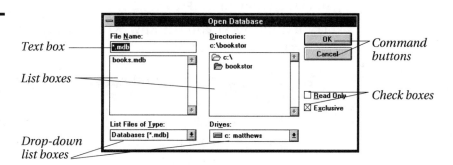

Figure 2-10

Access' Print Setup dialog box shows some other elements used in dialog boxes.

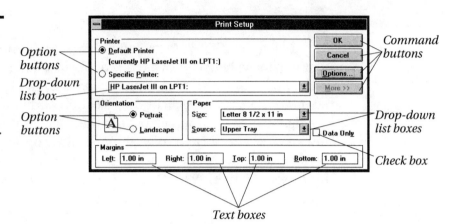

Most Windows commands can be entered from the keyboard. You can open a menu by pressing [Alt] and typing the underlined letter in a menu's name. For example, to open the File menu, you would press [Alt]-[F]. You can also just press [Alt] or [F10] to activate the menu bar, then, without holding down the key, use the [←] or [→] keys to move the highlight to the menu you want to open and press either [Enter] or [↓] to open the menu. To open the Control menu you press [Alt]-[Spacebar] for the active application window or [Alt]-[–] for the active document window.

With a menu open, you can choose an option by typing the underlined letter in the option name or by using the arrow keys to move the highlight to the option name and pressing [Enter]. To cancel a menu selection that you have started, without making a final selection, press [Esc].

Try using the keyboard now with these instructions in the Program Manager window:

1. Press [Alt] to activate the menu bar. Notice that the File menu is highlighted.

2. Press [→] slowly six times. The highlight moves through each of the menus including the two control menus and returns to the File menu.

3. With the highlight on the File menu, press [Enter]. The menu will open.

Table 2-3

Dialog Box
Elements and
Their
Functions

Element	Function
Check box	Allows you to turn features or options on or off.
Command button	Allows you to take an immediate action like completing and closing the dialog box (the OK button) or just closing the dialog box without taking any action (the Cancel button). A command button with an ellipsis (. . .) opens another dialog box and a command button with two greater-than signs (>>) expands the current dialog box.
Drop-down list box	Allows you, by clicking on the arrow, to open a list of items from which you can choose, possibly using a scroll bar to display the items. The currently selected item is displayed in the unopened box.
List box	Allows you to choose from a list of items, possibly using a scroll bar to display all the items. The currently selected item is highlighted.
Option button	Allows you to choose one option from a set of mutually exclusive options. A selection is changed by clicking on another option.
Text box	Allows you to enter text, like a filename, or edit existing text. In a text box, the mouse pointer is an *I-beam* which you can place between characters. When you click in a text box, you place an *insertion point* and anything you type appears to the left of the insertion point. Pressing [Delete] deletes selected characters or characters to the right of the insertion point, and typing replaces any selected characters.

4. Press [↓] eight times. The highlight moves through each of the options and returns to the original option.

5. Press [Enter] to choose the New option. The New Program Object dialog box will open.

6. Press [Esc] to close the dialog box and deactivate the menu bar.

7. Press [Alt]-[F] to open the File menu and type **r** to open the Run dialog box. Finally press [Esc] to close the dialog box and deactivate the menu bar again.

The Control Menu

In the upper-left corner of most windows there is a box with a bar in it called the Control-menu box as you have already read. When you click on this box or press Alt-Spacebar for applications windows or Alt-- for document windows, the Control menu opens as shown here:

The Control menu is used primarily to accomplish tasks with the keyboard that you can also do with the mouse. For example, moving, sizing, maximizing, and minimizing the current window can all be done by dragging or clicking the mouse. You can also do them through the Control menu using the keyboard. Not all control menus have the same set of options, but all the possibilities are described in Table 2-4.

Try using the keyboard and the Control menu with the following instructions:

1. Press Alt-Spacebar to open the Program Manager's Control menu.

2. Press ↓ three times to move the highlight to Minimize and press Enter to choose that option. The Program Manager's window will shrink to an icon.

3. Press Alt-Spacebar again. The Program Manager's Control menu should open unless you have another application running. If that is the case, press Alt-Esc to move from one application to another. Keep pressing Alt-Esc until the Program Manager's icon is selected. Then press Alt-Spacebar to open the Control menu and finally, press Enter to choose Restore. The Program Manager's window will be restored to its previous size.

Table 2-4

Control Menu
Options and
Their
Functions

Option	Function
Close	Closes the active window
Edit	Opens an Edit menu with the following options when running a non-Windows application in 386 Enhanced mode:
	Copy — Copies selected text to the Windows Clipboard
	Mark — Allows you to select text to be copied to the Clipboard
	Paste — Copies the contents of the Clipboard to the current insertion-point location
Scroll	Scrolls the active document window
Maximize	Maximizes the active window to fill the screen or the current application window that contains it
Minimize	Minimizes the active window to an icon
Move	Allows you to move the active window using the arrow keys on the keyboard
Next	Switches to the next open document window or document icon when you are in a document window (in an application window, this is replaced by Switch To)
Paste	Copies the contents of the Clipboard to the current insertion-point location in non-Windows applications in Real or Standard mode
Restore	Restores the active window to the size it was prior to being maximized or minimized
Settings	Allows you to enter settings to control multitasking for non-Windows applications in 386 Enhanced mode
Size	Allows you to size the active window using the arrow keys on the keyboard
Switch To	Switches to the next running application and if that application is an icon, the application window is opened

4.   Press [Alt]-[–] to open the Control menu for the active document window.

The only difference between a document Control menu and an application Control menu is that the last option on an application Control menu is Switch To, while the last option on a document Control menu is Next.

5. Type **m** to choose Move. The mouse pointer will change to a four-headed arrow telling you it is ready to move a window—you are going to use the keyboard, though.

6. Press the ⬅ three times and notice that a frame has extended from the active document window to the left. Press ⬆ two times and again you will see a frame extend up. The frame is telling you where the window will move when you press Enter as shown in Figure 2-11.

   While you are in the middle of the move, before you have pressed Enter, you can use the opposite arrow keys to return the window to its original position.

7. Press Enter to complete the move, press Alt - − to again open the active document's Control menu, and then type **s** to choose the Size option. Again the mouse pointer turns into a four-headed arrow.

   When you are sizing a window with the keyboard, the first press of an arrow key does not change the size, but rather selects the side that will be moved. So if you press the ➡,

Figure 2-11

When you move a window, a frame extends out from the original window to show you where the window will go.

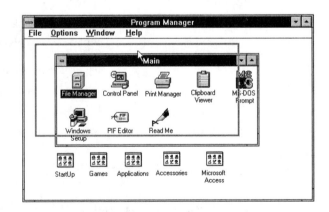

the right side will be selected. Then if you press the ⏵ again, the right side will be moved out and if you press the ⏴, the right side will be moved back. If you next press either the ⏶ or ⏷, the upper-left corner or lower-right corner will be selected, allowing you to size two sides.

8.   Press the ⏵ to select the right side and then press the ⏵ two more times to move that side out. Next, press the ⏶ and the upper-right corner will be selected. Press the ⏷ twice and the top side will move in. Press Esc to return the sides to their original position and quit sizing.

9.   Press Ctrl-F6 or Ctrl-Tab to move from one document window or icon to the next. Keep doing this until you have returned to the Main group document window or icon.

10. Use the Size option to size the Main group window so that you can see all of the application icons in the Main group. Your screen should look similar to Figure 2-11 but you might have different icons.

Shortcut Keys

On the right side of many Windows menus there are keystrokes opposite menu options. These keystrokes are *shortcut keys*; when you press them, the menu option they are opposite is executed. For example, pressing F7 is the same as choosing Move from the Program Manager's File menu. Not only do the Program Manager's menus have shortcut keys, most Windows applications have consistent shortcut keys. Some of the shortcut keys that are available in Access are shown in Table 2-5.

You will learn more about these shortcut keys and their functions in later chapters.

Windows Main Group Applications

The Windows Main group contains several utility applications that come with Windows. There are three applications that are useful when using Access. These are the File Manager, the

Table 2-5

Shortcut Keys
Available in
Access and
Their
Functions

Shortcut Key	Function
Ctrl-Z	Undoes the most recent operation
Ctrl-X	Cuts the selected item and places it on the Clipboard
Ctrl-C	Copies the selected item and places it on the Clipboard
Ctrl-V	Pastes the Clipboard contents at the insertion point
Delete	Deletes the selected item and does *not* place it on the Clipboard

Control Panel, and the Print Manager. Take a brief look at each of these in the following sections.

Using the File Manager

The File Manager provides the means of handling files on your computer. This includes copying, moving, deleting, searching, and renaming files; creating and deleting directories; and copying, labeling, and formatting disks. Open the File Manager now, look at some of its features and then create a new directory to hold the database you will build in the rest of the book.

1.   Double-click on the File Manager icon. The File Manager application window will open as shown in Figure 2-12. Your window will look different, reflecting the contents of your hard disk, your version of Windows, the File Manager settings that are set on your computer, and whether you have maximized your windows.

The standard File Manager window has a directory tree on the left and a list of files on the right. If your window does not look like that, you can change this with the View menu. The directory tree shows at least the directories off your root directory, and, depending on the settings in the Tree menu, it may show the subdirectories off of each directory. Each directory or subdirectory is represented by a file folder. If a file folder has a plus sign (+) in it, there are subdirectories under it. If a file folder has a minus sign,

Figure 2-12

The Windows
File Manager
lets you look at
and manipulate
files on your
disks.

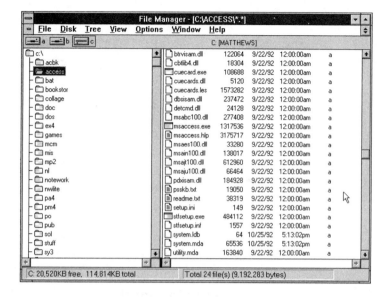

the subdirectories are displayed. One directory will be highlighted and the contents of that directory are shown on the right. You
can display the files of another directory by clicking on that
directory or using the arrow keys to move the highlight to the
new directory.

In the list of files on the right, data files are represented by a single sheet of paper with the upper-right corner folded over, while
program files (those with an .EXE, .COM, .BAT, or .PIF extension)
are represented by miniature windows. If you want to move a file
from one directory to another, you can drag it, using the mouse,
from its current directory on the right to a new directory on the
left. You can copy files between directories by holding down Ctrl
while using the same procedure as moving. If you want to copy,
move, delete, or rename a group of files at the same time, you
select the first file, press Shift and select the last file if they are in a
contiguous range, or hold down Ctrl while clicking on them if
they are not contiguous. You can then drag the highlighted group
or use the menus (see below) on the group the same as you can a
single file.

2. Click on the File menu and it will open as shown next:

The File menu provides the commands for manipulating files as you can see. In addition, one command allows you to create a new directory. Do that now and create a directory to store your database files. Since the sample database used in this book is for a bookstore, call the directory BOOKSTOR (you can only use eight characters).

3. Click on Create Directory in the File menu. A dialog box opens asking you the name of the new directory.

4. Type **c:\bookstor** and press Enter. You will see the new directory appear in the directory tree on the left.

5. Double-click on the File Manager's Control-menu box in the upper-left corner to close the File Manager and return to the Program Manager.

Using the Control Panel

The Control Panel, as its name implies, is where you set the defaults and other parameters that determine how Windows looks and behaves. You can customize Windows as you see fit through the Control Panel. Open your Control Panel now and look at some of the controls.

1. Double-click on the Control Panel icon in the Main group window. The Control Panel will open as shown in the illustration on the following page.

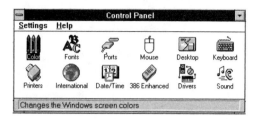

Depending on the version of Windows and the type of computer you are using, the Control Panel allows you to set some or all of the functions shown in Table 2-6.

Table 2-6

Control Panel Functions

Function	Description
Color	Changes the colors on your screen
Desktop	Determines how your desktop looks
Printers	Adds or removes printers
Fonts	Adds or removes fonts
International	Changes the standard date, time, number, and money formats
Date/Time	Changes the date and time
Ports	Sets the parameters for up to four communications ports (COM1 through COM4)
Mouse	Establishes how the mouse behaves (see below)
Keyboard	Determines the rate at which keys repeat and the delay before they do
Network	Establishes your network settings including passwords and the interrupt and port address of adapter cards
386 Enhanced	Sets the parameters for use of virtual memory and multitasking when in 386 Enhanced mode
Drivers	Adds and removes multimedia drivers
Sound	Determines whether or not your system emits a warning sound and the type of sound that you use for various events if you have a sound board

Try out the Control Panel by checking the setting for double-clicking the mouse, using these instructions:

2. Double-click on the Mouse icon. The Mouse dialog box opens as you can see here:

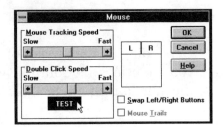

The Mouse dialog box allows you to swap the left and right buttons on your mouse in case you want to use your mouse with your left hand. It also allows you to set the tracking speed or the rate at which your mouse pointer moves on the screen and to turn on or off Mouse Trails—a momentary shadow of the mouse pointer that shows you for a brief time where the mouse has been. Finally, the Mouse dialog box allows you to test and set the rate at which two mouse clicks are considered a double-click.

3. Double-click on TEST in the Mouse dialog box. If TEST changes color, your double-click rate is set correctly to match your natural rate of double-clicking. If it does not change color, click on the slow or fast arrows to adjust the speed to your rate.

4. When the double-click rate is set for you, click on OK to close the Mouse dialog box.

If you find some things about Windows that irritate you, look at the Control Panel and see if there is a control function that allows you to make a change that better meets your needs. Windows should function the way you want.

Print Manager

The Print Manager initially stores your printing on your hard disk and then automatically prints it as your printer is available. It also allows you to connect to a network printer and share your printer on a network. The Print Manager is made available for use (enabled) or disabled using the Printers function in the Control Panel. See if your Print Manager is enabled with these steps (your Control Panel should still be displayed on the screen):

1. Double-click on the Printers icon. The Printers dialog box opens as you see here:

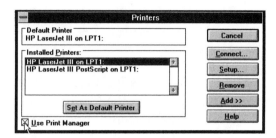

In the lower-left corner of the dialog box is a check box with the label "Use Print Manager." If this box is checked, your Print Manager is turned on.

2. If your Use Print Manager check box is not checked, click on it now. (If Use Print Manager is checked, you will be able to look at the Print Manager dialog box. If you do not want to use the Print Manager (you will see why you might not want to use it in a minute), you can come back and turn the Print Manager off after this exercise.)

3. Click on Close (or Cancel if you did not make a change) and you will be returned to the Control Panel. Then double-click on the Control Panel's Control-menu box to close the Control Panel and return to the Program Manager.

4. Double-click on the Print Manager icon in the Main group to open the Print Manager's window. If you have several printers and several jobs waiting to be printed, your Print Manager window will look like that shown in Figure 2-13.

The Print Manager allows you to change the order in which jobs are printed, to cancel jobs, to pause and resume printing, and to

Figure 2-13

The Print Manager queues your work to be printed and then prints it while you do something else.

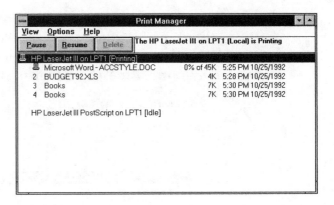

change the assignment of printers on a network. The Print Manager becomes important when you have a number of large printing jobs. With the Print Manager, you print these documents as you normally would, but instead of going to the printer, they are quickly written on disk, and then, while you are doing other work on your computer, the large print job is printed.

Tip

If you are only printing small documents, the Print Manager may actually slow you down because of the extra step of going out to disk.

5. Open the Print Manager's menus to see the options. They allow you to pause and resume printing, to change the order of documents to be printed and to remove documents from the print queue, and to change the window and its features. When you have finished looking at the menus, double-click on the Print Manager's Control-menu box to return to the Program Manager.

6. If you want to disable the Print Manager, double-click on the Control Panel again and then on Printers. Click on Use Print Manager to remove the × and then on Close. Finally double-click on the Control Panel's Control-menu box to close that window.

Starting and Switching Among Applications

To start a Windows application from the Program Manager, all you have to do is double-click on the application's icon. You have seen this demonstrated in several exercises earlier in this chapter. If you have an application running and want to start a second application without stopping the first, you must switch back to the Program Manager and then double-click on the second application's icon. To switch from an application to the Program Manager or to another application you can open the first application's Control menu and choose the Switch To option, or you can press and hold down [Alt] while pressing [Tab] several times to cycle through the applications that are running. Try starting several applications and switching among them using the following instructions:

1. Double-click on the Accessories group icon to open it, if it is not already open.

2. Double-click on the Write icon to start that application.

3. Click on the Control-menu box to open the Control menu and click on Switch To to open the Task List of applications that are running. Currently, based on the instructions here, it should have only Write and the Program Manager.

4. Double-click on the Program Manager to switch to it and then double-click on the Paintbrush icon to start that application.

5. Now, switch back to Write by pressing [Ctrl]-[Esc] to directly open the Task List (it should look like the Task List shown in the next illustration), pressing [↓] twice to highlight Write, and then pressing [Enter].

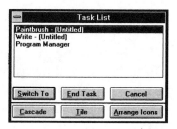

6. Switch back to Paintbrush by pressing [Alt]-[Tab] (pressing [Alt] and [Tab] switches you between the last two active applications).

7. Switch back to the Program Manager by pressing and holding down [Alt] and then pressing [Tab] repeatedly until a box appears that says Program Manager. Then release [Alt].

8. Using any of the above techniques, switch back first to Write and then to Paintbrush and put away each application by double-clicking on its Control-menu box. When both applications are closed, you should end up in the Program Manager automatically (it is the only application left running).

Leaving Windows

You have seen how you can double-click on the Control-menu box to close an application. You can do the same thing to leave Windows—double-click on its Control-menu box. You can also use the File menu and choose Exit Windows to leave Windows. Whichever way you choose, it is very important that you formally leave Windows and do *not* just turn off your computer. Windows and many Windows applications create temporary files and temporarily store information in memory instead of writing it on the disk. When you formally leave Windows or a Windows application, either by double-clicking on the Control-menu box or choosing Exit from the File menu, the temporary files are erased and the temporary information in memory is written out to disk. You can then turn off your computer and not risk losing information.

Before leaving Windows, you should arrange the Program Manager window, and at least the Access window the way you want them for on-going use. It is best to leave open those group windows you will be using often, like Access, and leave as icons those groups you will seldom use. This is a case of personal preference and there is no "right" answer.

One possible approach, if you are only going to be using Access for a while, is to have just the Main group and the Access group open and leave everything else as icons. Such a screen is shown in Figure 2-14.

Figure 2-14

If you are primarily using just Access, you only need to have the Access group and the Main group open.

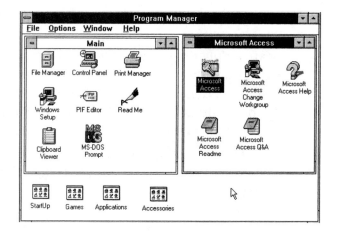

If you are using several applications frequently, another approach is to create a new group (see how below) called Applications, place the applications you are using in that group, and delete the separate groups that are created for the major applications. An example of this arrangement is shown in Figure 2-15.

Decide how you want to lay out your screen and then use the sizing and dragging techniques discussed earlier in this chapter to accomplish that layout. You can create a new group window using the File menu, choosing New, selecting Program Group and clicking on OK in the first dialog box, and then entering the name of the group window (for example, Applications) under

Figure 2-15

If you are using several applications, you can put them in an Applications group window.

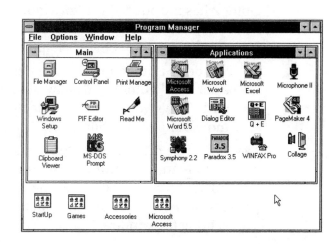

Description in the second dialog box, and again clicking on OK. To move applications from one group window to another, you can simply drag them. If you want to delete a program icon or a group window, select the icon or window and press (Delete). You will get a dialog box asking if you are sure you want to delete the item. If you do, click on Yes and the item is gone. If you delete an icon, the program file the icon represented is *not* deleted, only the icon is deleted.

When you have the windows arranged the way you want them, use the following instructions to leave Windows:

1.   Open the Options menu and make sure that Save Settings on Exit is checked. This saves the layout you just created. If it is not checked, click on Save Settings on Exit.

2.   Double-click on the Program Manager's Control-menu box. The Exit Windows dialog box will appear.

3.   Click on OK to finally leave Windows.

Windows provides a very powerful but easy-to-use environment in which Access can operate. You now know enough about this environment to begin learning about Access—the subject of the next chapter.

Summary

Chapter 2 has introduced you to Windows and looked at the features and functions of Windows that are used by Access. The major points brought out in the chapter are as follows:

◆   Windows is a graphical user interface (GUI) that provides a standard graphical display of information on the screen and allows you to communicate with it using both the mouse and the keyboard.

◆   Using the maximize button in the upper-right corner you can enlarge a window to fill the screen; using the minimize button to the left of the maximize button you can shrink the window down to an icon (a small picture representing the window).

◆ When you click the mouse (press and release the left mouse button) on an object, you will activate that object if it is a button or menu option, or select it for later use if it is something else like a file or some text.

◆ Scroll bars allow you to move the contents of a window in small fixed increments by clicking on the scroll arrows, in variable small to medium amounts by dragging the scroll box, and in large fixed increments by clicking on the scroll bars themselves.

◆ You can use your keyboard to select a menu by pressing [Alt] and the underlined letter in the menu name. You can then choose a menu option by typing the underlined letter in the option name.

◆ The Control menu, opened by clicking on the Control-menu box in the upper-left corner of most windows, allows you to perform tasks with the keyboard that you can also do with the mouse. This includes moving, sizing, maximizing, and minimizing windows.

◆ The Windows File Manager, located in the Main group, provides the means to perform most file- and disk-related operations. This includes copying, moving, deleting, searching, and renaming files; creating, deleting, and renaming directories; and copying, labeling, and formatting disks.

◆ The Control Panel, available in the Main group, allows you to customize how Windows looks and behaves. Among the customization that you can do is: change your screen colors, add or remove printers, change the date and time, and establish how the mouse behaves.

◆ The Print Manager, also in the Main group, provides the means to do printing while you are doing something else on your computer by temporarily storing your printing on disk and then doing the actual printing as computer and printing time are available.

◆ You start an application by double-clicking on the application's icon and you switch among applications by pressing and holding [Alt] while pressing [Tab] until you see the name of the application you want.

◆ You end an application and leave Windows by double-clicking on their Control-menu boxes. Formally leaving applications and Windows in this way is important so that you will not lose data in temporary files that Windows has written.

The next chapter will introduce you to Access itself and give you a tour of its menus, features, and capabilities.

The Access Environment

Access is a relational database management system, as you read in Chapter 1. Its purpose is to organize and provide easy access to the information which it stores. How Access does this, in an overview, is the purpose of this chapter.

The chapter begins by looking at the Access environment and how to enter it. The Access Database window is reviewed and the menus are discussed, along with some of the associated dialog boxes. The extensive help system that is available in Access is explored, including the many ways to use it. Then the six primary objects that are handled by Access are each described, including their purpose, how Access treats them, and where—later in this book—you can learn more about them. These six objects are tables, reports, forms, queries, macros, and modules. Finally, Access's toolbar and toolbox are introduced.

Entering the Access Environment

Access uses the standard Windows environment, so what you learned in Chapter 2 about Windows pertains directly to Access. This includes the display, as you can see in Figure 3-1, the use of menus, dialog boxes, and the mouse.

The Access window looks a lot like most other Windows displays. This is a significant asset because you probably already know the majority of the elements displayed on the screen. As shown in Figure 3-1, only three elements are not standard Windows features. These are the contents of the document window, which is a database table; the toolbar, which contains tools applicable to the currently active window; and the status bar, which displays message and status indicators. Both the toolbar and the status bar are common to other Microsoft Windows applications such as Word for Windows and Excel. The table-document window and the toolbar will be discussed further, later in this chapter.

The easiest way to learn about Access is to start it and look at Access for yourself. Do that now and follow along on your computer as you read here.

Starting Access

To start Access, you must first start Windows and have Access set up or installed on your hard disk. To start Windows, turn on your

Figure 3-1

The Access display has a very similar layout to most Windows displays.

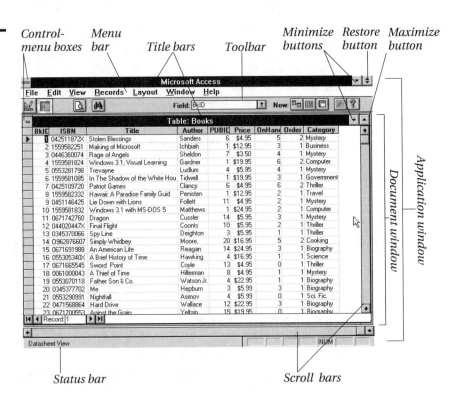

computer and, after you get a DOS prompt such as C:\>, type
win. (Windows might start automatically for you when you turn
on your computer if you or someone else has put Windows in
your AUTOEXEC.BAT file.) If you have not installed Access, first
start Windows and then follow these instructions:

1. Click on the Program Manager's File menu to open it and
   then choose the Run option. The Run dialog box will
   open.

2. Insert the first of your Access disks into one of your floppy
   drives.

3. Type **a:\setup** in the text box and press ⌷Enter⌷ or click on
   OK. If you used a floppy drive other than A, use that drive
   letter in this instruction. For example, if you placed the
   disk in drive B, type **b:\setup**.

   The Access Setup program will start and you will see a
   series of displays asking you questions and giving you
   information on the progress.

4. Answer the questions on the screen and insert the remainder of your Access disks as they are requested. You will be
   told when you have successfully installed Access.

When Windows has been started and Access has been installed,
you will see one of two things that tells you Access is available.
Either the Access group window will be open similar to what you
see here:

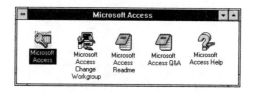

or the Access group window will be reduced to a group icon like this:

To start Access, follow these instructions:

1. If you have the Access group icon on your screen, double-click on it so it opens.

2. Double-click on the Microsoft Access application icon (on the far left in the Access group window illustration above) to start Access.

   As Access starts, you will first see a copyright message and then, if you or someone else has not turned it off during a previous sesson, you will see the Welcome to Microsoft Access window that is shown in Figure 3-2. This introductory window provides several guided tours of Access that are worth your time going through—but at another time; for now, continue on with this guided tour.

3. Click on Close. The welcoming window will disappear and you will be left with a virtually blank screen that is called the *startup window*.

To look at Access you must open a database. Thankfully, Microsoft has provided several sample databases to use for this purpose. Open one of these next using the startup window's File menu.

Figure 3-2

The Welcome to Microsoft Access window provides several ways for you to start using Access.

Using the Startup Window File Menu

To load an existing database or to create a new one, you use the File menu from the startup window. Click on that menu now and it will open as you see here:

Besides opening or creating a database, the startup window File menu allows you to do the following:

◆ **Compact** a database that has become fragmented over your disk, by restoring the database in as contiguous an area as possible. You must have room on your disk for both the original database and for the compacted copy. The name of the compacted copy can be the same as or different from the original.

◆ **Encrypt/Decrypt** a database so it cannot be read by text editors and word processors. The file is still usable through Access and you can separately establish security controls such as passwords, as needed, within Access. The encryption just prevents a file from being read outside of Access. Decryption is the opposite of encryption. You must have room on your disk for both the original database and for the encrypted copy. The name of the encrypted copy can be the same as, or different from, the original.

◆ **Repair** a database that has become corrupted by such things as a power failure or a hardware problem. If you always exit Access normally, the database you are using will not generally become corrupted. Access checks a file when it is opened, compacted, or encrypted to determine if it is corrupted. If it is, you will be asked if you want to repair the file. It is possible that a corrupted file will not be detected. So if you are experiencing some unusual behavior from a database, use the Repair Database option.

◆ **Exit** Access if you are done using it.

Between Repair Database and Exit are two dim menu options, Show Window and Run Macro, that allow you to display a hidden window and to run a macro you have written (see "Macros" later in this chapter). Of course, you must have a hidden window or a macro for these options to work. Also, there are up to four database filenames numbered 1 through 4. These are the last four files you have used. You can quickly return to one of these files by clicking on the one you want.

Loading a Database

To load a database and look around Access, continue on:

1. Click on Open Database in the startup window File menu. The Open Database dialog box appears as shown here:

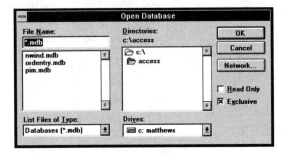

On the left side near the top of the dialog box, there is a text box where you can type the name of the file you want to use. Then you either press [Enter] or click on OK to open the file. Below the text box there is a list box with the list of Access database files in the current directory. These files have the .MDB extension. You can double-click on one of these files to open it. This is the easiest method of opening a file.

Below the list box on the left, there is a drop-down list box that allows you to determine the type of files that are displayed in the list box above it. The default type is database files with the extension of .MDB. You can also look at all files by clicking on the downward-pointing arrow on the right of the box and clicking on All Files in the drop-down list that appears.

In the middle of the Open Database dialog box there is a list box that shows the current directory and at least the directory above it. You can change the current directory by double-clicking on the directory above it and continuing until you are either at the root directory or as high as you need to be to come back down another path. Then double-click on as many directories below the current one as you need to get to the directory you want.

2. Make sure that you are in the Access directory or the directory in which you installed Access if it is not named "Access." Also, make sure that the selected file type is Databases (*.mdb).

3. Double-click on `nwind.mdb` to open this database. The Database window will appear as seen in Figure 3-3.

Using Access Menus

The Access menus, located in the menu bar near the top of the window, change to match the task being performed. With a database open, you have six menus available: File, Edit, View, Security, Window, and Help. Each of these are discussed in the next several sections.

The Database File Menu

When the Database window opens, the contents of the File menu changes to include the options necessary to work with databases. If a table or other object is opened, the contents will change

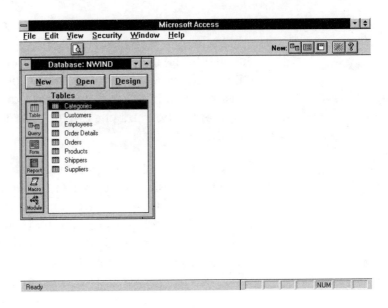

Figure 3-3

Figure 3-3

All work with
databases
begins with the
Database
window.

again. With only a database open, the File menu, whose options
and their uses are described in Table 3-1, looks like this:

The Edit Menu

The Edit menu has many of the normal Windows edit options
such as Cut, Copy, and Paste, plus ones unique to the Database
window as you see on the next page.

The Edit menu options and their uses are described in Table 3-2.

Table 3-1

File Menu
Options and
Their
Functions

Option	Function
New Database	Opens the New Database dialog box where you create and name a new database
Open Database	Opens the Open Database dialog box where you choose the name of an existing database you want to open
Close Database	Closes the Database window
New	Opens a submenu from which you can create a new table, form, report, query, macro, or module
Rename	Lets you give a new name to the selected object in the Database window
Import	Brings in objects from other Access databases and from other applications
Export	Copies tables to other Access databases or to other applications
Attach	Links tables from other applications so they can be read and edited in Access and still be used in the original application
Imp/Exp Setup	Allows you to create a specification to use when importing or exporting fixed-width text files
Print Preview	Shows you how an object will look when it is printed
Print	Prints an object from the database
Print Setup	Allows you to set the parameters for printing (it is available in the menu only when there is something to print)
Run Macro	Lets you select and run a saved macro associated with the open database
Exit	Allows you to close Access when you are finished with it

The View Menu

The View menu, shown below, primarily duplicates the object buttons found on the left side of the Database window:

The View options or the object buttons determine what type of object is currently displayed in the Database window—tables, queries, forms, and so on. Additionally, the Options option allows you to customize the Access environment. This includes changing the key assignments on the keyboard, setting the margins for printing, tailoring the way the window looks, and adjusting the display of the different Access objects.

Table 3-2

Edit Menu Options and Their Functions

Option	Function
Undo	Reverses the last command given to Access unless the Can't Undo command is displayed, which indicates there is no command to undo
Cut	Copies the selected text to the Windows Clipboard and then removes it from its current location
Copy	Places a copy of the selected text onto the Clipboard but does not remove it from its current location
Paste	Copies the contents of the Clipboard to the current pointer location (Paste is only available if you have previously performed a Cut or Copy)
Delete	Removes the selected object from the Database window, or the selected text or field from other windows
Relationships	Permits you to determine the relationship between tables in a database to be a one-to-one or one-to-many relationship

The Security Menu

The Security menu contains options that restrict user access to databases with passwords associated with user names and group designation. The Security menu looks like this:

The Security menu options and their uses are described in Table 3-3.

The Window Menu

The Window menu is standard in Windows, with the top three options, Tile, Cascade, and Arrange Icons controlling the way the window is displayed. The next two options, Hide and Show, are described in Table 3-4. At the bottom of the Window menu there is a numbered list of open windows. To switch from one window to another, you can open the Window menu and click on one of the other windows or type the number of the window you want to become active. The Window menu is shown here:

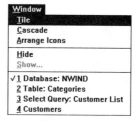

The Help Menu

All the Access help features are available from the Help menu, seen here:

Option	Function
Permissions	Allows you to grant permission to users and groups to have access to each database object you create. When Access is first installed the default is for all users to have full access to all database objects. Permissions are changed in the Permissions dialog box, which is shown below, and can only be changed by the author of the object or a member of the Admin group (people who have been identified as "Admin"):

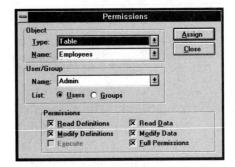

Option	Function
Users	Shows the Users dialog box where user names are added to the system. The names must be added here before they can be added to a group.
Groups	Allows you to add group names using the Groups dialog box. This makes it easier to control the access to databases by different departments of your company.
Change Password	Opens the Change Password dialog box where you change your own password. When a new user is added to the system, Access assigns a blank as the password. Change the password by leaving the Old Password box blank and typing a new one of up to 14 characters in the New Password box.

Option	Function
Hide	Allows you to hide a database object even though it is open. For instance, you can open a table, hide it, then open another.
Show	Shows the hidden windows and is available only after you use the Hide option.

Since Help is such an important feature, the next section is devoted entirely to this subject.

Using Access Help

Access Help is one of the most important features of Access. It provides extensive help that is always available with the mouse or keyboard. You can get help by clicking on the help button in the toolbar, by pressing [F1] on the keyboard, or by clicking on Help in the menu bar or in most dialog boxes.

Help from the Toolbar

The help button on the right end of the toolbar has a question mark as its icon. Clicking on this button produces a help window that is context sensitive; that is, it pertains to what you are doing at the time. You get this same help window when you press [F1] on the keyboard.

Help from the Menu Bar

The Help menu is always available, no matter what task you are performing. It contains three options that provide three ways to get help: Contents, Search, and Cue Cards. Additionally, the About Microsoft Access option tells you the version of Access you are using and gives you some facts about your computer, as well as your Access license.

Help Contents

Help Contents is used to obtain help when you are not sure of exactly what you want. This option allows you to browse through a wide range of subjects.

See how this works by following these steps:

1. Open the Help menu and choose Contents. The Help Table of Contents window appears as shown in Figure 3-4.

2. Click on Databases to see the Databases How To's window.

3. In the How To's window you can click on any underlined item to see detailed help on the selected subject. For instance, click on Creating and Administering a Database and you see an additional window with a list of subjects that are described in detail.

4. Click on Designing a Database and you see a window, shown in Figure 3-5, containing a list of all the items to consider in designing a new database.

5. When you are finished perusing the help windows, click on Back in the toolbar to return to the How To's window, then click on Back again to return to the Help Table of Contents window.

The Help Table of Contents window (see Figure 3-4) includes a section called Reference, where you can find answers to questions on Access database subjects. This section contains the Glossary, from which you can choose any one of almost 450 different terms and get its definition.

As you see in the Help Table of Contents window in Figure 3-4, and in all other help windows, the menu bar contains a File

Figure 3-4

The Help Table of Contents window allows you to choose from a number of subjects.

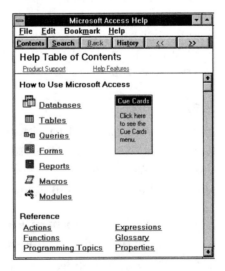

Figure 3-5

Using the help
system you can
get to this
window that
shows you all
the things to
consider when
designing a
database.

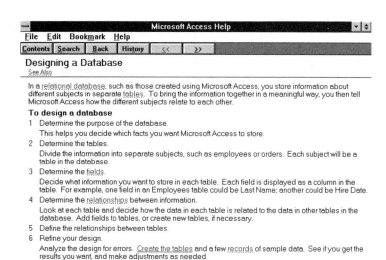

menu. This File menu has a print option that allows you to print
help topics. You see the Help File menu here:

For example, if you click on Glossary in the Help Table of Contents
window and then on Print Topic in the File menu of that window,
you get a printed list of all the terms in the Glossary.

Searching Help

The Search option in the Help menu is used to get help based on
a keyword or phrase. Try the Search option using these steps:

1. Choose Search from the Help menu and the Search dialog
    box appears. Use this box to select the subject on which
    you need help.

2. Type the topic you want help on in the text box with the
    flashing insertion point on its left. To get the same help

Figure 3-6

Figure 3-6

The Search
dialog box
allows you to
enter a subject
on which you
want help.
Access then
searches for
that subject.

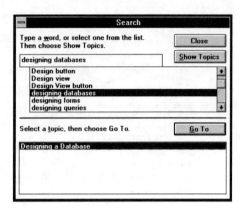

window you got using the Contents command, type **design.**
Notice the topics in the window scroll around as you type
each letter; when the **d** is typed the first of the alphabetical listing for *D* appears.

3.   Click on "designing databases" and then on the Show
     Topics button. The topic is displayed in the Select a topic
     list box as you can see in Figure 3-6.

4.   Click on Go To and the help window for Designing a Data-
     base appears as you saw in Figure 3-5.

5.   When you are finished with the help topic, double-click
     on the Control-menu box to return to the Access window.

Getting Help from Cue Cards

Cue Cards give detailed help in the form of specific steps you use
to create tables, forms, reports, and queries in Access. When you
create these objets for the first time, it is helpful to use the Cue
Cards. The cards remain in the window alongside your work until
they are put away. Call up the Cue Cards now using these steps:

1.   You bring up the Cue Cards in one of two ways depending
     on where you are when you make the choice: either
     choose Contents in the Help menu and click on the Cue
     Cards icon, or choose Cue Cards in the Help menu. Which-
     ever way you choose Cue Cards, their menu window opens
     as shown in Figure 3-7.

2. Click on the > button to the left of Build a Database with Tables and the first Cue Card in this stack will appear. The Cue Card will remain on the screen alongside your work until you call the next one or you put away the stack. From this point on, change the Cue Cards one at a time and they will show you the steps for the function you are performing.

3. When you finish with the Cue Cards, double-click in the Cue Card Control-menu box to put them away and return to the Access window.

Databases and Database Objects

There are two types of objects used in Access, system objects and database objects. *Systems objects* are those that are already defined by Access and are usually used to write Access Basic programs. Programming and system objects are beyond the scope of this book. *Database objects*, on the other hand, are objects you create to use in the Database window and include tables, reports, forms, queries, macros, and modules.

Figure 3-7

Select a task from the Cue Cards menu and get a detailed series of steps for carrying out the task.

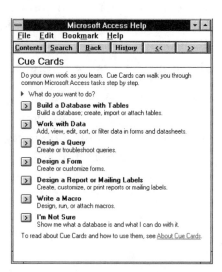

An Access database is a DOS file with the extension .MDB and is where Access puts all the database objects that you create. Besides using a database to receive Access objects, you must also have a database open to receive any imported or attached files from other applications. You can create an empty database by selecting New Database in the File menu and then giving it a name in the New Database dialog box that you see here:

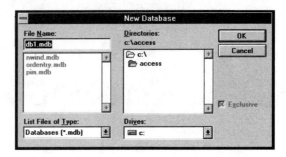

The database name can be up to eight characters long excluding the extension .MDB, which Access automatically adds.

Tables

The information contained in an Access database is stored in *tables* that you create. Each table contains all the data about one particular subject. For instance, a table of employees might contain fields with their names, addresses, home phone, and social security numbers.

The steps necessary to create an Access table are as follows:

1.   With the Database window open and the Table button selected, click on New in that window or choose New in the File menu. An empty table appears in Design view, as you see in Figure 3-8.

      A table is defined by the fields or columns it contains. Each field has a field name, a data type, a description, and a set of field properties.

Figure 3-8

Tables are defined by naming the fields in the table, selecting the data type of each field, entering the field properties, and typing descriptions for the fields.

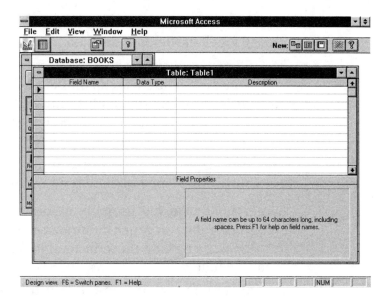

2. Since the insertion point is by default in the text box for the first field name, type a field name of up to 64 characters, which can include blanks. It must not duplicate any other field's name.

3. Press (Enter) or click in the Data Type text box to the right of the Field Name and a drop-down arrow appears. Click on it and you can select the field's data type from the drop-down list box. Data types include text, number, data/time, and currency.

4. Press (Enter) and type the field description of up to 255 characters.

5. Press (F6) or click in the first field properties box in the lower half of the Design view window. Make the necessary changes. Field properties differ with different data types but include field size, format, and default value. Press (Tab) to go to the next field property or click in its text box. Change or enter the field properties as needed.

6. Press (F6) to return to the field name.

7. Press ⬇ to go to the next field and repeat steps 1 through 6 for all the fields in the table.

8. When you have created the necessary fields for the table you are building, click on the datasheet view button, second from the left on the toolbar. Answer Yes, you want to save your table design, and you will be switched to Datasheet view where you can enter data into your table.

9. After completing the work on the table, double-click on the Control-menu box to return to the Database window.

Chapter 4 will take you through the process of creating a table and entering data in much more detail and explain the many alternatives, especially those in the Field Properties section of the Table window.

Creating a table is quite simple, but the design of the tables requires a great deal of thought and planning, as you learned in Chapter 1.

Reports

Reports are printed documents that you create to present data in a logical and readable form with data brought together from one or more tables or queries. Reports can contain percentages, totals, and the grouping of information.

There are two ways to create reports: manually in the design window and more automatically with the Access ReportWizards. Using the design window and starting from scratch can be very laborious and time-consuming; on the other hand, using Access ReportWizards is fast: you only have to answer a few questions. With the ReportWizards you have a choice of three kinds of reports, the fields to include, and the sorting and grouping of data to use. The following steps demonstrate how to use the ReportWizards:

1. With the Database window open, click on the Report button and click on New or choose New in the File menu and then click on Report. The New Report dialog box appears.

2. Click on the drop-down list arrow on the right of the Select a Table/Query box and then choose a table from the drop-down list box. The selected table is the one on which the report will be based. Click on the ReportWizards button and the first ReportWizards dialog box appears as you see here:

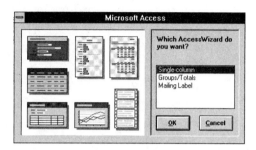

3. Choose one of the three available types of ReportWizards and click on OK or press [Enter]. In the remaining dialog boxes that appear, follow the directions that ReportWizard gives you.

4. In the last ReportWizard dialog box, you can click on the Print Preview button to see the results of your work on the screen. You see that you and the ReportWizard have created a very creditable report.

    ReportWizards reports can be used just as they are created, or changes can be made using the design window. You open the design window by clicking on the Design button in the last ReportWizard dialog box.

5. Double-click on the Control-menu box in the Report window to close it and then on Yes when asked if you want to save.

Chapter 5 provides a detailed explanation of using the ReportWizards to produce both a typical report and mailing labels, as well as using the design window to modify the ReportWizard report.

Forms

Forms are database objects you create to use as a means of entering data into or displaying data from tables. Using an Access form is much like using a printed form, except you use the keyboard to fill in the blanks and the screen to view it.

As with reports, you can create a form from scratch using the design window or Access will create the form with you using the FormWizards. Also like reports, using the design window can be very time-consuming. The FormWizards, though, are an excellent choice because the forms you create with FormWizards can be used just as they are, or can be modified using the design window. The FormWizards give you four choices for the form's format and five different styles in which to present the form. You choose the form that is easiest to use with the data that you have in the table. The steps to use the FormWizards are:

1. With the Database window open and the Table button selected, click on the new-form button (fourth from the right) on the toolbar. The New Form dialog box opens.

2. In the Select a Table/Query box, click on the drop-down arrow to see the list of available tables and select the table on which you want to base the form.

3. Click on the FormWizards button and you get a dialog box where you select the form's format. Select the format you want and click on OK. Chapter 6 discusses the different formats.

4. In the series of dialog boxes that follow, select the fields you want (click on the >> button to use all fields), the look you want, and the title for the form. When you finally click on Open after completing the dialog boxes, your form will appear. Figure 3-9 shows a sample Employees form from the NWIND database.

5. You can use a form to look at or edit existing data and to enter new data. Press Ctrl-Pg Up or Ctrl-Pg Dn or click on the left or right arrows in the lower left of the form to go from record to record. You can also press Ctrl-Home or Ctrl-End or click on the left and right arrows with lines to go to the first and last record respectively.

Figure 3-9

The single-column form shown here is one of four types of forms you can create with FormWizards.

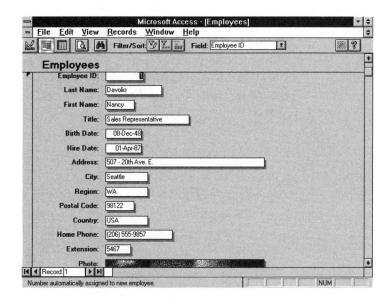

To go from field to field within a record, press the ↓ or ↑, click in a field text box, or select a field in the Field drop-down list box in the toolbar.

To enter a new record, go to the next record after the last record currently in the table and you will get a blank form that you can fill in.

6.   After you are done using the form, close it by double-clicking on its Control-menu box and clicking on Yes when asked if you want to save the form.

Chapter 6 provides a detailed discussion of creating forms with FormWizards and then modifying them in the design window.

Queries

A *query* is a database object you create that brings together a particular set of records and data you request. The value of a query is in its ability to furnish information from more than one source (table or other query) and to provide just the information you want. This data is displayed in Datasheet view but actually it is in a temporary location called a *dynaset*, which contains only the source information for the data you requested. The dynaset is temporary and exists only while the query is open. You can work with data in a dynaset as if it were a regular table, but the records remain in their original locations. When you close the query, the dynaset is deleted until the next time you open the query.

The steps to create a query are:

1. With a Database open and the Table button selected, click on the table you want to query.

2. Click on the new query button in the toolbar (fifth from the right end). The Select Query dialog box appears in Design view where you select the fields you want to appear in the query.

3. Double-click on each field in the table that you want to appear in the query. For instance, you might want first name, last name, and birth date in a database of employees. When you select these fields, the screen will appear as you see in Figure 3-10.

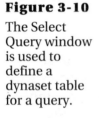

Figure 3-10

The Select Query window is used to define a dynaset table for a query.

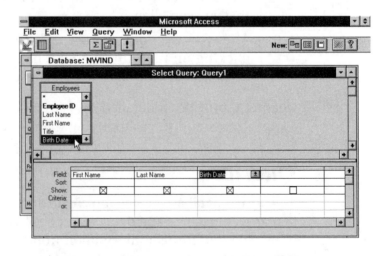

4. Click on the second button from the left in the toolbar to switch to Datasheet view and see the dynaset or data selected by your query.

5. Close the Select Query window by double-clicking on its Control-menu box and then choose Yes when asked if you want to save the query.

Queries are covered in depth in Chapter 7.

Macros

A *macro* is an Access database object that contains instructions to carry out specific tasks in Access. Each task you put in the macro is called an *action* and is placed in the macro through the Macro window.

To build a macro use these steps:

1. With the Database window open and the Macro button selected, click on New. The Macro window appears and you can select the action and the action arguments and enter the necessary comments.

2. Click on the drop-down arrow in the Action column of the Macro window to display a list of possible actions.

3. Using the drop-down list of actions, scroll down to the action you want and click on it, as you see in Figure 3-11.

Once an action is selected, the boxes in the Action Arguments section at the bottom of the window present arguments for that action. The box on the right side gives a description of the action, and the box on the left is where you change the arguments using drop-down lists.

When you have entered the actions and arguments that you need, you can save this set of macro commands like other database objects, using Save in the File menu. Later you can run the macro by clicking in the toolbar on the button with an exclamation point as its icon or choose Run Macro in either the File or Macro menus.

Figure 3-11

Use the Macro
window to add
a list of actions
to a new macro.

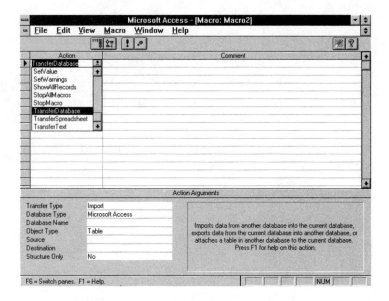

Chapter 9 gives you a detailed look at macros and how they are
constructed.

Modules

A *module* is a collection of Access Basic programming procedures
that are stored in a database. Almost everything you need to do
with a database can be done without programming; however, to
completely automate a process or when the operation is too complex for a macro, a module can be used. Modules are created by
selecting the Module button in the Database window and then
clicking on New.

Programming methods are not within the scope of this book, but
are covered in the *Microsoft Access Language Reference*, supplied
with the Access program.

Using the Toolbar and Toolbox

Each Access window has its own *toolbar* across the top of the
window directly under the menu bar. The toolbar contains the
tools needed for the task being performed in that window.

Buttons in the toolbar are shortcuts for the commands in the menus. The *toolbox*, on the other hand, is the only method for selecting the components of forms and reports that are represented by the icons in it. The toolbox is normally available in the Report window and the Form window. If it does not appear in these windows, you can open it by choosing Toolbox in the View menu.

Use Help for more information on the individual buttons in the toolbar and toolbox. Do that by following these steps:

1. From any Access window, click on Search in the Help menu, then type **toolbar** in the box provided in the Search window.

2. Click on Show Topics and the names of all the different toolbars appear in the bottom half of the window.

3. Click on one of the toolbars to select it and then click on Go To. The toolbar you selected will appear. You can then click on the individual toolbar buttons in the help window to get information on each of them.

4. Follow these same steps but type **toolbox** to see the toolbox help window.

5. Double-click on the help window Control-menu box to return to the Access window where you started.

Tools in the Toolbar

You perform many different database management tasks in Access and each of them has its own toolbar containing buttons needed for the particular task. When you are working with tables, forms, reports, queries, and macros there are different toolbars displayed. There are even different toolbars displayed when you are working with tables in Design view and in Datasheet view. To know what tools are available, you must take into account what you are doing.

When Access opens, the toolbar is blank except for the help button (the question mark on the right end). The help button appears on all the toolbars of the various Access windows. These toolbars are described and shown in the next several sections.

Database Toolbar

The database toolbar has five buttons in addition to help, one of which, the undo button (second from the right), is seen on all the remaining toolbars. The database toolbar is seen below. The other buttons are, from left to right, print preview and the New buttons: query, form, and report.

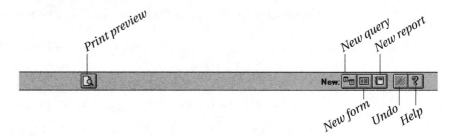

Tables Toolbar in Datasheet View

The tables toolbar in Datasheet view appears when you open a table. This toolbar adds buttons for working in the Design and Datasheet views of the table. The first button on the left is the design view button, which allows changes to the structure of the table you have open. Next, the datasheet view button allows work on the data in the open table. After the print preview button is the find button (the binoculars icon). Find opens the Find in Field dialog box where you enter a string of characters you want to locate in the selected field. The Field box lets you select the field in which to work. The tables toolbar in Datasheet view is shown here:

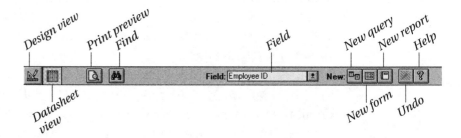

Tables Toolbar in Design View

The tables toolbar in Design view adds the properties button (third from left) and next to it, the primary key button as you can see below. The properties button opens or closes the properties dialog box and the primary key button makes the selected field the primary key.

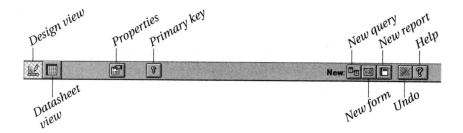

Queries Toolbar in Design View

The queries toolbar in Design view adds the totals button (third from left) and next to the properties button, the run button (fifth from the left). The totals button displays or hides the total row in a query window and the run button executes the query. You can see the queries toolbar in Design view next:

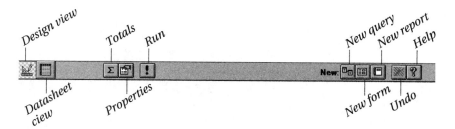

The toolbar for queries in Datasheet view is the same as the toolbar for tables in Datasheet view.

Form Toolbar in Design View

The form toolbar in Design view is available when you are creating or editing the design of a form. The buttons in this toolbar are design view, form view, datasheet view, print preview, properties, field list, and palette. When a text field is selected in a form or a text button is selected in the toolbox, font, font size, style (bold, italic, or underline), and align text buttons (left, center, right, or general) also appear, as shown here:

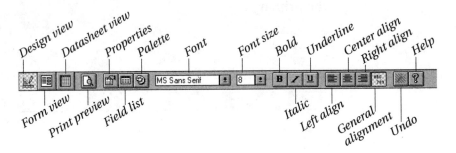

Form Toolbar in Form or Datasheet View

The form toolbar in Form or Datasheet view has three unique filter/sort buttons in the middle as you can see below. These are, from left to right, the edit filter/sort button which opens the Filter window, the apply filter/sort button which makes the current Filter window contents take effect, and the show all records button which turns off the effects of the Filter window.

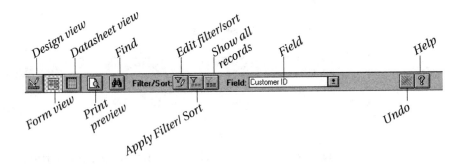

Report Toolbar

The report design toolbar (there is no datasheet view for reports), as it appears fully displayed with a text item selected, contains only one button you have not seen above. This is the sorting and grouping button which is the second button from the left. You see such a report design toolbar here:

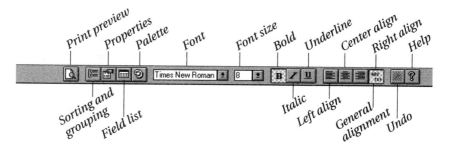

Macro Toolbar

The macro toolbar has four new buttons as shown below. The first two allow you to show or hide the Macro Names and Conditions columns in a Macro window. Then next, the run button, runs the macro and the last, the single step button, runs the macro one step at a time to find the errors.

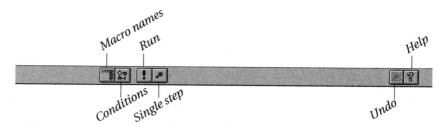

Tools in the Toolbox

The toolbox appears in the Form and Report design windows and contains a group of icons that add items to forms and reports. By clicking on the different buttons, you can use the mouse to drag the items where you want them in a form or report. These include such things as lines, rectangles, label boxes, text boxes, and all the other items you might use to design a report or form. For example, you use the text box control tool to set up the location where text is to be entered. The toolbox with its buttons identified is shown in the illustration on the following page:

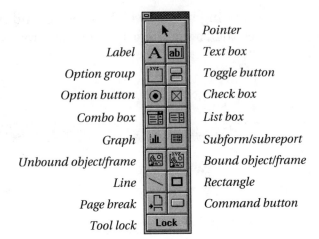

			Pointer
Label			Text box
Option group			Toggle button
Option button			Check box
Combo box			List box
Graph			Subform/subreport
Unbound object/frame			Bound object/frame
Line			Rectangle
Page break			Command button
Tool lock			

The tools in the toolbox are covered in greater detail in Chapters 5 and 6.

Summary

This chapter has introduced you to Access and its major components. Among the items discussed in the chapter were the following:

◆ Begin using Access by starting Windows, double-clicking on the Access icon in the Access group window, and then opening or creating a database from the File menu.

◆ The Help menu provides general help and covers most subjects. The help button on the toolbar, like the F1 key, is context sensitive so the help is for the task being performed.

◆ The Help Table of Contents window, from the Help menu, provides help on how to use Access. At the bottom of the Table of Contents window is the Reference section which provides information on a wide range of functions. This section also contains a glossary of terms.

◆ Databases are DOS files that Access uses to store all the objects that pertain to a given subject. To move, copy, or delete the file, you use DOS or the File manager in Windows.

◆ Tables are the objects that contain the data you enter into Access.

◆ Reports are the objects that bring together the data you request and print it in the format you want.

◆ Forms are objects you create for entering data into tables and displaying that data on the screen.

◆ Queries are objects that are used to select specific data from one or more tables, databases, or even other queries.

◆ Macros are database objects that contain a group of instructions or commands. The commands are carried out when you run the macro.

In the next chapter you will see how to create a database and its tables.

Creating a Database and Its Tables

In the first three chapters you have gotten a good overview of databases, Windows, and Access. It is now time for some hands-on practice in creating a database and its related tables. In this chapter, you will create the sample bookstore database that was introduced in Chapter 1. Included in this database will be three tables: one for books, one for customers, and one for suppliers. In subsequent chapters, you will refine these tables and add reports, forms, and queries and even some additional small tables to this database.

Creating a Database

Imagine that you are the owner of a small bookstore. You want to keep track of the books in stock and on order. You would like to be able to find books from a certain author or publisher, or be able to list all books in a certain category. You also want to keep track of supplier and customer information and to access that information in various ways.

The inventory of the store can be maintained in a single table, since the only product that the store sells is books. A table for the books in the store will contain detailed information about the books themselves (for example, author, title, publisher, and price) as well as inventory data such as quantity on hand and quantity to order. The Books table can be used to answer questions such as, Are there any books on order from a certain publisher?

Customer information such as name, address, phone number, and credit limit should be stored in another table. The Customer table can be used to find when a customer last placed an order or how much money a customer owes the store.

A third table should contain the information about the bookstore's suppliers. In addition to the names and addresses of the suppliers, the names of sales and accounting contacts and their phone numbers can be stored in the Supplier table.

These three tables will be stored in a new database named Books. Create this new database now with the following steps:

1. If it is not already running, start Access by double-clicking on its icon in the Windows Program Manager. If the Welcome to Microsoft Access window appears, click on Close. You should be left with the blank Access window and only the File and Help menus visible.

2. Open the File menu and choose the New Database option. The New Database dialog box opens, as shown in Figure 4-1.

3. If necessary, change the directory in the Directories list box to the Bookstor directory you created in Chapter 2 or the directory where you want to store your database file. Do this by clicking on the directory above the current directory until you are at or above the directory you want, and then, if needed, click on the subdirectory you want.

4. Type the name **books** in the File Name text box. You can make this either lower- or uppercase and you do not need to type in a period or an extension. Access automatically adds .MDB to the filename you enter. Filenames can be up to eight characters long and cannot contain any spaces.

Figure 4-1

The New
Database
dialog box
allows you to
name a
database and
determine
where to
store it.

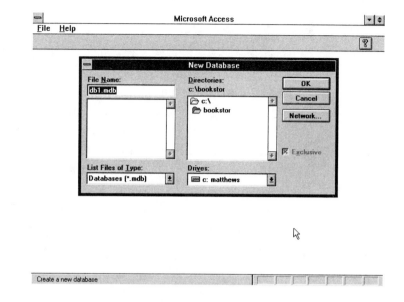

5.   Click on the OK button or press [Enter]. The Database window opens, as shown in Figure 4-2.

Figure 4-2

The Database
window is
where you
switch among
tables, reports,
forms, queries,
macros, and
modules.

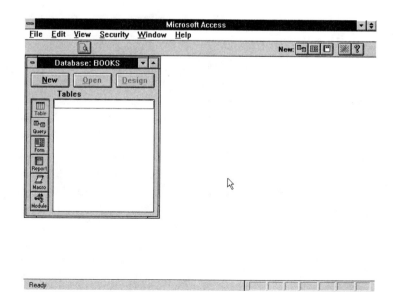

Creating Tables

With the database created, the next step is to create tables in which to store the data. The tables you create define the structure of your database as you learned in Chapter 1. The importance of carefully laying out this structure cannot be overemphasized. In this chapter you can use part of the structure that was developed in Chapter 1 to build a simple database. This database will be refined and developed further in subsequent chapters.

You create a table in the Table window, which you can open from where you are in the Database window. If it is not already depressed, click on the Table button on the left side of the Database window, then click on the New button. A new Table window opens, as shown in Figure 4-3.

The Table Window

The Table window is divided into two sections. The top section is used to define the fields in the table and is called the *field definition* section. The bottom section of the window allows you to set

Figure 4-3

The Table window is used to create a new table.

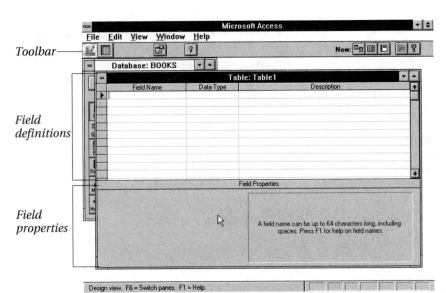

Toolbar—

Field definitions

Field properties

field properties for each field. Field names, data types, and descriptions are entered into the top part of the Table window; and field size, format, default value, and other parameters are set in the Field Properties area, located in the bottom part of the Table window. Before actually creating the fields for the table, it is important to understand the different components of a field definition.

Field Names

The *field name* can be up to 64 characters long and should describe the type of information that will be stored in the field. The name should be long enough to identify the information that the field contains and short enough to be fully displayed in an appropriate column width. The description (discussed below) can be used to further describe the field so the field name does not need to say everything about the field. Spaces can be used in the field name.

Data Types

The *data type* specifies the type of data that will be stored in the field. You have a choice of eight data types: text, memo, number, date/time, currency, counter, yes/no, and OLE-object. Look at each of these in the next several sections.

Text and Memo Data Types   The *text* and *memo* data types are alphanumeric fields that can contain any combination of letters, numbers, and special characters. A text field can store up to 255 characters. A memo field can store 32,000 characters. Memo fields are used for long descriptions, notes, or comments.

Number Data Type   The *number* data type stores integers (whole numbers) or fractions (numbers with decimal places). You cannot put letters or special characters in a number field. When you choose the number data type, the field properties *format* and *field size* are often set to customize the number field. Field properties are discussed in detail later in this chapter.

Date/Time Data Type   The *date/time* data type stores dates and times from the year 100 through the year 9999. Dates and times are not stored as text, but rather as a special number. Storing dates and times in the date/time data type allows you to use dates in calculations like subtracting two dates to determine the number of days between them. You do not see the number on the screen because it is formatted in one of several normal date and/or time formats. Formats are discussed in the "Field Properties" section later in this chapter.

Currency Data Type   The *currency* data type is used to store monetary values. Currency fields store positive and negative numbers that have up to fifteen digits to the left of the decimal point and four digits to the right of the decimal point. You can use any number format to display a dollar amount, but the currency format is the one most commonly used. See the "Field Properties" section later in this chapter for detailed information about formatting.

Counter Data Type   The *counter* data type is a numeric field that is automatically incremented for each record entered. Counter fields are useful for indexing. A counter field in the first record would contain the value 1, the second record would contain the value 2, and so on. You cannot change the value in a counter field since the value is automatically assigned by Access as records are added.

The primary key or index of a table is often a counter field. Setting up a field as a primary key where the values are automatically entered by the computer avoids many potential problems. Chapter 1 explains how primary keys are used. In this chapter you will learn to set up primary keys for the tables you are creating for the bookstore.

Yes/No Data Type   The *yes/no* data type defines a field to be Boolean. A Boolean field stores one of two values: yes or no, on or off, true or false, 1 or 0. Use the format option in the Field Properties portion of the Table window to control how values in the field are displayed.

OLE-Object Data Type   An *OLE* (object linking and embedding) object is data or graphics created in other programs that can be linked to or embedded in an Access database. Objects are linked through controls on a report or form.

Description

The description is an optional entry in the Table window that describes the field more specifically. The text you enter into the description will appear in the status bar when you are entering data. Descriptions should help the person entering the data understand more about what kind of information the field should contain, or how the information should be entered.

Field Properties

The lower part of the Table window contains a number of settings called *field properties*, as you can see here:

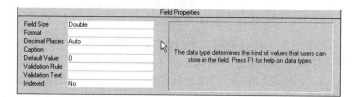

Field properties allow you to define a field more specifically. For example, you can change the size of a field or change the way that the values in a field are displayed. The various data types have some or all of the following field properties: field size, format, decimal places, caption, default value, validation rule, validation text, and indexed. Each of these field properties is described next.

Field Size

The *Field Size* property allows you to control the size of a field, if the data type is either text or number. Text and number fields have default field sizes that may not be the best choices for what is being stored in the fields. Try to set the field size as small as possible. Your database file will be smaller and some operations will work faster when field sizes are compact.

The default field size for a text field is 50 characters. If the longest text string that you will be storing in the field is 15 characters long, having a field size of 50 characters wastes space. When adjusting the field size for a text field, try to figure out the length of the longest string that you will be storing in that field. Set the length of the field a little longer than you think you need to give yourself a margin of error.

There are five possible field sizes for a number field. Just as with text strings, you want to choose a field size that is big enough without wasting space since the field size controls how a number is stored. Each field size available for a number field stores a specific range of integers or real numbers. Table 4-1 summarizes the possible number field sizes.

Format

The *Format* field property allows you to control how a field is displayed if the data type is a number, currency, or a date or time.

Number or Currency Formats There are six built-in number formats that can be set in Field Properties and used for either numbers or currency. Number formats only control how the entry is displayed, not how the entry is stored. Table 4-2 summarizes the built-in number formats.

You can also create custom number formats by replacing the name of a built-in format in the Field Properties Format box with a custom format. These custom formats are built with a combination of the codes shown in Table 4-3.

A custom format has four parts. The first part defines the format used if the value in the field is positive. The second part defines the format used if the value is negative. The third part defines the

	Field Size	Range	Type	Bytes
Table 4-1 Size Options for Number Fields	Byte	0 to 255	Integer	1
	Integer	-32,768 to 32,767	Integer	2
	Long Integer	-2,147,483,648 to 2,147,483,647	Integer	4
	Single	-3.402823E38 to 3.402823E38	Real	4
	Double	-1.79769313486232E308 to 1.79769313486232E308	Real	8

	Format	Description	Decimals (Default)	1000s Separator	Negatives
Table 4-2 The Built-in Number Formats	General Number	As entered	varies	No	- sign
	Currency	Dollars	2	Yes	parentheses
	Fixed	Two decimal places	0	No	- sign
	Standard	1000s separated	2	Yes	- sign
	Percent	Percent sign	2	No	- sign
	Scientific	Scientific notation	varies	No	- sign

format used if the field contains zero, and the fourth part defines the format used if the field contains nothing. The four parts are separated by semicolons.

It is not necessary to define all four parts. For example, if you enter the single custom format $#,000.0000, positive and negative numbers as well as zero and blank values will all be formatted in this way:

♦ The data in the field will be displayed with at least three digits to the left of the decimal place and zeros will be used if other digits are not present.

♦ Additional digits to the left of the decimal place will be displayed if the number is large enough, and a comma will be used to separate thousands.

♦ Four digits will be displayed to the right of the decimal place and zeros will be used if other digits are not present.

♦ A dollar sign will be displayed to the left of the number.

The value 23.45 is displayed as $023.4500, 12345.678912 is displayed as $12,345.6789, -678.456 is displayed as -$678.4560, and zero and blank values are displayed as $000.0000.

If you want negative numbers and zero and blank values formatted differently, you can specify their formats individually. For example, the custom format $#,000.0000;($#,000.0000) [Red];$0;"Blank" displays positive numbers as described above.

Table 4-3

Format Codes
That Can Be
Used in
Custom
Formats

Code	Description
.	Adds a decimal separator
,	Adds a thousands separator
0	Displays a digit or a zero
#	Displays a digit only if it exists
$	Adds a dollar sign
+ or -	Adds a plus or minus sign to all numbers independent of whether they are positive or negative
( )	Adds parentheses
[*color*]	Displays the number in the *color* which can be black, blue, cyan, green, magenta, red, white, or yellow
"*text*"	Displays any text between quotation marks as a literal string without the quotation marks
\	Displays the character following the backslash as a literal character; the \ is not displayed
%	Multiplies a number by 100 and adds a percent sign
*	Fills any empty space in a field with the character following the asterisk; the * is not displayed unless it is repeated
E- or e-	Displays number in scientific notation with only negative exponents signed
E+ or e+	Displays number in scientific notation with either positive or negative exponents signed
space(s)	Adds the number of literal spaces that are included in the custom format

Negative numbers are displayed in the same format, except they are enclosed in parentheses and are red. Zero values are displayed as $0 if the Decimal Places field property is set to Auto (see "Decimal Places" below). If the field contains nothing, the word Blank is displayed.

Date and Time Formats   There are a variety of formats that are available for the date/time data type. Table 4-4 summarizes the built-in date/time formats. In Table 4-4, the right column shows the appearance of 1:00 PM on January 1, 1993, given the standard U.S. settings on the Windows International Control Panel.

Custom date/time formats can be created by replacing the name of a built-in format in the Field Properties Format box with a custom format. Custom date formats consist of combinations of codes, just like custom number formats. Table 4-5 contains a list of the custom format codes for dates and times.

Decimal Places

The *Decimal Places* field property allows you to change the number of digits that are displayed to the right of the decimal point, if the field is a number or currency field. There can be up to 15 digits displayed to the right of the decimal point. Each number format has a default number of digits to be displayed. If you want the format that you choose to determine the number of digits displayed, the Decimal Places field property should be set to *Auto*. If you want to choose a setting other than the default, type in the number of digits that you want displayed, or click on the number from the drop-down list box in the Decimal Places setting.

Table 4-4

Built-in
Date/Time
Formats

Format	Appearance
General Date	1/1/93 1:00 PM
Short Date	1/1/93
Medium Date	01-Jan-93
Long Date	Friday, January 01, 1993
Short Time	13:00
Medium Time	01:00 PM
Long Time	1:00:00 PM

Table 4-5

Custom
Date/Time
Format Codes

Code	Description	Type	Digits	Range
:	Separator	Time	1	n/a
/	Separator	Date	1	n/a
d	Day of the month	Date	1-2	1-31
dd	Day of the month	Date	2	01-31
ddd	Day of the week	Date	3	Sun-Sat
dddd	Day of the week	Date	6-9	Sunday-Saturday
w	Day of the week	Date	1	1-7
ww	Week of the year	Date	1-2	1-52
m	Month of the year	Date	1-2	1-12
mm	Month of the year	Date	2	01-12
mmm	Month of the year	Date	3	Jan-Dec
mmmm	Month of the year	Date	3-9	January-December
q	Quarter of the year	Date	1	1-4
y	Day of the year	Date	1-3	1-365
yy	Year (last 2 digits)	Date	2	01-99
yyyy	Year	Date	4	0100-9999
h	Hour	Time	1-2	0-23
hh	Hour	Time	2	00-23
n	Minute	Time	1-2	0-59
nn	Minute	Time	2	00-59
s	Second	Time	1-2	0-59
ss	Second	Time	2	00-59
AM/PM, am/pm	Upper- or lowercase pair of letters for the part of the day	Time	2	n/a
A/P, a/p	Upper- or lowercase letter for the part of the day	Time	1	n/a
AMPM	Designator in the Windows International Control Panel for the part of the day	Time	Varies	n/a

Caption

The *Caption* field property allows you to label the field for use on reports and forms. Normally, the field name is used as the label for reports and forms. If you want something other than the field name to be used on reports and forms, enter the label in the Caption box.

Default Value

If you want a field to be filled in automatically with a particular value when you add a new record, enter that value in the *Default Value* field property box. If a value is entered for a new record, that value will replace the default; otherwise, the field will contain whatever you place in the Default Value box. If you do not enter a default value, Access makes the default value 0 for numbers and currency. The Default Value field can contain a certain value or a formula that is evaluated. For example, you may want the current date to be entered automatically into a field. To accomplish this, enter the formula =DATE() in the Default Value box. (See Chapter 9 for more information on formulas and expressions.)

Validation Rule and Validation Text

The *Validation Rule* field property allows you to restrict the values entered into the field. The *Validation Text* field property contains text that is displayed when an entry does not meet the validation rule. Values that cannot be validated using the validation rule are not allowed and cause the validation text to be displayed. For example, you can restrict a date field to allow only dates between 1/1/93 and 12/31/93, or restrict a number field to allow only values smaller than 1,000. The validation text in these cases might say "Please enter a date in 1993" or "Enter a number less than 1,000."

The validation rule must be entered as a formula or expression. An expression can contain a mixture of values, field identifiers, operators, and functions. Expressions can be very simple or extremely complex. For our purposes, this section will merely introduce expressions as validation rules. Chapter 9 will more fully explain expressions. Here you will look at the different components of an expression and then work through some examples.

Operators provide a means of comparing two values, or performing some function on the *operands* (numbers on which the operators operate). Table 4-6 summarizes the available operators.

An example of a validation rule would be >=100. This simple validation rule would ensure that values entered into the field are greater than or equal to 100. The validation text for this might be "Values must be larger than 99."

There are also built-in functions that can be used in validation rules. For example, the date function mentioned under the Default Value entry can also be used in a validation rule such as <Date(). This ensures that a date entry is prior to the current date. The validation text for this might be "Date entry must be prior to today." Chapter 9 will discuss the built-in functions further.

Sometimes you may want to create a validation rule using a value from another field. In that case you can use the field name as an identifier in an expression. For example, if you have a field named "Credit Limit" that stores the credit limit for a customer and another field named "Balance Due" that stores the customer's current balance due, you can validate that a new purchase does not cause the customer to exceed his or her credit limit. The validation rule <=[Credit Limit]-[Balance Due] in a new purchase field would force values entered into that field to be less than or equal to the customer's remaining credit. The validation text in this case might be "Purchase exceeds remaining credit."

| Tip |

Field names in a validation rule always need to be in square brackets ([ ]) as in the above example. In some other uses of expressions, such as on forms and reports, if the field name is a single word like Title or Author, it does not have to be in brackets. This is not true in validation rules or query criteria.

Like the square brackets around field names, literal dates or times have number signs (#) around them. If the date in a validation rule is in a field formatted as a date or time, Access will automatically add the number signs for you. For example, if you type

Operator	Description
=	Equal
<	Less than
>	Greater than
<>	Not equal to
<=	Less than or equal to
>=	Greater than or equal to
And	Logical AND which joins two objects
Or	Logical OR which excludes one or the other of two objects
Eqv	Logical equivalence
Imp	Logical implication
Not	Logical NOT
Xor	Logical exclusive OR
Between	Is the value between two values?
In	Is the value in the given list?
Is	Is the value equal to a value or expression?
Like	Checks strings for patterns
&	Concatenates two strings
*	Multiplies two values
+	Adds two values
-	Subtracts one value from another
/	Divides one floating-point number by another
\	Divides one integer by another
^	Raises a number to a given power
Mod	Returns the remainder of a division operation

Table 4-6

Available
Operators

>10/31/93and<12/1/93 to ensure the dates being entered are in November, 1993, Access will automatically change this to >#10/31/93#And#<12/1/93#. If the validation text for such a field were "Date must be in November '93" and you entered a date not in November 1993, you would get this message box:

You can tell if Access recognizes the keywords you enter, such as the logical AND in the validation rule just discussed, by typing them in lowercase. If Access recognizes them, it will convert them to leading-capital letters.

When you use text in a validation rule, the text must have quotation marks (") around it unless the text is a single word without spaces or punctuation, in which case Access will add the quotation marks for you. An example of using text in a validation rule is ensuring that a name, say Smith, not be entered. The validation rule for this is <>"Smith" (you do not have to type the quotation marks).

Indexed

The last field property, *Indexed*, allows you to identify a field as being indexed or not and, if indexed, whether you will allow duplicates. If you are going to search a table often on a particular field, indexing that field will speed up the searches. On the other hand, an index will slow down adding or changing a record. You therefore need to consider if an index is worthwhile before adding it. You can have indexes in several fields, but the more you have the slower the updating will be.

If you choose to have unique indexes, so as not to allow duplicates, Access will not allow the entry of a record with a duplicate value in the indexed field. This is a major restriction and needs to be carefully considered. It is right in some circumstances and not in others. Only your knowledge of the database you are building can determine which is right for you.

Creating the Fields for the Books Table

Now that you have learned how to create fields in a table, continue on with the bookstore's Books database and table and add fields for the ISBN (International Standard Book Number), title, author, publisher, price, category, the number of books on hand, the number of books on order, and the book number.

Follow the steps below to add these fields to the Books table. If your pointer is not already there, use your mouse to click on the first Field Name box.

1. Type **ISBN** in the Field Name box and press (Enter). The pointer moves to the Data Type field.

2. The default value for Data Type is *Text*. Since the ISBN field is a text field, press (Enter) again. The pointer moves to the Description box.

3. Type **Enter the ISBN for the book** and press (Enter). This message will be displayed in the status bar when data is being entered. When you press (Enter), the pointer moves to the second Field Name box.

You have just defined the first field in the Books table. The Title and Author fields are also text fields. Define these two fields the same way that the ISBN field was defined above. When you are done, your Table window should look like Figure 4-4.

If you find that you have made a mistake and want to go back and correct a field name or description that you have completed (one for which you have already pressed (Enter)), highlight the field by moving the pointer to it or by clicking on it. Moving the pointer with the arrow keys highlights the entire field; once you begin to type, you will replace *everything* that was previously in the field. You can also change just a few characters by pressing (F2) and using the arrow keys to move the pointer to the characters you want to change, or you can click the mouse where you want to make the change. You can use the (Delete) key to delete characters to the right, the (Backspace) key to delete characters to the left,

Figure 4-4

The Table
window with
the first three
fields defined

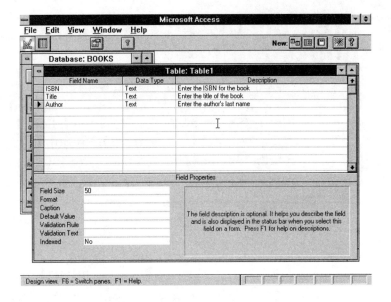

or you can drag over characters to highlight them and then type
their replacement text. When you are done making a correction,
press Enter to complete the editing.

The next field is the Publisher ID field. You will create a Publisher
table later in this chapter. The Publisher ID field will link the
Books table with the Publishers table. The Publisher ID is a unique
number that identifies a particular publisher. To create the
Publisher ID field, follow these steps:

1. Type **PubID** in the next Field Name box and press Enter.
    The pointer moves to the Data Type box.

2. Click on the down arrow on the right side of the Data Type
    box and then click on Number in the list that drops down.

    Notice that the Field Size box in the Field Properties area
    of the window reads Double. This is the default field size
    for the data type Number. With this field size, the Pub-
    lisher ID field can contain real numbers in the range of
    $-1.79769313486232E308$ to $1.79769313486232E308$. It
    takes eight bytes to store a number with a Double field
    size. A field of this size is overkill in this situation. Since
    this field will only contain integers, it makes more sense

to change the field size to Integer. A number field with the field size of Integer is stored in two bytes and can contain integers in the range of -32,768 to 32,767.

3. Click on the Field Size box in the Field Properties portion of the window.

4. Click on the down arrow and then click on Integer.

5. Click on the Description box in the upper portion of the window, type **Enter the ID of the book's publisher** and press ⌐Enter¬. The pointer moves to the next Field Name box.

The Price field is a currency field, so its definition is slightly different than the first four fields. The steps below will lead you through creating this field:

1. Type **Price** in the Field Name box and press ⌐Enter¬. The pointer moves to the Data Type box.

2. Click on the down arrow on the right side of the Data Type box. A drop-down list box appears with the possible data types listed.

3. Click on Currency in the drop-down list.

4. Click on the Format box in the Field Properties portion of the window.

5. Click on the down arrow on the right side of the Format box and then click on Currency.

6. Click on the Description box, type **Enter the retail price of the book** and press ⌐Enter¬.

The next two fields, OnHand and Order, are numeric fields. They should be entered with the data type Number and the field size Integer, just like the PubID field.

The last field, Category, is a text field. When you are finished defining the fields, your Table window should look like Figure 4-5.

Defining a Primary Key

A *primary key* is a field that contains a unique value. There is only one primary key for each record and it is never repeated in a table—there is a 1:1 relationship between a primary key and the record it represents. When records are displayed in a form or table, they are automatically sorted by the primary key. An index is created for the primary key in which duplicates are not allowed. The primary key speeds up queries and manipulations of the data.

Since the primary key field must be unique, no two records can be entered with the same value in the primary key field. It is convenient to set up the primary key field as the *counter* data type so that Access automatically numbers each record sequentially. This primary key field can be treated as an internal ID number for the record.

Add a book ID number to the table you are building and identify it as a primary key using these instructions:

1. Select the ISBN field name by clicking on it with your mouse. An arrowhead moves to the left of the ISBN field, indicating that the ISBN field is selected.

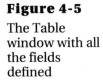

Figure 4-5

The Table window with all the fields defined

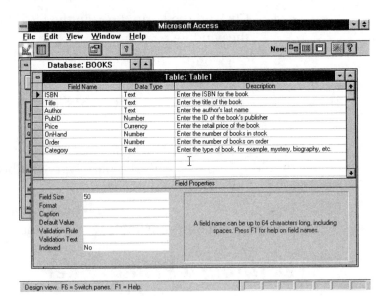

2. Choose Insert Row from the Edit menu. A new field is inserted above ISBN.

3. Type **BkID** in the Field Name box and press ⌈Enter⌋. The pointer moves to the Data Type box.

4. Set the data type to Counter and press ⌈Enter⌋.

5. Type **Internal book ID number** in the Description box.

 6. Click on the primary key button, fourth from the left in the toolbar and shown at the left here.

A small key appears to the left of the BkID field name, telling you this is the primary key. Also, the Indexed field property now reads "Yes (No Duplicates)." This completes all field entries for the first table.

Naming the Table

Before you start entering data into the table, name and save the new table, even though the table is still empty. When you save a table for the first time, you can name it. Once you name the table, you can simply choose the Save command from the File menu when you feel you need to save your work, and the table will be saved under the existing name. If you want to save the table under a different name, you need to choose the Save As option from the File menu. To name and save the table you have created, follow these steps:

1. Choose the Save option from the File menu and the Save As dialog box opens, as shown here:

2. Type the name **Books** in the Table Name box, and press ⌈Enter⌋ or click on OK. The table is now saved with the name Books. Figure 4-6 shows the completed Books table.

Figure 4-6

The completed
Books table

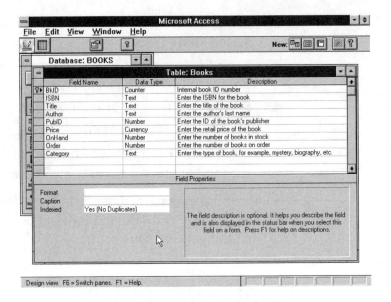

Setting Up the Suppliers Table

The next table needed for the bookstore's database is a table of the store's suppliers—in this case, publishers. First you will need to open a new table. Your screen should look like Figure 4-6.

1. Click on the Database window to bring it to the front.

2. Click on the Table button if it is not still selected, then click on New. A new database window appears on your screen, as shown in Figure 4-7.

The first field in the database will be an identification field. You will set up this field so that a unique number will automatically be assigned to each new record as it is added. This is the number that you will use in the Books table to identify the publisher, so the field is called PubID to match the name you used in the Books table. Follow these steps to set up the PubID field:

1. Type **PubID** in the first Field Name box and press (Enter). The pointer moves to the Data Type box.

2. Click on the down arrow on the right side of the Data Type box, select Counter, and press (Enter). The pointer moves to the Description field.

Figure 4-7

The second
new Table
window
will be used
to build the
Suppliers table.

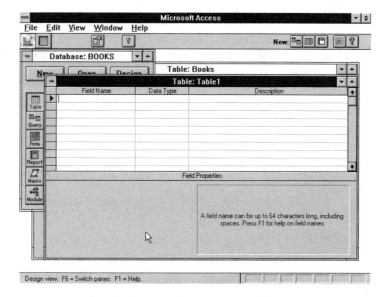

3.   Type **This field contains the publisher ID number** and
     press (Enter). The pointer moves to the next Field Name
     box.

4.   Click on the PubID field name, then click on the primary
     key button to make the PubID field the primary key.

5.   Choose Save from the File menu, type **Suppliers** in the
     Table Name box, and press (Enter) or click on OK.

6.   Click on the up arrow in the upper-right corner of the new
     Table window so that the window fills the entire screen.

7.   Enter the remaining fields as shown in Figure 4-8.

Figure 4-8

The completed
Suppliers table

Field Name	Data Type	Description
PubID	Counter	This field contains the publisher ID number
Name	Text	Enter the name of the publisher
Address1	Text	Enter the first line of the publisher's address
Address2	Text	Enter the second line of the publisher's address
City	Text	Enter the publisher's city
ST	Text	Enter the two digit abbreviation for the state
ZIP	Number	Enter the publisher's ZIP code
Order Phone	Text	Enter the order phone number in the format 999-555-1212
Admin Phone	Text	Enter the adminstrative phone number in the format 999-555-1212
Discount	Number	Enter the publisher's standard discount rate
Order Contact	Text	Enter the name of the person to contact for orders
Admin Contact	Text	Enter the name of the person to contact for administrative items
Subject	Text	Enter the publisher's primary subject, for example art, textbooks, general, etc.

Most of the work creating the Suppliers table is done. Some of the fields need additional attributes set. These attributes are controlled in the Field Properties area of the window.

The field that contains the state abbreviation code only needs to be two characters long. Follow these instructions to change the field size of the ST field:

1. Click on the field name ST.

2. Drag across the number 50 in the Field Size box in the Field Properties area.

3. Type **2** for the new field size.

The ZIP field is a number field that contains a five-digit ZIP code. The default field size is Double, which requires eight bytes of memory. Since you do not need to store numbers that large, a long integer field size is sufficient (long integers take four bytes of memory to store).

1. Click on the field name ZIP.

2. Click on Field Size in the Field Properties area.

3. Click on the down arrow on the right side of the Field Size box, and select the Long Integer field size.

The two fields that contain phone numbers are text fields. Since phone numbers can be stored in 12 characters, change the field sizes of Order Phone and Admin Phone:

1. Click on the field name Order Phone.

2. Drag across 50 in the Field Size area of the Field Properties.

3. Type **12** as the new field size.

4. Click on the field name Admin Phone.

5. Drag across 50 in the Field Size area of the Field Properties.

6. Type **12** as the new field size.

The Discount field needs to be defined as a percent format. The field size should also be reduced to store the information in a more efficient manner:

1. Click on the field name Discount.

2. Click on Field Size in the Field Properties area.

3. Click on the down arrow on the right side of the Field Size box and select Integer.

4. Click on the Format box, then click on the down arrow on the right side of the Format box.

5. Click on Percent.

Before going on, restore the window to its normal size by clicking on the restore button in the upper-right corner of the window. Then save your work as you did above.

Setting Up the Customers Table

The third and last table that needs to be built is the Customers table. It will store information about the bookstore's customers, such as names, addresses, phone numbers, credit limits, and account balances. Create the Customers table now with the following instructions:

1. Click on the Books Database window to bring it to the front.

2. Click on the Table button if it is not currently selected, then click on New. A blank Table window will appear, similar to those you have seen earlier in this chapter.

The first field in the Customers table is a customer ID field which will be used as the primary key. Follow these instructions to set up the CusID field:

1. Type **CusID** in the first Field Name box and press (Enter).

2. Click on the down arrow on the right side of the Data Type box, select Counter, and press (Enter).

3. Type **This is the Customer ID number** in the Description field, then click the mouse on the primary key button and press Enter. The CusID field has been defined as the primary key.

4. Choose Save from the File menu, type **Customers** in the Table Name box, and click on OK.

5. The next step is to enter the rest of the fields. Click on the maximize button in the upper-right corner of the Customers Table window and enter the fields as shown in Figure 4-9. Once you enter the fields, modify the field size for the ST, ZIP, and phone number fields just as you did for the Suppliers table. The Credit Limit and Bal Due fields should be formatted as Currency. When you are finished, restore the Customers table to its original size and save your work.

Entering Data

A database table can be viewed in two ways: Design view and Datasheet view. When setting up the fields for the table, you are in Design view. To add records to the table, you need to change to the Datasheet view. There are two buttons on the left side of the toolbar that change your view. The leftmost button is the design

Figure 4-9

The completed Customers table

Field Name	Data Type	Description
CusID	Counter	This is the Customer ID number
Last Name	Text	Enter the customer's last name
First Name	Text	Enter the customer's first name
Company	Text	Enter the name of the company, if applicable
Address1	Text	Enter the first line of the customer's address
Address2	Text	Enter the second line of the customer's address
City	Text	Enter the customer's city
ST	Text	Enter the customer's state abbreviation
ZIP	Number	Enter the customer's ZIP code
Phone (Day)	Text	Enter the customer's daytime phone number in the format 999-555-1212
Phone (Nite)	Text	Enter the customer's nighttime phone number in the format 999-555-1212
Last Order	Date/Time	Enter the date of the customer's last order
Credit Limit	Currency	Enter the customer's credit limit
Bal Due	Currency	Enter the customer's balance due

view button and the button to its right is the datasheet view button, as shown here:

Whenever you switch from Design view to Datasheet view, Access will prompt you to save the changes you have made to the table if you have not already saved your work. With the Customers table active, click on the datasheet view button (second from the left). Your screen should look like Figure 4-10.

Now you can begin to enter data. The first field in the Customers table is the CusID field, which is a counter field. Access automatically enters a value in this field for you if you simply press ⌐Enter¬. Complete the remainder of the first record in the Customers table with these instructions:

1.   Press ⌐Enter¬ if you have not done so already. Access enters a 1 into the CusID field and moves the pointer to the Last Name field.

Figure 4-10

The Customers table in Datasheet view

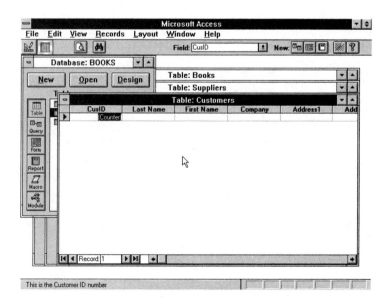

2. Type **Cummings** in the Last Name field and press Enter.
   The pointer moves to the First Name field.

3. Type **Richard** in the First Name field and press Enter. The
   pointer moves to the Company field.

Enter the remaining information for this record as shown in
Table 4-7.

When you press Enter after entering the balance in the Bal Due
field, the pointer moves to the beginning of the next record. Enter
several more records from the information given in Figure 4-11.

In the same way, enter several records for both the Suppliers table
and for the Books table. Figure 4-12 shows the information that
can be entered into the Suppliers table and Figure 4-13 shows the
information that can be entered into the Books table.

As you enter data, you might find mistakes that you have made in
previous entries. As was discussed earlier in entering field names,
you can use your mouse, Delete, Backspace, or F2 and the arrow
keys to correct any errors that you see.

Table 4-7

Information to
Be Entered into
the First
Record of the
Customers
Table

Field Name	Data to Be Entered
Last Name	Cummings
First Name	Richard
Company	Horizon Manufacturing
Address1	11415 W. 15th S
Address2	
City	Seattle
ST	WA
ZIP	98151
Phone (Day)	206-555-7654
Phone (Nite)	206-555-1892
Last Order	5/15/92
Credit Limit	$100.00
Bal Due	$27.95

Figure 4-11

The data for the Customers table

Customers Table

CusID	Last Name	First Name	Company	Address1	Address2	City	ST	ZIP	Phone (Day)	Phone (Nite)	Last Order	Credit Limit	Bal Due
1	Cummings	Richard	Horizon Manufacturing	11415 W. 15th S.		Seattle	WA	98151	206-555-7654	206-555-1892	5/15/92	$100.00	$27.95
2	Potter	Sarah		1582 S Beacon		Edmonds	WA	98040	206-555-1234		8/22/92	$0.00	$0.00
3	DeMuth	Donald	DeMuth Fabrics	4516 E. Pine		Seattle	WA	98113	206-5551236	206-555-7823	9/9/92	$200.00	$57.56
4	Vanderbilt	Jeanette	Pacific NW Trading	Pacific Trade Center	4115 Western A.	Seattle	WA	98151	206-555-9753	206-555-2364	1/15/93	$100.00	$0.00
5	Farquhar	Eric	Fashions Supreme	C/O Fashion Mart	2237 Fourth Ave.	Seattle	WA	98112	206-555-3579	206-555-4274	3/16/93	$100.00	$0.00
6	Fakkema	Edwin	Evans and Fakkma	3497 Westend Ave.		Lake City	WA	98206	206-555-5436	206-555-5456	3/5/93	$0.00	$0.00
7	Rondell	Mary		5517 Lighthouse Dr		Clinton	WA	98236	206-555-1513	206-555-6512	8/19/93	$50.00	$0.00
8	Eskenazi	Ralph		1956 Dalphin Lane		Langley	WA	98260	206-555-6328		8/3/92	$0.00	$0.00
9	Stevens	Thomas	Blanchard Mem. Hospital	416 Ninth Avene		Bellevue	WA	98004	206-555-5111	206-555-5589	6/3/93	$100.00	$0.00
10	Anderson	John		53 Summitt Drive		Redmond	WA	98060	206-555-5459		11/4/92	$100.00	$0.00
11	Dailey	Stephan	Minning Machinery	415 Dark Mountain R		Black Diam	WA	98627	206-555-9891	206-555-9943	11/9/92	$0.00	$0.00
12	Martinez	Susan		5654 Wispering Pine		Bow	WA	98435	206-555-5532		4/26/93	$50.00	$24.00
13	Sato	Yas	Empire Graphics	32 Sentinal Avenue		Renton	WA	98334	206-555-7372		11/22/92	$100.00	$0.00
14	Barton	Barbara	Western Antiques	735 Elliot Avenue		Seattle	WA	98151	206-555-1121	206-555-1132	7/4/92	$50.00	$0.00
15	Gallagher	Linda		92 Vancouver Drive		Bellingham	WA	98532	206-555-6647		3/28/93	$0.00	$15.75
17	Devereaux	Shelly	NW Stone and Concrete	6758 Hwy 553 E.		Kent	WA	98456	206-555-5331	206-555-0953	4/15/93	$0.00	$0.00

Figure 4-12

The data for the Suppliers table

Suppliers Table

PubID	Name	Address1	Address2	City	ST	ZIP	Order Phone	Admin Phone	Discount	Order Contact	Admin Contact
1	Prima Publishing	1830 Sierra Garden, Suite 130	P. O. Box 1260	Rocklin	CA	95677	916-786-0426	916-786-0426	20.0%	Helen Duncanson	Nancy Martinelli
2	St. Martin's Press	175 Fifth Avenue		New York	NY	10010	800-325-5525	212-674-5151	33.0%	Jeanette Zwart	Jane Siebert
3	Ballantine Books	201 E. 50th St.		New York	NY	10022	800-733-3000	212-751-2600	25.0%	Steve Black	
4	Bantam	666 Fifth Avenue		New York	NY	10103	800-223-5780	800-223-6834	44.0%	Don Weisberg	John Cornetta
5	Doubleday	666 Fifth Avenue		New York	NY	10103	800-223-5780	800-223-6834	40.0%	Don Weisberg	Lee Swenka
6	Berkley Publishing	200 Madison Ave.		New York	NY	10016	800-223-0510	212-951-8800	20.0%	Norman Lidofsky	Donna Jaszquit
7	Warner Books	666 Fifth Avenue		New York	NY	10103	800-726-0600	212-484-2900	25.0%	Bruce Paonessa	
8	HarperCollins Publishers	10 E. 53rd St		New York	NY	10022	800-242-7737	212-207-7000	30.0%		
9	Knopf, Alfred (Random House)	201 E. 50th St.		New York	NY	10022	800-733-3000	212-751-2600	25.0%	Maury McClelland	Linden Grantham
10	Dell (Doubleday)	666 Fifth Avenue		New York	NY	10103	800-233-5780	212-765-6500	44.0%	Don Weisberg	John Cornetta
11	Signet Books (Penguin)	375 Hudson St.		New York	NY	10014	800-526-0275	212-366-2000	20.0%	Tim Glass	Laura Cascina
12	Wiley, John & Sons	605 Third Avenue		New York	NY	10158	800-225-5945	212-850-6276	20.0%	Rich Freese	Maryann Lauda
13	Pocket Books	1230 Avenue of the Americas		New York	NY	10020	800-223-2336	212-698-7000	44.0%	Sally Dedecker	Susan Krivit
14	Simon and Schuster	1230 Avenue of the Americas		New York	NY	10020	800-223-2336	212-698-7000	25.4%	Therese Burke	Terri Schwartz
15	Summit Books	1230 Avenue of the Americas		New York	NY	10020	800-223-2336	212-698-7000	25.0%	Therese Burke	Terri Schwartz
16	McKay (Random House)	201 E. 50th Street		New York	NY	10022	800-733-3000	212-751-2600	25.0%	Maury McClelland	Linden Grantham
17	Morrow, William & Co.	105 Madison Ave.		New York	NY	10016	800-843-9289	212-889-3050	20.0%	Larry Norton	Darleen Federica
18	Open Court Publishing	P. O. Box 599		Peru	IL	61354	800-435-6850	815-223-2520	20.0%	Christine Sampson	
19	Ten Speed Press	P. O. Box 7123		Berkeley	CA	94707	800-841-2665	510-845-8414	20.0%	George Young	Torri Randall
20	Saratoga Publishers	1581 West Links Way		Oak Harbor	WA	98277	206-675-9592	206-675-9592	40.0%	Deborah Skinner	Laura Moore

Figure 4-13

The data for the
Books table

Books Table

BkID	ISBN	Title	Author	PubID	Price	OnHand	Order	Category
1	042511872X	Stolen Blessings	Sanders	6	$4.95	5	2	Mystery
2	1559582251	Making of Microsoft	Ichbiah	1	$12.95	3	1	Business
3	0446360074	Rage of Angels	Sheldon	7	$3.50	4	1	Mystery
4	1559581824	Windows 3.1, Visual Learning	Gardner	1	$19.95	6	2	Computer
5	0553281798	Trevayne	Ludlum	4	$5.95	4	1	Mystery
6	1559581085	In The Shadow of the White House	Tidwell	1	$19.95	3	1	Governme
7	0425109720	Patriot Games	Clancy	6	$4.95	6	2	Thriller
8	1559582332	Hawaii: A Paradise Family Guide	Penisten	1	$12.95	2	1	Travel
9	0451146425	Lie Down with Lions	Follett	11	$4.95	2	1	Mystery
10	1559581832	The Power of Windows and DOS	Matthews	1	$24.95	2	1	Computer
11	0671742760	Dragon	Cussler	14	$5.95	3	1	Mystery
12	044020447X	Final Flight	Coonts	10	$5.95	2	1	Thriller
13	0345370066	Spy Line	Deighton	3	$5.95	1	1	Thriller
14	0962876607	Simply Whidbey	Moore,	20	$16.95	5	2	Cooking
15	0671691988	An American Life	Reagan	14	$24.95	3	1	Biography
16	055305340X	A Brief History of Time	Hawking	4	$16.95	1	1	Science
17	0671665545	Sword Point	Coyle	13	$4.95	0	1	Thriller
18	0061000043	A Thief of Time	Hillerman	8	$4.95	1	1	Mystery
19	0553070118	Father Son & Co.	Watson Jr.	4	$22.95	1	1	Biography
20	0345377702	Me	Hepburn	3	$5.99	3	1	Biography
21	0553290991	Nightfall	Asimov	4	$5.99	0	1	Sci. Fic.
22	0471568864	Hard Drive	Wallace	12	$22.95	3	1	Biography
23	0671700553	Aginst the Grain	Yeltsin	15	$19.95	0	1	Biography
24	0679505288	The Rise & Fall of the DC10	Godson	16	$19.95	0	1	Business
25	0553292714	The Fourth K	Puzo	4	$5.99	1	1	Thriller
26	055329461X	The Difference Engine	Gibson	4	$5.99	0	1	Sci. Fic.
27	0446513857	Discovery of the Titanic	Ballard	7	$29.95	1	1	Exploratio
28	0688066631	Whirlwind	Clavell	17	$22.95	2	1	Adventure
29	0385116284	Final Approach	Stockton	5	$7.95	0	1	Flying
30	0446512516	Megatrends	Naisbitt	7	$15.50	2	2	Social Sci
31	0385182694	Overdrive	Buckly	5	$16.95	0	1	Biography
32	0385191952	Hackers	Levy	5	$17.95	1	1	Computers
33	0875483100	There's No Such Thing as a Free	Friedman	18	$9.95	0	1	Economics
34	0385234104	Fatherhood	Cosby	5	$14.95	2	3	Children
35	0345303067	2010	Clarke	3	$3.95	1	2	Sci. Fic.
36	0394405102	Classic Italian Cookbook	Hazan	9	$15.95	1	2	Cooking
37	0913668680	Moosewood Cookbook	Katzen	19	$9.95	1	2	Cooking

Locating particular records in the table can be accomplished by
using the Find option in the Edit menu or clicking on the find tool
in the toolbar (the binoculars). The Find dialog box is shown here:

To use the Find dialog box, type the information you want to find
in the Find What text box and click on Find First. The first occur-

rence of the information you want to find will be highlighted. You can then click on Find Next to find the next occurrence or you can click on Close if the first occurrence is what you wanted.

More sophisticated methods for locating records are available when using forms. Forms also provide the ability to enter data more easily, to group records based on certain criteria, and to sort the data in a table. Chapter 6 discusses these capabilities in depth.

Summary

You have now completed the process of creating a database and entering its data. The major points that have been brought out while doing this are as follows:

- You create a new database by selecting New from the File menu, entering the name of the new database, and then selecting the directory in which it will be stored.

- Tables are initialized by clicking on Table and New in the Database window. This produces a blank Table window.

- You can specify a default value to automatically fill in a field when a new record is created. This default value can include a formula or expression.

- You can also specify a validation rule to ensure that the information entered into a field fits certain specifications. If it does not, Access will open a message window with validation text you have specified for that field.

- One or more fields may be indexed and the indexes can allow duplicates or not as you choose.

- One field may be identified as a primary key which cannot allow duplicates.

- You can edit field names, descriptions, and data that have been entered into tables either with the mouse by clicking or dragging across where you want to make a change, or by highlighting the field, pressing F2, and using the arrow keys. In either case, you can then use Delete, Backspace, or the arrow keys.

◆ You can look at a database table in two ways: the Design view where you can create and change the field definition and field properties, and the Datasheet view where you can enter and edit data. These views are selected with a pair of buttons on the left of the toolbar.

◆ You can find a particular entry in a database by choosing Find in the Edit menu or using the find tool and using the dialog box that opens.

In the next chapter, you will use the data you entered into your database to create, modify, and print several reports.

Creating Reports and Labels

After spending the first four chapters learning about and creating databases, it is time to start using them.

Access gives you the ability to create and print a report in almost any format you choose by bringing together information from several different tables and queries. In this chapter you will learn to create and print reports using the tables you designed earlier in the book. A report can display all or part of the information from one or many different sources. Some examples of reports are phone lists, address lists, sales analyses, inventory summaries, labels, and almost anything that you need to present in a readable format. You may not consider a mailing label to be a report, but think of it as information taken from a database and presented in readable form. Labels will be covered in depth later in the chapter.

Creating and Changing Access Reports

There are two ways to create a report: with Access's ReportWizards and manually on your own. Both options are available from the New Report dialog box.

◆ *ReportWizards* create reports by asking you questions and using the information you supply. ReportWizards can create three different types of reports: a group with totals report, a single column report, and a mailing label report. You can use these reports as is or you can use them as a starting point for creating customized reports that are better suited to your needs.

◆ Manual reports are created from scratch using the Blank Report option. This option allows you to design any report format you wish, but it might take substantial time to complete.

Using ReportWizards

Since the ReportWizards are the easiest and fastest to use, create your first report with them. You are given the choice of several different formats as you work your way through a report. These include whether the report will be in a single column or in a table and what the report should look like when printed.

Assume you need to produce a list of the books in stock that is by the category in which the book is found. You want to use this report to quickly tell a customer if the book is on hand and if so, where it is located.

Try a ReportWizard now by following along in this exercise (Windows and Access should be running and the Books database loaded):

1. Open the Database window and click on the Table button to activate both, if they are not already activated.

2. Choose the table you want to use to create the report; in this case use Books. Your choice is now highlighted.

3. Click on the Report button in the toolbar (third button from the right). Your screen should appear as shown in Figure 5-1.

Figure 5-1

The New
Report dialog
box allows you
to select the
table or query
and method of
creating the
report.

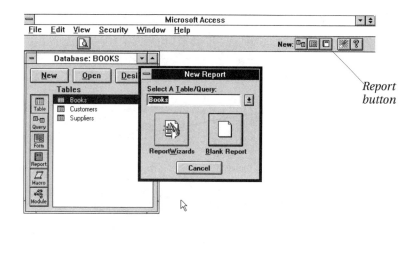

4.   In the New Report dialog box, click on ReportWizards. A
      dialog box appears, allowing you to choose the type of
      report you want to make. The choices are:

      ◆ **Single-column**, which puts all the fields of a record
        into a single column

      ◆ **Groups/Totals** assembles like items into groups and
        gives a total for columns containing numbers

      ◆ **Mailing Label** is a report that extracts name and ad-
        dress information from a table or query and puts it
        into the label you specify

5.   Choose Groups/Totals and then click on OK. This will
      produce a report illustrating the ReportWizard's ability to
      group like items. If you had chosen to create a single-col-
      umn report, all the fields would have been in one column
      down the center of the page. With Groups/Totals, the
      ReportWizard window will appear as shown in Figure 5-2.
      From this point on, you just answer the questions asked
      by the ReportWizard.

The first question you must answer relates to the fields you want to appear on your report. The available fields are listed on the left. To move a field item from the left to the Field order list box on the right, choose the field by clicking on it and then click on the button with a greater-than (>) sign. If you want to move it back for any reason, click on the field in the right list and click on the < button. To move all the fields at one time, use the >> button, and to return all click on the << button.

6. Scroll down to the Category field in the left-hand list, click on it, and then click on the > button. Continue by choosing Title, Author, Price, and OnHand and click on the > button for each of them. These fields will appear in the right-hand list and will be on your report. Click on Next.

7. A dialog box appears and asks the question: Which field(s) do you want to group by? Choose the Category field, click on > and then on Next. This will group the titles by the categories into which you entered them in your database.

Figure 5-2

The ReportWizard dialog box is used to select fields for the report.

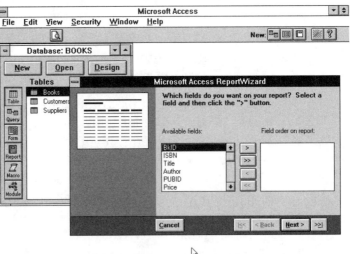

8.   Another dialog box appears and asks: `How do you want to group data in each field?` Normal is already selected and what you want, so you only need to click on Next. As stated in the dialog box, Normal groups together all records with the same value, in this case the same category.

9.   The next question asks: `Which field(s) do you want to sort by?` Move the Title field to the Sort order list box by clicking on > and then click on Next.

10.   The ReportWizard asks: `What kind of look do you want for your report?` You are given three choices, Executive, Presentation, and Ledger. Executive and Presentation are similar, with both having an open table format. Their main differences are in the lines separating the title and the lines separating the column headings. Ledger is also a table format, but has lines to separate the columns and the rows.

   In order to make a report that is easier to read across the columns, choose Ledger by clicking on its option button and then click on Next.

11.   Finally, you are asked: `What title do you want for your report?` The ReportWizard shows a title in the Report Title box and you can accept it or change it. For this exercise type **Book List by Category**. Click on the Print Preview button and you will see the resulting report, which looks similar to Figure 5-3.

The ReportWizard, by default, gives you a total for any column that has numbers in it. You can see that a total in these columns is not appropriate in this report and should be deleted. You will make these and other changes in the section, "Manually Changing the Report Design."

Saving and Closing a Report

It is a good idea to start saving a report very soon after you start working on it and to save often during the project. You might have invested a good deal of time that could be lost with a power or equipment failure. You can save a report with these steps:

Figure 5-3

A report
designed by
ReportWizards

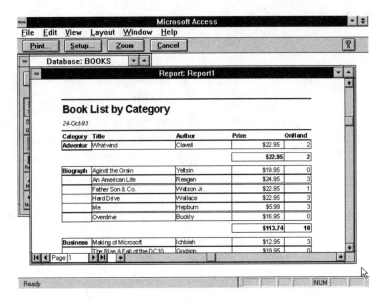

1. Click on Save in the File menu. The first time a report is saved, the Save As dialog box appears with a default name of Report1.

2. You can type a report name of up to 50 characters, replacing the name Report1. For now, type **Book List by Category**.

3. Click on OK. After the report is saved, the name will appear in the window title bar.

To close the report and remove it from the screen, do one of the following steps:

♦   Click on Close in the File menu.

♦   Double-click on the window Control-menu box.

If the report has not been saved before you close it, a dialog box will appear that asks if you want to save before closing.

Deleting a Report

Reports are not stored as normal DOS files, so you cannot use DOS or the File Manager to delete them; you must use Access for that purpose. Use these steps to delete a report:

1. In the Database window, click on the Report button. The window displays the list of reports associated with the open database.

2. Select the name of the report you want to delete.

3. In the Edit menu, choose Delete or press ⌜Delete⌟ on the keyboard. A dialog box will ask you if you are sure you want to delete the named report.

Manually Changing the Report Design

As you have seen from the previous exercise, the ReportWizards are a very good choice for the first-time user and for anyone making simple reports. Many reports can be used just as the ReportWizards created them. These reports can also be modified and, in that way, be used as a starting point for custom reports.

Deciding What to Change

With possible modification in mind, take another look at the Book List by Category report and decide what changes you want to make to the report. You can make changes in the appearance as well as add or remove fields. For instance, looking at the report, say you decide it needs the following changes in appearance and content:

♦   Remove the totals for the groups and remove the grand total since they have no meaning.

♦   Add an additional column containing the ISBN of each book on the report for possible reference purposes.

♦   Lengthen the lines across the report header and the page header to match the increased report width due to adding the ISBN, and change the lines to a thickness of one point for aesthetics.

♦   Center the report title in the report header.

♦   Remove the lines from the Category column. You want to try this just to see how it will look.

Of course you can make some of these changes by going back through the ReportWizard again, but others require the design window. To learn more about changing a design, go through the following exercise in the design window. Remember to save the new report with a different name so you still have the original report for comparison. Access uses the names Report1, Report2, and so on. These are fine as long as you keep track of which one you are using. Finally, save often so that if a step does not work out, you can discard the report in the window and reopen the last one you saved.

Setting Up the Design Window

Now you are ready to set up the design window as a workspace to make the changes you want. Use the following steps as a guide. The BOOKS.MDB database should be open and the Database window should open with Books selected.

1. Click on the Report button to select it. The report you created and saved with the ReportWizard, Book List by Category, should be highlighted; if it is not, then select it.

2. Click on the Design button and the design window will appear as you see in Figure 5-4.

3. Click on the maximize button in the title bar where you see Report: Book List by Category, and the design window fills the work area.

4. When the design window appears, the toolbox also appears with the pointer selected. The pointer is the default tool and will always reappear after any other tool is used. You use the pointer to edit the objects in the report, such as moving, sizing, or selecting them. It is a good idea to drag the toolbox out of your work area now. Point on the toolbox title bar and drag it to the right side of the screen.

The Design Window   The design window is the workspace for creating reports from scratch and for making changes to any report regardless of how it was created. The window contains

Figure 5-4

The design
window allows
you to make
changes to a
report.

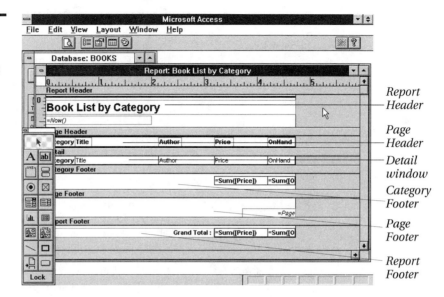

several tools to help you design a report that presents the necessary information and looks professional when printed.

The design window is made up of several areas for working on
the different sections of a report as you see in Figure 5-4. These
are described in Table 5-1.

The header and footer windows are activated from the Layout
menu. When you choose Page Hdr/Ftr or Report Hdr/Ftr, a check
mark is added or removed in the menu and the header/footer is
added to or removed from the design window.

Another feature in the design window is the ruler across the top
of the window and on the left side of each section of the report.
The rulers are activated from the View menu and show the size of
the items when printed. When the mouse button is held down in
the report, you see a mark on both the horizontal and vertical
rulers to indicate the exact position of the pointer. With the
pointer anywhere in the window, click and hold the mouse button and you will see this for yourself.

The Mouse Pointer   The mouse pointer will usually take on the
look of the tool that is selected in the toolbox. You can see this
when you click on the pointer tool. But even this changes as you

Table 5-1

Design
Window Areas

Area	Description
Report Header	Contains the name or title of the report. The Report Header appears only on the first page.
Page Header	Contains the column names that appear at the top of each page. This consists of label boxes which contain text you enter.
Detail window	Contains the fields or controls to produce the body of the report. These controls normally consist of text boxes which are linked to fields in a table or query.
Page Footer	Contains anything you want to appear at the bottom of each page, such as a page number. The Page Footer window will appear only if you have a page header.
Report Footer	Contains objects you want to appear only at the end of the report. The Report Footer window appears only when you have activated the Report Header.

use the pointer for different jobs. Try these steps to see the changes for yourself.

1.   Click in the middle of the box that contains the report title in the Report Header. Notice that the mouse pointer changes to an I-beam for working with text. Notice also the small squares that appear at each corner and in the center of each side. These are called *sizing handles* and indicate that the box is selected. You can see that the upper-left handle is larger than the others; this is called the *moving handle.*

2.   Place the pointer on the moving handle and the pointer will change to a hand with a pointing finger. With the finger on the moving handle, hold the mouse button and drag the box to the right as you see here:

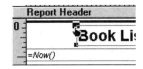

With the box moved away from the side you can see the moving handle much better. Now drag the box back to its original position.

3. Place the pointer on any of the lines forming the selection box and the pointer will change to a flat hand. You can also move the box with this hand by dragging the hand in any direction.

4. Place the pointer on a corner sizing handle and the pointer will change to a two-headed arrow pointing at a 45-degree angle. When you drag this arrow you can see the size change in two directions as shown here:

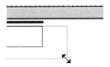

The center handles are also for sizing, but only in one direction at a time, horizontal or vertical.

5. Click outside the selection box and it will be deselected. Place the pointer on the bottom edge of the Report Header area. The pointer will change to a cross with arrows on its vertical bar. You can change the window size by dragging up or down.

Using the Design Window Toolbar

The design window is like a desk top where you can spread out your work to design a report. The tools needed to design or change the design of a report are available in the design window's toolbar. There are two groups of tools: design-related tools which are always available, and text-related tools which are available when you are working on text fields. You select a tool by clicking on the proper button in the toolbar.

Design-Related Tools   The design-related tools either display the report the way it will be printed or they open one of four dialog boxes that give you control over some aspect of the report. The design-related tools and their buttons are described in Table 5-2.

The properties button, after the print preview button, is the next most heavily used while working in the design window. Look at it next with these steps:

1.   Select the label box in the Report Header containing the title `Book List by Category` by clicking anywhere in the box. The handles appear on the box, indicating it is selected.

Table 5-2

Design-Related Tools

Button	Description and Use
	The *print preview* button is the first button from the left, and probably the most used on the toolbar. You can click on this button at any time to see how your report will look when it is printed. When you want to return to the design window, click on Cancel.
	The *sorting and grouping* button is second. It presents a dialog box with a list of the fields that can be used for sorting or grouping in the report. This button is used when creating a report from scratch. You will not use it in this exercise.
	The *properties* button is third and is used when changing a design. All objects in a report have a set of properties and they can be viewed and edited with this button.
	The *field list* button is the fourth button from the left. Use this button to see and select from a list of the available fields for the table in use.
	The *palette* button is fifth and last. It is used to choose a color, to create special effects such as depth, and to choose a line width.

Figure 5-5

Figure 5-5

The properties
dialog box is
used to set or
change the
values of an
object on a
report.

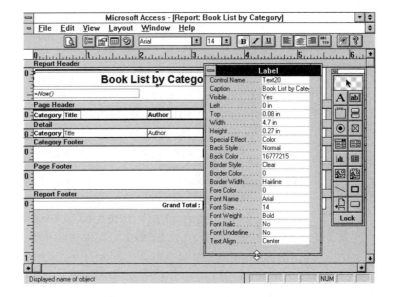

2. Click on the properties button in the toolbar (third button
    from the left) and a properties dialog box will appear.
    Drag the properties dialog box to the top of the screen
    and drag the bottom edge down to expand the box. You
    can see all the options now, as shown in Figure 5-5. You
    can also use the scroll bar on the side of the box to see the
    full list of properties.

Notice the information in the status bar at the bottom of the
screen; as you click on each item in the properties dialog box an
explanation appears. After you take a good look at the dialog box,
return it to a smaller size by dragging the bottom upward and the
right side inward so that it doesn't take up as much workspace.
You can drag and size any of these boxes to make more room in
the workspace or to see more of the dialog box. Once you size
and locate one of these boxes and then leave the Access report-
design function with the box that way, it will still be that size and
in that location the next time you return to report design.

While you have the label box in the Report Header selected and
the properties dialog box in front of you, try changing the align-
ment of the text:

1. Click on the last item in the dialog box, Text Align; an arrow appears at the right to indicate that there are more choices.

2. Click on the arrow, then click on Center. Watch the text, `Book List by Category`, move to the center of the label box. The title on the report will now be centered on the printed page. Select print preview (first button on the left) to see this change in the report.

Text-Related Tools The buttons for the text-related tools appear only when you are working with text or label boxes. They allow you to change the properties of text just as you can with the properties dialog box. Once you are familiar with the various editing functions available, you might find that you prefer to use these buttons instead of the properties dialog box. The text related buttons, which are located to the right of the design buttons, are shown and described in Table 5-3.

Table 5-3

Text-Related Buttons

Button	Description and Use
Arial	The *font name* button is used to assign a font
14	The *font size* button is used to assign a font size
B	The *bold* button is used to make text bold
I	The *italic* button is used to make text italic
U	The *underline* button is used to underline text
≡	The *left alignment* button left-aligns text
≡	The *center alignment* button aligns text in the center
≡	The *right alignment* button right-aligns text
ABC 789	The *general alignment* button aligns text on the left and numbers on the right; this is the default alignment

These text-related buttons are used interchangeably with text and label properties dialog boxes to set and change the appearance of text in your report.

Using the Toolbox

The toolbox in the design window contains a group of tools used to create objects or controls in both reports and forms. In Access, the term *control* is used to indicate all the objects (text and label boxes, rectangles, and lines) you place in a report. These controls are either *bound* or *unbound* to a field. For instance, a label box containing the title of a report is unbound since it has text you type and it is not connected to a field in the table. On the other hand, a text box is bound since it is connected to a field in a table. The information displayed in a bound text box will come from the designated field in the related table.

In order to see more information on the individual tools in the toolbox, open the Help menu, and then click on Search. Type **toolbox** and press (Enter), then click on Toolbox in the list at the bottom and click on Go To. The screen you get should look like Figure 5-6. A brief description of the tools used with reports is provided in

Figure 5-6

The Toolbox help window provides help on each of the tools in the toolbox.

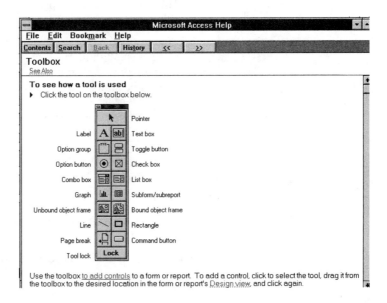

Table 5-4

Toolbox Tools

Button	Description and Use
	The *pointer* is used to choose menu commands and to select and edit report objects. This is the default tool and it returns after you use any of the other tools.
	The *label* button is used to create unbound text boxes in which you type text. The box expands as you type.
	The *text box* button is used to create text boxes that are bound to some item in the underlying table.
	The *graph* control displays a graph on a report.
	The *subform/subreport* creates a control that displays a subreport in another report.
	The *unbound object frame* control displays a picture or other objects from a source other than an Access table.
	The *bound object frame* control displays a picture or other objects from an Access table.
	The *line* control places a straight line on a report. You click the line crosshair at the starting point to make a line the length shown in the default properties box. You can also click and drag the line to any length.
	The *rectangle* control places a rectangle on the report to contain like items or to emphasize parts of a report.
	The *page break* control places a page break where you want it on a report.
Lock	The *tool lock* locks the other toolbox controls so they will stay active. Without the tool lock the toolbox buttons function once each time they are selected and then the pointer becomes active again. To turn the lock off, click the tool lock again.

Table 5-4. You can also click on the tools in the help window to see additional information.

The remaining tools (option group, toggle button, option button, check box, combo box, list box, and command button) are all used only on forms and will be described in the next chapter.

Making Your Changes

You now have the work area set up and you have briefly looked at the available tools. You know what changes are needed (see the earlier section, "Deciding What to Change"), so you can begin to make them by working in the design window.

You can use the print preview button at any time to check your progress in the design screen. Do this with these steps:

1. Click on the print preview button in the toolbar. The report, as it will be printed, is shown on the screen. Notice the mouse pointer is in the shape of a magnifying glass. This is the zoom tool and can be used to view the whole page. Click on the screen to zoom out and click again to zoom in. You can use the scroll bars to center the report in the window.

2. Click on Cancel to go back to the design window.

Removing the Totals   The totals should be removed from the Price column and from the OnHand column because it is not appropriate to add these items. The text boxes that calculate totals contain expressions that begin with an equal sign, for example =Sum(. . .). You can see these in the Category Footer window and the Report Footer window. Remove them by using these steps:

1. Select each box containing =Sum(. . .) and press Delete. To shorten this process you can select all of these text boxes at one time by pressing Shift while you click on each one. When you press Delete, all the selected boxes are removed.

2. There is still a box left in the Report Footer that contains the label Grand Total; click on this one and press Delete.

3. If you should make a mistake and delete the wrong object, choose Undo in the Edit menu, press its shortcut key Ctrl-Z, or click on the undo button (second from the right in the toolbar). Choose Undo now to see the box returned to the window. The Undo feature is your safety net.

Select the Grand Total box again and delete it.

4. Click on the print preview button in the toolbar. You can see there is space between the groups that must be closed. This space is caused by removing the total text boxes from the Category window. Click on Cancel to return to the design window.

5. The unwanted space is corrected by dragging the bar with the title `Page Footer` in it up to the Category Footer, closing the empty workspace. Do this by moving the mouse pointer to the top of the bar with `Page Footer` and when the pointer changes to a double-vertical arrow, drag it up as far as you can. Check the print preview window to see the changes.

Adding a Field A column containing ISBN could be added simply by running the ReportWizard again. In this exercise, though, try these steps to see how to add it manually using the design window.

1. Click on the text box button in the toolbox, on the right side of the second row from the top, as shown in Figure 5-6. The pointer will change to the text box icon with a crosshair attached.

2. The crosshair should be placed where you want the upper-left corner of the new text box. Here, place the crosshair in the Detail window on the upper-right corner of the OnHand text box and click. Your new box appears and is labeled `Unbound`.

3. If the properties dialog box is not already in the window, then with the new text box still selected, click on the properties button (third from the left). The Text Box dialog box will appear. Scroll the dialog box until you see Control Source. Click on Control Source, then on the arrow. The available fields will appear. Scroll the fields until you see ISBN.

4. Click on ISBN and it appears in the box you created, replacing the word *Unbound.*

Changing Line Properties   *Lines* are objects in the report that can be edited like any other object. Some differences exist in the way that lines are described, such as *width* meaning the length of a horizontal line and *height* meaning the length of a vertical line. The lines in this report need to be made longer to adjust for adding ISBN and thinner for aesthetics. Use these steps to do that:

1. Click on the top line in the Report Header to select it. The line now has handles to show it is selected. In the print preview window you can see that the line does not reach the right edge of the report.

2. In the properties dialog box, scroll down to the Border Width box and you see that this line has a border width of 2 points. This is the size or thickness of the line. Do not confuse border width with line width, which is the length of the line. Click on Border Width and an arrow appears on the right to indicate there are additional choices. Click on the arrow and then choose the 1 point option. The line changes when you make the selection.

3. In order to change the length of the line to include the width of the ISBN text box, you have to know the width of the report. Find this out by adding the length of the ISBN text box to the original length of the line.

    Select the ISBN text box and look at the properties; you see the left side of the box is at 4.74 inches from the left side of the report (yours might be different) and the box is one inch in width. Therefore the new line width will be 5.74 inches or what your left side position plus the box width turns out to be.

4. Once more select the top line and look at the properties. Scroll down to Width, click on it, and then change the width by typing **5.74** (or your number, if different) and pressing ⌷Enter⌷.

5. Change the two lines in the Page Header by following the same steps. You might have some trouble selecting the

bottom line; if you do, use the pointer to drag down the Detail header to expose it as you see here:

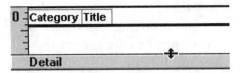

Changing Control Properties Another desired change is to remove the lines in the Category column. These lines are formed by the text box around the Category field. Remove them with these steps:

1. You can see there are two boxes containing the word *Category*, one in the Page Header and one in the Detail window. Click on the Category text box in the Detail window. The properties dialog box changes to reflect a text box as you see here:

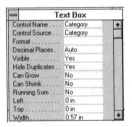

2. In the properties dialog box, scroll up or down until you see Border Style. Click on Border Style, then on the arrow to the right, and finally on Clear. This will cause the text box border to be transparent on the report.

3. Click on the print preview button. The preview window appears and it looks like there are still boxes around the Category column. Usually changing the border style of a text box to Clear is enough to cause the box to disappear, but the ReportWizard put this text box in a rectangle, so you are still seeing the rectangular border. It will continue to have a border until you make some more changes. Click on Cancel to return to the design window.

4.   Drag the Category Footer bar down so you can see the bottom line of the rectangle around the Category box. Now click on the line. Your properties dialog box should now have Rectangle in the title bar. Scroll down to Border Style and change it to Clear as you did in Step 2.

5.   Move the Category Footer bar back up even with the bottom of the Detail boxes. If this step is omitted, each row in your report will be separated by the distance you dragged the Category Footer bar.

6.   Now click on the print preview button to view your progress. Your screen should appear as you see in Figure 5-7.

Solving the Remaining Problems

With the print preview window still showing, you can see there are still some obvious problems with the report, including the following items:

◆   You need a heading for the new ISBN column.

◆   The numbers in the ISBN column need to be right-justified so that they are separated from the OnHand column.

◆   The report title is not centered.

Correct each of these items next.

Making Column Headings   The column heading is designed using a label box created with the label tool in the toolbox. Create a new heading now using these steps:

1.   Click on Cancel to return to the design window and then click on the label tool in the toolbox. This is the button with an *A*. When you move the pointer out of the toolbox and over to the Page Header area, it will change to a crosshair with the label icon attached.

2.   Place the crosshair on the upper-right corner of the OnHand label box in the Page Header and click. Notice the box is very narrow, but it will stretch when you start to type. You can also see that the crosshair changes back to the pointer when you click.

Figure 5-7
You can follow
the progress of
changes on the
preview screen.

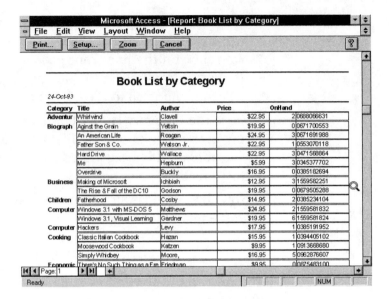

3. Type the letters **ISBN** and the box gets bigger to accommodate them. When you finish, click outside of the box. That is all there is to making label boxes.

   Your box took the font and other characteristics of the boxes already in the Page Header. Of course, you can change it any way you want using the properties dialog box to make the changes.

4. Select the ISBN label box again and then in the properties dialog box scroll down to Border Style and choose Clear, so the column heading will not be enclosed by a visible box.

Completing the Report   There are two more things to do to complete the report: center the heading and right-justify the ISBN column. To center the title in the Report Header, follow these steps:

1. Click on the label box containing the text, `Book List By Category`.

2. Place the pointer on the right-center sizing box and drag the side of the box to the right edge of the report. Since

you centered the Report Header in an earlier step, the title will automatically move to the center when you resize the box.

To right-justify the ISBN column use the following instructions:

1. Click on the ISBN box in the Detail window. The properties dialog box changes to Text Box.

2. Scroll to the Text Align box and choose the Right option. (You could alternatively have chosen the right-align button in the toolbar.) The column of numbers will now be aligned to the right edge of the report.

   An additional step you can take, if you wish, is to center the heading labels over the columns. Do this by selecting each label box and then dragging it to the center of the column. If you followed these steps including centering the headings, and selected page preview, your screen should appear like the one you see in Figure 5-8.

3. Save the report by choosing the Save option in the File menu.

4. Close the preview window by clicking on Cancel or double-clicking on the Control-menu box.

5. Close the report window by double-clicking on its Control-menu box. You will return to the database window.

Creating Mailing Labels

Access provides the means to create and change mailing labels using a ReportWizard, just as you created the report in the first part of this chapter. Making mailing labels is one of the simpler tasks you will perform while using Access. You can create mailing labels with these steps:

1. Open the database and table you plan to use for the name and address information. For this exercise use the Customers table in the Books database by clicking on Table and then Customers.

Figure 5-8

The redesigned
ReportWizard
report

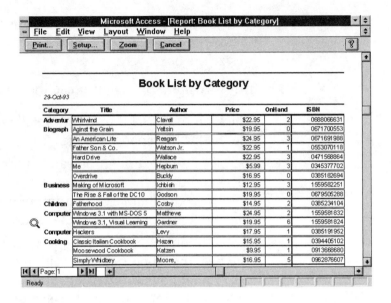

2. In order to remind you of the field names that are appropriate for labels, click on Open. The table appears and you
   see that a label can use First Name, Last Name, Address 1,
   City, ST, and ZIP. (Address 2 and Company could also be
   used but will not be here to keep it simple.)

3. After you decide on the fields to use, double-click on the
   Control-menu box for the table window to close it.

4. In the database window, click on the Report button and
   then on New. The New Report dialog box appears.

5. Click on the scroll arrow in the Select A Table/Query box and
   a list of the available tables will appear as you see here:

6. Choose Customers and the name appears in the Select A Table/Query text box.

7. Click on ReportWizards. A dialog box appears. Choose Mailing Label and then click on OK. The ReportWizard dialog box appears as shown in Figure 5-9.

This dialog box is similar to the ReportWizard dialog box seen in Figure 5-2. However, there are several added buttons and a window that allows you to add your own text to a label. You use the buttons in the window for navigating around the label. For example, after you choose a field and move it from the Available fields window to the Label appearance window, you must use the return (↵) button in the window (not the one on your keyboard) to move down one line. Try this with the following steps:

1. Click on First Name in the Available fields list and then on > to move the field over to the Label appearance window.

2. Click on Space to add a space after First name, then click on Last Name and move it across with the > button. You can see that both fields appear on the same line.

Figure 5-9

The label
ReportWizard
dialog box
allows you to
choose the
fields for the
mailing label.

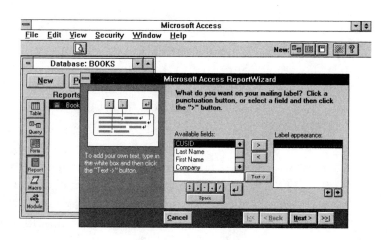

If you move another field now it will go on the same line, unless you move to the next line with the return (↵) button. To double-space, click the return button a second time.

3. Click on the return button to move the highlighted line down.

4. Choose Address 1 and move it across to the Label appearance side by clicking on the > button.

5. Again move the highlight down one line with the return button, then choose City and move it across to the highlighted line.

6. Form the rest of this line in the label by clicking on the comma and Space buttons, then on ST. Finish the line with two spaces and ZIP.

7. Click on Next. The next dialog box asks: Which field(s) do you want to sort by? Assume you want to sort the labels by ZIP code. In this case, scroll down to ZIP, select and move it across to the Sort order side, and then click on Next.

8. A dialog box appears and asks: What label size do you want? The size and type of label will depend on the ability of your printer. Access presents a list of Avery label numbers from which to choose. Scroll through this list and choose the style of label you want. For instance with a laser printer you might use the Avery number 5160. Click on your choice and then on Next.

9. Choose Print Preview to see the labels as they will be printed or the Design button if you want to change the ReportWizard design. If you clicked on Print Preview, then click anywhere in the window to zoom out so you can see the entire page. Your screen should look like that shown in Figure 5-10.

10. Save the mailing labels as a report by clicking on Save in the File menu. Give the report a name by typing a name

Figure 5-10

The preview
window, after
being zoomed
out, displays
the page layout
of the mailing
labels.

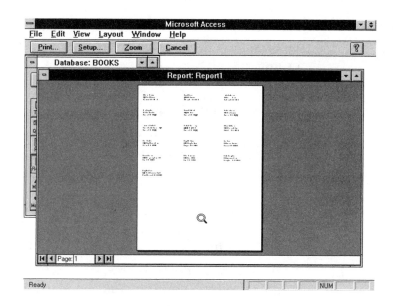

such as **Customer Mailing Label** in the Save As dialog box
as you see here:

11. Click on OK, then close the preview window by clicking
     on Cancel or double-clicking on the Control-menu box.

12. Close the report window by double-clicking on its
     Control-menu box.

With these steps you have created and saved a mailing label
report that is ready for printing.

Printing Reports and Labels

The reports you created and changed with Access in the previous
exercises demonstrate the ease with which you can do this. The
reports look great in the preview window but you only have an

audience of one. It is time to move the reports from your computer screen to a printed page. The first step is to set up your printer.

Printer Setup

Access uses Windows to control your printer. All the printers you installed in Windows are available to Access through the print options in the File menu. Usually you decide which printer will be the default and set that up with the Printers dialog box reached through the Windows Control Panel (see Chapter 2). You only need to make this setting once and it remains in the Windows setup information until it is changed.

Once you start work in Access, there is no need to think about the Windows printer controls. You can reach the printer dialog boxes using either the buttons on the toolbar or the options in the File menu.

Printer Setup from Print Preview

You can reach the Print Setup dialog box any time you are working in the print preview window by using these steps:

1. Select a report in the Database window, and click on the Preview button in that window or the print preview button in the toolbar. Either button opens the print preview window and adds four new buttons to the toolbar: Print, Setup, Zoom, and Cancel.

2. Click on the Setup button to get the Print Setup dialog box and then click on the More >> button to expand the Print Setup dialog box to include the item setup across the bottom of the box, as seen in Figure 5-11. You will look at this dialog box in more detail in the next section.

Printer Setup from the File Menu

There are times when you want to print a report that is stored in the database and you have no need to preview it. In these cases,

Figure 5-11

The Print Setup
dialog box with
the More >>
option chosen

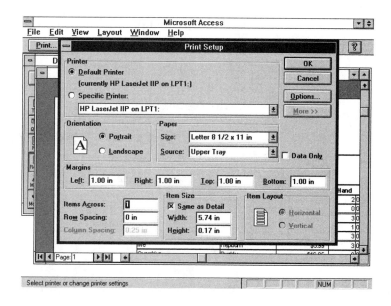

select the report in the Database window and then select Print
Setup in the File menu as you see here:

The Print Setup dialog box will appear and you can change the
setup just as you can from the preview window. Among the
changes you can make in the Print Setup dialog box are the following:

◆ You can change to another printer by clicking on the arrow
in the Specific Printer window. This arrow shows a list of all

the printers installed in Windows. Use the default printer or choose one by clicking on it in the list.

◆ You can change the print quality (if it is changeable on your printer) by choosing the Options button and getting the dialog box you see here:

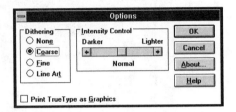

◆ You can change the orientation of printing on the page with the Orientation option buttons. These allow you to specify whether you want to print across the long side of the page (Landscape) or across the short side (Portrait). Click on the option button for the orientation that fits your print job.

◆ You can change the margins by clicking in each Margins box and replacing or editing the default numbers.

◆ You can change the spacing and size of labels using the text boxes and other controls across the bottom of the dialog box. These are different for different reports. For instance if you are previewing mailing labels, the Item Size area shows the size of the label you selected from the Avery list.

When you have made all the changes and the options are the way you want them, click on OK.

Printing Your Document

With the printer set up, you can now print using these steps:

1. Click on the Print button in the toolbar when the print preview window is active or use the File menu and click on Print. The Print dialog box appears as you see here:

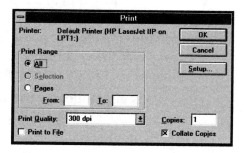

2. You can set the Print Range to print all pages or just the ones you want. To print less than all the pages in a report, click on the Pages option button. In the From box, type the starting page number; then click on the To box and type the last page number you want to print. For instance if you want to print only page 2, then in the From box type **2**, and in the To box type **2**. The print quality can be set from the highest density your printer will handle down to draft quality.

3. Set the number of copies by typing the number in the Copies box. When you click on OK in this dialog box the printer will print your report.

Summary

Chapter 5 has shown you how to create, change, and print reports and labels based on data in Access tables. The major points brought out in this chapter are as follows:

- In Access you can create reports both with the ReportWizards and manually using the Blank Report option.

- To delete a report you have to use Access since reports are not separate DOS files.

- A ReportWizard report can be edited in the design window, using the toolbox and toolbar tools.

◆ All the information in a report is produced by the controls you put there. *Control* is the term used by Access to indicate the objects you place in a report such as fields, text, and lines. These objects are either bound to a field in a table or are unbound, allowing you to type in the contents.

◆ The design window is the workspace used to create and change reports and is made up of the header, detail, and footer windows.

◆ The toolbox contains all the controls you can place in a report, including text boxes, label boxes, rectangles, and lines.

◆ After making changes, use the print preview option to view your progress and to see how the report will look when it is printed.

◆ The ReportWizards can be used to create mailing labels. Make the labels by answering the questions, such as which fields to place in the label. Use the buttons in the ReportWizard dialog box to place the fields where you want them.

◆ Printing reports and labels is accomplished by Access using Windows printer setup and dialog boxes and the print commands in the File menu.

The next chapter will show you how to create and change forms that you can use for data entry into the Access tables you have built and to get sorted and calculated information out of those tables onto your screen.

Creating and Customizing Forms

A *form* is a database object that allows data entry to, and displays data from, a table in a format similar to a paper form. The typical database form shows all the fields in the table and includes the field names and values in a single column; however, an Access form can be customized to present the data for a table in any format you choose.

A form is convenient to use because it usually allows you to see all fields in the table at the same time, making it easier for you to add or change data in a single record. A form can be designed to resemble paper forms that are familiar to the user. When you design a form, you can change the location of the fields that show data from the table, and you can also display additional information that is only part of the form design and is not be saved in the table. For example, you may want to include calculated totals, or you can insert graphs or other forms that show additional information. You also can add lines and borders and change the colors in which the data is displayed. In addition to displaying the data in an attractive format on the screen, you can also use a form to print the data for distribution.

Using a form does not necessarily restrict you to viewing one record at a time. You can switch from Form view to Datasheet

167

view, which displays multiple records as they are shown in a table. You will learn how to do this later in this chapter.

Creating Forms

There are two ways to create your own forms: You can use the FormWizards, which prompt you for the type of layout you want, or you can design the form on your own, starting with a blank form and placing all the fields manually. Using the FormWizards and then modifying the form they create is much easier than trying to create the forms from scratch and is what will be covered in this chapter.

Using the FormWizards

Using the FormWizards is an easy way to create a form and it is much like using the ReportWizards. You are asked what type of layout, which fields, and what style you want to use for the form. The layout choices are single-column, tabular, graph, and main/subform. After choosing the type of layout you want, you are asked to specify which fields are to be included in the form. Next, you choose the form style in which you want the information displayed. The style choices are standard, chiseled, shadowed, boxed, and embossed. In addition to choosing the layout, fields, and styles, you also enter a title for the form.

Use the FormWizards now to create a form for the Books table and learn more about the options. Windows and Access should be running, and the Books database should be open.

1. Click on the Form button to activate it as shown here:

2. Click on the New button to display the New Form dialog box that you see here:

3. Click on the down arrow to the right of the Select A Table/ Query box (or press ↓) to display the list of tables in the database. Choose Books. The name of the table is now displayed in the text box.

4. Click on the FormWizards button to display the first FormWizards dialog box, shown in Figure 6-1a, which shows the layout choices for the form. Table 6-1 describes each of the layout choices and how they affect the form.

5. Keep the default single-column layout, which is the most frequently used, and click on OK. The screen now displays the second FormWizards dialog box, shown in Figure 6-1b. This dialog box contains the list of fields that can be used in the form.

   To choose which fields will be in the form, you click on the field name and then click on the greater-than (>) symbol to the right of the list of field names. You will then see the field name in the box on the right indicating that it will be in the form. If you want to include all fields in the form, click on the button with the double greater-than symbols (>>). If you want to remove a field that you had previously chosen, click on the less-than (<) symbol, or if you want to remove all the fields you selected, click on the double less-than (<<) symbol.

6. Click on the double greater-than (>>) symbol to select all of the fields and then click on the Next button to display the third FormWizards dialog box, shown in Figure 6-1c. This dialog box contains a list of styles.

Figure 6-1

The FormWizards dialog boxes assist you in creating forms.

a)

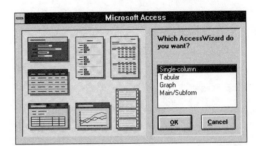

b)

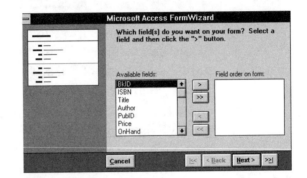

c)

d)

Table 6-1

Layout Options

Type of Layout	Effect on the Form
Single-column	The values in each field in a record are displayed in a single column. Only one record at a time is displayed.
Tabular	The values in each field are in columns similar to the way data is displayed in a table. Multiple records are displayed in this layout.
Graph	The data is displayed in a graph. You can choose from among several different types of graphs: bar, line, pie, area, or lines and markers.
Main/subform	This layout combines forms to display a one-to-many relationship. A single-column format is used for the main form (the "one" side of the relationship), and a tabular format is used to show the subform (the "many" side of the relationship).

When a style is chosen, an example of that style is displayed in the box at the left. Table 6-2 lists the styles and describes how they affect the appearance of the form.

7.   Accept the default Standard style and then click on Next to open the fourth FormWizards dialog box, shown in Figure 6-1d. Use this dialog box to enter the title of the form.

8.   Type **Book Inventory** for the title that will be displayed on the form.

Table 6-2

Style Options

Style	Effect on the Form
Standard	The values are displayed directly after each field name without additional enhancements
Boxed	A border is added around both the field name and the value
Chiseled	A line is added under the value to create a three-dimensional effect
Embossed	The value is displayed in a raised box
Shadowed	A shadow is added behind the box containing the value

9. Click on Open to see the data displayed in Form view. Click on the maximize button to zoom the form window to full size. Your screen should look like that shown in Figure 6-2.

Viewing Data

Once you have created a form, you can view the data in the form in both Form view and Datasheet view. Form view displays one record at a time while Datasheet view shows multiple records in the familiar table format. You can also use print preview to see how the form will look when it is printed. Look at the information in these various views before saving the form to see if you need to make changes to the layout:

◆ To change from Form view to Datasheet view, click on the datasheet view button, third from the left in the toolbar, as shown at left.

The familiar Access table is now displayed.

◆ To return to Form view, click on the form view button, second from the left in the toolbar. It looks like the button shown at left.

Figure 6-2

The Book Inventory form shows all the fields in a single record.

Microsoft Access - [Book Inventory]	

File　Edit　View　Records　Window　Help

Filter/Sort　Field: BkID

Book Inventory

BkID:	1
ISBN:	04251187
Title:	Stolen Blessings
Author:	Sanders
PubID:	6
Price:	$4.95
OnHand:	5
Order:	2
Category:	Mystery

Record: 1

Form View

Printing the Form

Before printing a form it is a good idea to look at it with print preview. As you saw with reports, print preview allows you to see how the form will look when it is printed. Print preview also can be used to zoom in, or magnify, the display so you can read it more easily. To see how the form will look when it is printed:

1.   Click on the print preview button, fourth from the left in the toolbar, or choose Print Preview from the File menu.

2.   Click on the Zoom button to magnify the display in the print preview window. You can also move the mouse pointer to any spot in the page display and click to magnify that particular area.

3.   Click again on the Zoom button to return to the original size.

4.   Click on the Cancel button to leave the print preview window.

You can print a form from the print preview window, or you can print it from Form view. These are the steps for each:

◆   To print the form from the print preview window, click on the Print button on the left of the toolbar. You can also choose Print from the File menu.

◆   To print from Form view, choose Print from the File menu.

Saving the Form

After you have created a form, if you try to close it, you will be asked if you want first to save the form. You can save it at that time or you can save the form before you try to close it. In either case, you have a choice of saving the form with the default name, Form#, or giving it a name of your choice. For the form you created above, save it with a unique name before closing the form. From the File menu, choose Save Form As. In the dialog box that appears, type **Book Inventory** and then click on OK to save the form.

Closing the Form

When you are finished using a form, it can be closed and, if saved, opened later when you want to use it again. To do that, follow these steps:

1. Double-click on the Control-menu box at the left end of the menu bar in the Form window, or choose Close from the File menu.

2. If you have not saved the form before trying to close it, a dialog box will appear and ask you if you want to save the form now. You can answer Yes to save the form before closing, No to not save the form and continue to close it, or Cancel to neither save nor close the form.

3. If you choose Yes to save the form, a dialog box is displayed where you can either accept the suggested name—Form#—or enter a new name. In either case, click on OK to complete saving and closing the form.

When the form is closed, it is no longer on the screen, and the form name is displayed in the database list.

Deleting a Form

If you no longer want a form, you can reclaim the space it was taking on your hard disk and remove its name from the list in the Database window by deleting it. Do that with these steps:

1. Click on the form name in the Database window and press Delete. A dialog box, as shown below, will be displayed asking if you want to delete the form. (Do not delete the Book Inventory form.)

2. Click on Cancel in this case; but if you wanted to delete a form, you would click on OK, the form would be deleted,

and the form name would no longer be displayed in the database list.

Customizing Forms

The layout of the fields on a form can be changed to present the data in a format that is more logical and convenient to view or enter. You can also change the labels and add borders and lines to enhance the appearance. In addition, information that is not in the table can be inserted, such as calculated totals based on other fields in the table; or you can add check boxes and buttons, lists, objects, or change the colors used on the form.

You use the toolbox that is displayed in Design view to customize your form. Chapter 5 covered some of the tools in the toolbox (pointer, label, text box, graph, unbound object frame, bound object frame, line, rectangle, page break, and tool lock). The remaining tools (option group, toggle button, option button, check box, combo box, list box, and command button) are used to add their respective objects to a form. Table 6-3 describes the use of the object on the form. The toolbox is shown here:

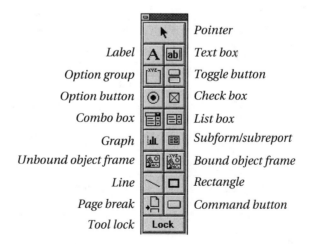

Toggle buttons, options buttons, and check boxes are all *exclusive*; that is, only one in a group can be selected. This is unlike Windows dialog boxes where check boxes are not exclu-

Table 6-3

Toolbox Tools
Used in Forms

Tool	Use of the Resulting Object on the Form
	An *option group* is used when you want to group together more than one check box, option button, or toggle button (see below) on a form. An option group gives the user of the form a choice of one of several items.
	A *toggle button* allows the form's user to make a yes-or-no, or on-or-off choice. A toggle button is a rectangle with text or a picture on it (see next page). It can be used alone or in a group where the form's user can select one item from a group of items. In a form, the toggle button appears to be pressed down when it is selected or on, and appears up otherwise.
	The *option button*, like the toggle button, allows the form's user to make a yes-or-no, or on-or-off choice and can be used by itself or in a group to select one item from a group of items. An option button is a circle and shows a dot in the middle when it is selected or turned on (see next page). Option buttons are also called "radio buttons" because they work like the buttons on a car radio.
	The *check box*, like both a toggle button and an option button, can be used by itself to make a yes-or-no, or on-or-off choice, or it can be used in a group to choose one item from a group of items. A check box contains an × when it is selected, or turned on, and it is clear when it is turned off.
	The *list box* displays a list of choices from which the user can select a value. The list of values is always displayed on the screen, usually with a scroll bar.
	The *combo box* displays a list of choices similar to a list box; however, in a combo box the form's user can also type a value in the text box at the top of the list. The list is not displayed on the screen until the user clicks on the down arrow at the right of the text box.
	The *command button* allows the form's user to perform a command or a set of commands. For example, a command button might be used to save and close a form similar to an OK command button in a Windows dialog box.

sive. In an Access form the only difference among the three objects is how they look—you can see the differences here:

Modifying the Layout

The fields in a form can be moved to new positions to make the form easier to use or more attractive. For example, in a form for a customers table, you can rearrange fields for the first name, last name, and parts of the address to resemble the layout used in an address on a letter or on an envelope—a format that is more familiar to users.

In the next exercise, rearrange the fields in the Book Inventory form. You will use the Design button in the Database window to display the form in Design view and then place several short fields on one line and group other fields into logical areas on the form. Access should be running with only the Database window open and the Books database active.

1. Click on the Form button if it is not already active. The Book Inventory form should be selected.

2. Click on the Design button in the Database window. If the Form window is not maximized already, click on the maximize button in the upper-right corner to make the form fill the window. It is easier to work on the form when it is larger. The form is displayed in Design view as shown in Figure 6-3.

3. Drag on the title bar of the toolbox to move it to the right side of the window as shown in Figure 6-3.

Table 6-4 describes how the parts of a form in Design view are used.

Figure 6-3

When the Book Inventory form is in Design view you can rearrange the fields, change labels, and add text as needed.

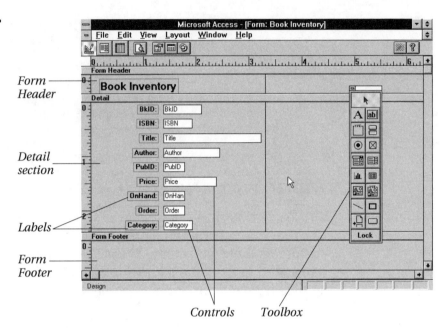

Moving the Controls and Attached Labels

You can move controls with their labels to new positions, or you can move the controls separately from their labels. You can also change the size of both the text boxes and the labels, and add or change the text displayed in the labels.

Now move the BkID field to the left, and then move the ISBN field up and to the right of the BkID field using the following steps:

1. Move the mouse pointer to any spot in the BkID control (anywhere in the BkID label or data field) and hold down the mouse button. The pointer changes to a hand like this:

2. Drag the control to the left.

3. In a similar fashion, move the ISBN field up and to the right of the BkID field. Be sure when you point on the con-

Table 6-4

Parts of a Form

Part	Use
Form Header	Displays the title of the form that will appear at the top of your finished form. This header will not appear on subsequent pages. If you want a header on all pages, you can turn one on by using the Page Hdr/Ftr option in the Layout menu. You will then see two additional bars in the form Design view window where you can enter text and graphics that will appear at the top and/or bottom of each page.
Detail	Shows the fields in the form and their attached labels. When you display or print the form, the detail section will be repeated for each record, as many times as will fit on a page.
Form Footer	Displays text or graphics that will appear only at the very end of the form. If you want a footer on each page, you can turn one on by using the Page Hdr/Ftr option discussed above for the Form Header.
Controls	Display data or perform an action when the form is used. Most objects in the Detail section of the form are controls including fields with their labels, buttons, and lines. In the initial Design view, the field name is shown in both the label on the left and the text box (seen in white in Figure 6-3); however, when the form is used, actual data will show in the text box—the field name will only show in the label.
Labels	Display the field name or other descriptive text to identify a field. The field names or other text in labels will be shown both in Design view and when the form is used. For example, the label for the first text box in the Books Inventory form is BkID.
Toolbox	Contains the tools used to add other controls, borders, groups, and lists to a form. It is displayed by default in the lower-left corner of the design window. In Figure 6-3 the toolbox has been moved so that the other sections of the design window are more easily seen. The toolbox can be closed by clicking on its Control-menu box in the upper-left corner of the toolbox's title bar. To display the toolbox again, choose Toolbox from the View menu.

trol that the pointer changes to a hand, not an I-beam. You may have to click on the Detail section background and then click again on the control to display the hand.

4. Practice moving other fields to new positions as shown in Figure 6-4. You can drag the vertical line shown in the center of the window to the right if you need more space; however, it will be moved automatically if you move a control to a position that requires more space. You can also drag the Form Footer bar down to enlarge the Detail section.

 Note Controls in a form can be copied as well as moved. First select the control and choose Copy from the Edit menu. Then choose Paste from the Edit menu. The copy will overlap the original control. You can then drag the copy to a new location.

Separating the Labels and Controls

You may want to move the labels so they are above the controls rather than on the same line. The following exercise shows how

Figure 6-4

The Book Inventory form in Design view shows controls that have been moved.

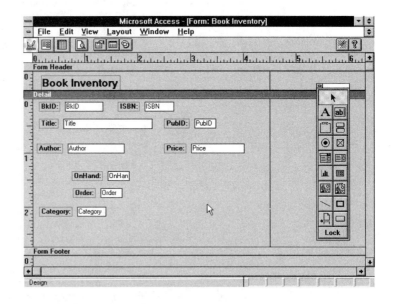

Figure 6-5

This Book Inventory form shows controls with their labels on different lines.

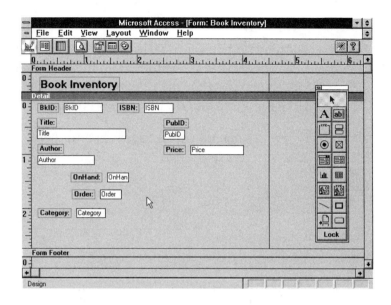

to position the controls and the labels for Title, Author, and PubID fields so that your form resembles the Book Inventory form shown in Figure 6-5.

1. Move the Title text box below its accompanying label by pointing on its move handle in the upper-left corner, as shown here:

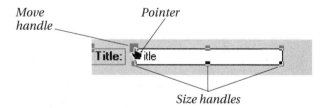

When you use the move handle, the pointer becomes a hand with a pointing finger.

2. When the pointer becomes the pointing finger, drag the Title text box down to a position below the label.

3. Repeat Steps 1 and 2 for the Author and PubID fields so that your form resembles that shown in Figure 6-5.

Resizing Controls

It may be helpful to change the size of a text box in order to display all the data. The following steps show how to change the size of the text box for the title by dragging the size handles located at the right end and on the top and bottom lines of the box:

1. Click on the Title text box to display the size handles that you see here:

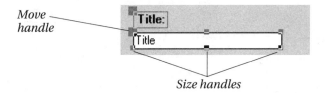

Move handle

Size handles

2. Position the pointer on one of the size handles at the right end of the box. The pointer will become a two-headed arrow pointing at a 45-degree angle. Drag the end of the box to the right to increase its length.

3. Make the box slightly taller by positioning the pointer on the size handle in the center of the bottom line and dragging it down.

If you want to change size both vertically and horizontally at the same time, point to any corner except the upper-left corner and drag the corner diagonally away from the corner.

Selecting Several Controls at Once

When you select several controls, the screen shows a rectangle (when you hold down the mouse button) around the ones you have selected. This is an easy way to move or realign several controls at once.

To move the OnHand and Order text boxes to the left by selecting both controls at once, use the following steps:

1. Move the pointer slightly above and to the left of the OnHand label—it must be outside of the OnHand label box.

2.   Hold down the mouse button and drag the pointer diagonally so that a rectangle is drawn around both the OnHand and the Order controls.

3.   Release the mouse button. Both controls are now selected, but the rectangle now does not appear on the screen.

4.   Then point anywhere in the area that was selected in the rectangle. Hold down the mouse button to display a hand. The rectangle will now also be displayed on the screen.

5.   Drag the rectangle to the left, the same way you move a single control.

Modifying Labels

You can edit the text shown in labels, and you can also add labels that are not attached to any control. These freestanding labels may be used to provide additional instructions for entering data in the table or add any other information that you may want to display in the form.

Editing a Label

You can expand or change the text that is displayed in a label so that it is more easily read. For example, in the Book Inventory form it would be helpful to change the label BkID to read Book ID. Follow these steps:

1.   Slowly click twice (do not double-click) on the BkID label to select the text. Be sure no handles are showing.

2.   Click the insertion point between the *B* and the *k* and type **oo**.

3.   Move the insertion point in front of the *I* and press (Spacebar) to insert a space between *k* and *I*.

4.   Move the text box to the right and adjust the size of the label so that the characters in Book ID are on one line, like this:

Book ID: BkID

Adding a Freestanding Label

To add text that is not attached to a control on the form, use the label tool in the toolbox.

Add the information *See Suppliers table* to the right of the PubID text box using the following steps:

1. Click on the label tool in the toolbox. It looks like the tool shown at left.

2. Point about 1½ inches to the right of and on a level with the PubID label and click. A small rectangle will be displayed as you see here:

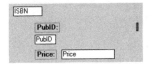

   The small rectangle is where you will type the text for the new label. The box is positioned at the far right of where you want the text because the text will move to the left as you type.

3. Type **See Suppliers table** in the new label box. You may have to move the label to the right or left to position it relative to the PubID label.

Adding and Changing Lines and Borders

You can enhance the appearance of the form by adding lines to separate one group of fields from another, or you can add a border to make a logical group of several related fields.

Adding and Changing a Line

You can insert a line to separate various sections of the form. For example, you may want to insert a line to separate the form's header from the other sections. If the form is printed, this can enhance the appearance of the information. Both horizontal and vertical lines can be inserted at any position in the form.

To insert a horizontal line below the form's header:

1. Increase the size of the Form Header area in the design window by pointing on the top of the Detail line (the mouse pointer becomes a horizontal bar with a vertical double-headed arrow) and drag the line down about ⅛ inch.

2. Click on the line tool (shown at left) in the toolbox.

3. Point on the left side of the Form Header area about 1/16 inch below the first letter in the title.

4. Press and hold (Shift) and drag the mouse pointer to the right side of the form (the vertical line at about 4¾ inches). Release the mouse button and only then release (Shift).

    Holding (Shift) down assures that the line will remain horizontal. If you do not hold (Shift) down and inadvertently move the mouse pointer up or down, you will insert a diagonal line.

Your new line should be selected with the size handles displayed (if not, click on the line).

To change the length of the line:

1. Point on the right end of the line so the mouse pointer becomes a two-headed arrow pointing at a 45-degree angle. Drag the line to the left to shorten it and release the mouse button when the line is equal in length to the title.

    When you are sizing a line after you have completed drawing it, (Shift) no longer helps you keep the line horizontal so you must be more careful moving the mouse.

2. If your line tool is still active, click on the pointer tool at the top of the toolbox to activate it.

Now that you have changed the layout and added a line, see how the form looks by first switching to Form view and then to print preview:

1. Click on the form view button, second from the left in the toolbar, as you see here:

    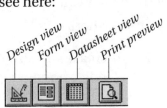

2. To see how the form will look if you decide to print it, click on the print preview button (fourth from the left). In the print preview window, click on Zoom and then adjust your window with the scroll bars so you can see the first record, as shown in Figure 6-6.

    Notice several things about the form as it currently exists in Figure 6-6: the ISBN field is too small to display the full ISBN; the Book ID field is too large; it is not easy to see where one record ends and another starts; the OnHand and Order numbers do not command your attention the way they should; and you are lacking a field that displays the value of the inventory by multiplying the quantity on

Figure 6-6

Using print preview shows you what a form will look like when you print it.

hand by the price. This is the purpose of looking at print preview at this stage—to determine what needs to be changed to produced a polished form.

3. Click on Cancel to return to Form view and then on the design view button (on the far left of the toolbar) to return to the Form design window, where you can make your changes.

Changing the Field Widths and Adding a Separating Line

The first changes to make are to adjust the two field widths and add a separating line at the bottom of the form. Do that with these instructions:

1. Click on the Book ID text box to display the size handles.

2. Point on the lower-right corner so the two-headed arrow appears. Drag that corner to the left to shorten the text box so it is only about ½ inch wide.

3. Click on the ISBN text box and drag its lower-right corner to the right to lengthen the text box so it is about ¾ inch wide.

4. Drag the Form Footer down so that there is at least ¾ inch between it and the Category control.

5. Click on the line tool in the toolbox, press and hold ⌈Shift⌉, and then draw a line between the left and the right margins halfway between the Category control and the Form Footer (about ⅜ inch below the Category control). Release the mouse button before releasing ⌈Shift⌉. Your screen should look something like Figure 6-7.

Adding and Formatting Borders

The next task is to add a border around the OnHand and Order fields to call attention to their important information. You will then format the border with one of three special effects: a three-dimensional look which can be either raised or sunken, or a shadow effect.

Figure 6-7

The Design
view window
looks like this
after changing
the field widths
and adding a
line at the
bottom.

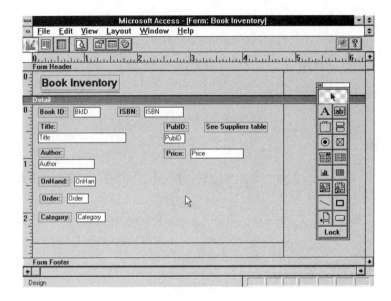

Start by adding a border around the OnHand and Order fields
with these steps:

1. Click on the rectangle tool (shown at left) in the toolbox to
    activate it.

2. Point on a spot slightly above and to the left of the OnHand
    label. Then hold down the mouse button and drag down
    and to the right to create a rectangle which includes the
    OnHand and Order controls and their labels. When you
    are slightly to the right of these fields, release the mouse
    button.

3. The rectangle will cover the controls. To correct that, open
    the Layout menu and choose Send to Back to display the
    controls and the attached labels. This border now shows
    handles. You can resize it the way other parts of the form
    can be resized.

Next use the palette tool to format the border with a raised
three-dimensional effect. Follow these steps to do this:

1. If the border is not already selected, click anywhere within
    or on the border, but not on the fields. You may have to

click first somewhere outside the border, then click on it
again.

2.   Click on the palette button in the toolbar to display the
palette shown here:

Palette button

Palette

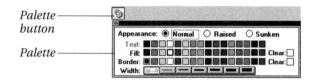

3.   Click on the Raised button in the palette. The design window now shows a different effect for the border.

4.   Click on the print preview button in the toolbar to see how
the form will look when it is printed. Your screen should
look like Figure 6-8.

5.   When you are done looking at the form, click on Cancel to
return to Design view.

6.   Close the palette by double-clicking on its Control-menu
box.

Figure 6-8

Now the Book
ID and ISBN
fields are better
sized, and you
can easily
distinguish
between
records; the
OnHand and
Order fields
stand out, too.

Adding and Changing Calculated Fields

One of the advantages of using a form for data is that you can enter a control that displays the results of adding, subtracting, multiplying, or dividing values in existing controls. For example, in the Book Inventory form, it would be helpful to display the current value of the inventory for each of the books on hand. To do this, an arithmetic expression can be inserted in a control text box that multiplies the value in the Price field by the value in the OnHand field.

Inserting a New Calculated Field

When you add a new field in Design view, that field will be displayed in Datasheet view as well as in Form view. You first create the new text box and then use its properties dialog box to enter the expression that will perform the calculation.

Creating the Text Box for the Calculated Field   The first step in adding a calculated field is to insert a new text box that will display the results of the calculation:

1. Click on the text box tool in the toolbox, as shown at left, to activate it.

2. Click below the Price field to insert the new control. A control and attached label containing a field number are displayed. Access automatically assigns a field number and yours may be different than the one shown here:

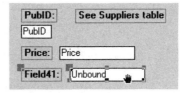

3. Move the mouse pointer until it is an open hand and then drag the new field so that it is aligned with the Price field as shown above.

Entering the Calculation Expression   To insert the expression in the text box, you need to display the properties dialog box for the control.

1. Double-click on the new text box or choose Properties from the View menu to display the properties dialog box. If the new text box is not already selected, click on it. Your screen should now resemble Figure 6-9.

You can also display the properties dialog box by clicking on the control text box and then clicking on the properties button in the toolbar.

2. Drag across the existing name in the Control Name text box in the Text Box dialog box and type **Inventory Value**. This new name will replace the field number in the label.

3. Move the pointer down to the text box for Control Source and type this expression: =[**price**]*[**onhand**]. This will show, in the Inventory Value field, the result of multiplying the value in the Price field by the value in the OnHand field. Be sure to enclose each field name in square brackets ([ ])

Figure 6-9

The properties for the new text box are shown in the Text Box dialog box.

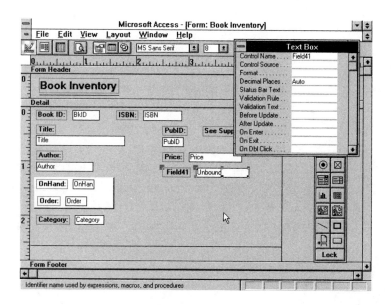

4. Move the pointer down to the Format drop-down list box. Notice that a down arrow appears when you move into the box. Click on the down arrow to display the list of formats. Scroll through the list and choose Currency as the format to be used for this control.

5. Leave Decimal Places at Auto and clear the Text Box dialog box from the window by double-clicking on its Control-menu box. The expression now appears in the new text box in the form like this:

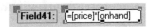

Entering Text for the New Field's Label   You can now change the text in the label for the new field to show the function or use of the new field:

1. Slowly click twice on the label until no handles are displayed.

2. Drag across the existing field name and type **Inventory Value**.

3. Move the label and control text box to the right so they are aligned under *Price*.

Viewing the Form   See how the form now displays the calculated field:

1. Click on the form view button (second from left in the toolbar). The results of the calculation are displayed as shown in Figure 6-10.

2. Click on the design view button (at the far left of the toolbar) to leave Form view and return to Design view.

Changing the Calculated Field

The calculated field can be moved or resized the same way that any other control or attached label is changed. You can also change the expression so that it produces different results. You

Figure 6-10

The form now shows the inventory value in the new calculated field.

```
─                  Microsoft Access - [Book Inventory]          ▼ ▲
─  File  Edit  View  Records  Window  Help                        ▲
 ☒ ▣ ▥ ▢ ☒  Filter/Sort: ☒ ☒ ☒  Field: BkID    ▣         ☒ ?

    Book Inventory
 ▶  Book ID:    [  1]   ISBN:  [042511872X]
    Title:                      PubID:     See Suppliers table
    [Stolen Blessings        ]   [   6]
    Author:                     Price:      [    $4.95]
    [Sanders        ]
                                Inventory Value  [   $24.75]
    OnHand:    [   5]
    Order:     [   2]

    Category:  [Mystery]


 ┃◀ ◀ Record:1  ▶ ▶┃
 Form View
```

do this by just editing the text that is displayed in the text box; you do not have to display the properties dialog box again.

Suppose you want to modify the expression that multiplies the price of a book by the amount of the orders so that you can see the total value of the orders for each book (be sure you are in Design view to do this):

1. Slowly click twice in the text box for the new Inventory Value field. Be sure the pointer is an I-beam and that the size and move handles are not showing.

2. Place the pointer in the text box containing the expression and drag across *onhand*.

3. Type **order**. Be sure you did not delete or type over the brackets or the multiplication sign.

4. To see the results, click on the form view button in the toolbar. The field should now display the results of the edited expression. Then return to Design view.

5. Follow Steps 1 through 3 to restore the expression to =[price]*[onhand] for the Inventory Value.

Adding and Using Option Buttons and Check Boxes

Option buttons and check boxes are used to get yes/no decisions or to have one item chosen from among several items in a group. In the following exercises you will add both a single check box and a group of option buttons.

Adding a Check Box

In the Book Inventory form, it would be helpful to indicate when it is time to reorder a specific book. You can add a check box that will be turned on automatically when the value in the OnHand field is at zero (or any other amount that is appropriate). To do this, insert a check box with an expression that produces this result:

1. Click on the rectangle around the OnHand and the Order controls to select it.

2. Drag the middle size handle in the right border roughly ½ inch to the right so the new control can be inserted in it.

3. Click on the check box tool (shown to the left) in the tool-box to activate it.

4. Click to the right of and in line with the Order control to insert the check box.

5. Double-click on the check box text box, or select Properties from the View menu, to open the Check Box properties dialog box.

6. In the Control Name box, type **Reorder**.

7. In the Control Source box, type the expression =**[onhand]=0**. Leave the other properties as they are.

8. Slowly click twice on the label for the new field. Be sure no size or move handles are showing. An I-beam should be displayed in the box. Drag across the existing name and type **Reorder** as the text for the label.

9. See how the check box works by clicking on the form view button in the toolbar. Then move the pointer to the OnHand field, delete the value that is displayed there, and type **0**. Click on the print preview button in the toolbar. An × should now be showing in the Reorder box as you can see in Figure 6-11.

10. Click on Cancel to return to the Form view, restore the value in the OnHand field to 5, and click on the design view button.

Adding an Option Group

An option group consists of a label and a frame into which you can insert check boxes, toggle buttons, and option buttons. You can also add text that will be displayed in the status bar explaining each button or check box. The option group can be bound to a field, unbound, or it can contain an expression. The value entered in the database when a button or check box is selected on the form is always numeric. The default values are 1 for the

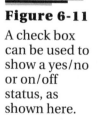

Figure 6-11

A check box can be used to show a yes/no or on/off status, as shown here.

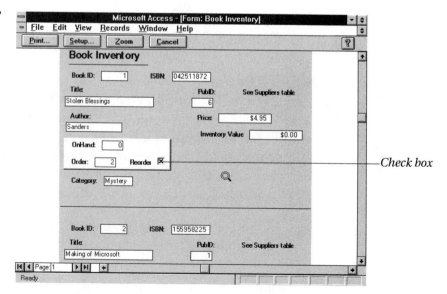

first button, 2 for the second button, 3 for the third button, and so on. You can, however, change these to different numeric values using the properties dialog box. The value corresponding to the button selected is then displayed in the table in the field to which this control is bound.

Here, add an option group that specifies the reading level of each book. Four reading levels (Easy, Average, Difficult, and Hard) will be displayed in the labels for option buttons that are included in the group frame, and the status line will define the grade levels for each.

Adding a New Field to the Books Table　You will need to add a new field, Reading Level, to the Books table so that the option group can be bound to that field. Do that with these steps:

1.　Close the form by double-clicking on its Control-menu box. When prompted to save the form, click on Yes.

2.　Click on the Table button in the Books database, select Books, and click on Design.

3.　Add the new field, Reading Level, at the end of the list of fields. Choose Number as the Data Type and Integer as the Field Size. Then double-click on the Table window Control-menu box to close it, answer Yes to save the table revision, and return to the Database window.

Creating a Bound Option Group　You are now ready to add an option group to the form that is linked or bound to the field you just added. This will be done by selecting the option group tool from the toolbox, opening a list of fields, and then dragging the Reading Level field where you want to place the option group. It is very important that you do the procedure in this order. Otherwise you will not attach, or *bind*, the field to the option box:

1.　In the Database window, click on Form (Book Inventory should already be selected) and click on Design to go to Design view for the Book Inventory form.

2.　Click on the option group tool (shown at left) in the toolbox.

3.   Click on the field list button in the toolbar (shown below), or choose Field List from the View menu, to display the list of field names in the Books table.

4.   Scroll down the field list until you see Reading Level.

5.   Point on Reading Level in the field list, and press and hold the mouse button while dragging the small rectangle—representing the Reading Level field—to a position on the form beneath the Inventory Value where you want the option group to sit. Release the mouse button. The option group frame will appear with Reading Level as its label, similar to what you see in Figure 6-12.

| Tip |

By dragging a field from the field list with the option group tool to the group's intended location, you attach the field to the group.

Figure 6-12

A new option group that is attached to the Reading Level field has been dragged from the field list with the option group tool.

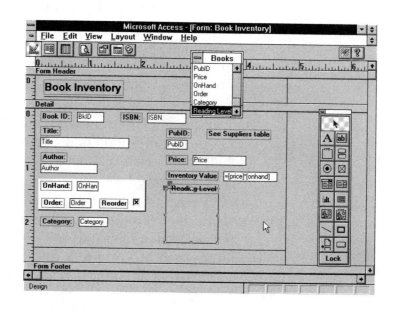

6. Use the size and move handles to adjust the frame and label so that the frame is moved down, shortened, and stretched out to the right, as shown here:

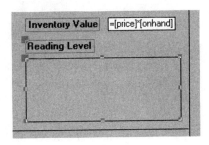

Adding Option Buttons   Next add the option buttons, change their labels and properties, and add their status bar text with the following instructions:

1. Click on the option button tool (shown at left) in the toolbox. Then click on the place in the option group frame where you want the first option button to appear (the crosshairs represent the upper-left corner of the button, and the label will stick out to the left). Figure 6-13 shows how the option buttons are placed in the group.

2. Repeat Step 1 for the three additional option buttons.

3. Click on each label, drag across the existing label text, and then type: **Easy** for the first button, **Average** for the second button, **Difficult** for the third button, and **Hard** for the fourth button. Figure 6-13 shows how the form will look with the correct labels.

4. Look at the properties of each button and change its option value to correspond to the label you just entered. To do that, double-click on the Easy *button* (not the label) to display the properties dialog box. Type **4** in the Option Value box as the value of that option.

5. Move the pointer to the Status Bar text box where the text to be displayed in the status bar will be typed. To make it easier to enter the text, press [Shift]-[F2] to expand the text box. Type **Grade 4 through 6 reading level**.

Figure 6-13

The Form design window shows the option group containing four option buttons.

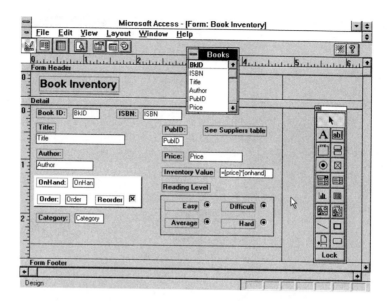

6. Repeat Steps 4 and 5 for the remaining buttons. Click on each to display its properties (or double-click if the properties dialog box is not already displayed) and enter the following: for the Average button, enter **7** as the Option Value and type **Grade 7 through 8 reading level** for the status bar text; for the Difficult button, type **9** and **Grade 9 through 12 reading level**; and for the Hard button, type **13** and **Grade 13 through 17 reading level**.

7. To see how the option group works, click on the form view button. In the first record, click on the Average button. Notice the status bar displays the text defining the reading level.

8. Repeat Step 7 for the other books, choosing an appropriate reading level. Then click on the datasheet view button to view the Reading Level field in the table layout with the new entries you just made on the form. The Reading Level value for the first book is displayed as 7, as shown in Figure 6-14, which is the value that you entered for the Average button.

Figure 6-14

In the
Datasheet view
of the Book
Inventory form,
you can see the
inventory
values, reorder
check boxes,
and reading
levels for
several records
at once.

Author:	PubID	Price:	OnHand	Order:	Category:	Inventory Value	Reorder	Reading Level
Sanders	6	$4.95	5	2	Mystery	$24.75		7
Ichbiah	1	$12.95	3	1	Business	$38.85		9
Sheldon	7	$3.50	4	1	Mystery	$14.00		4
Gardner	1	$19.95	6	2	Computer	$119.70		4
Ludlum	4	$5.95	4	1	Mystery	$23.80		7
Tidwell	1	$19.95	3	1	Governmen	$59.85		7
Clancy	6	$4.95	6	2	Thriller	$29.70		7
Peristen	1	$12.95	2	1	Travel	$25.90		4
Follett	11	$4.95	2	1	Mystery	$9.90		9
Matthews	1	$24.95	2	1	Computer	$49.90		7
Cussler	14	$5.95	3	1	Mystery	$17.85		4
Coonts	10	$5.95	2	1	Thriller	$11.90		9
Deighton	3	$5.95	1	1	Thriller	$5.95		13
Moore,	20	$16.95	5	2	Cooking	$84.75		7
Reagan	14	$24.95	3	1	Biography	$74.85		9
Hawking	4	$16.95	1	1	Science	$16.95		13
Coyle	13	$4.95	0	1	Thriller	$0.00	☒	9
Hillerman	8	$4.95	1	1	Mystery	$4.95		13
Watson Jr.	4	$22.95	1	1	Biography	$22.95		7
Hepburn	3	$5.99	3	1	Biography	$17.97		7
Asimov	4	$5.99	0	1	Sci. Fic.	$0.00	☒	7
Wallace	12	$22.95	3	1	Biography	$68.85		7
Yeltsin	15	$19.95	0	1	Biography	$0.00	☒	13
Godson	16	$19.95	0	1	Business	$0.00	☒	9
Puzo	4	$5.99	1	1	Thriller	$5.99		7
Gibson	4	$5.99	0	1	Sci. Fic.	$0.00	☒	13

9. Click again on the design view button to return to the Design view.

Adding a List Box

A box showing a list of choices is helpful in maintaining consistency in entering values into the database. For example, in the Category field in the Books table, many of the categories are repeated. It would be helpful if the user could choose from a list when indicating the category in which a specific book belongs.

You can use either the list box tool or the combo box tool for that purpose. If you use the list box tool, the entire list will be displayed on the screen. This is appropriate if you have a short list. If you have a long list, the combo box is a better choice. It will display the list only when you click on the arrow beside the text box, thus taking up less space in the form. Also, a combo box allows the user to type the first characters of the value, and Access will scroll through the list to find the matching characters.

In this exercise, you will replace the Category field with a combo box that displays the list of category names when it is opened:

1. Click on the Category text box and its label, and press [Delete] to delete that control.

2. Click on the combo box tool (shown at left) in the toolbox.

3. Click on the field list button in the toolbar to display the list of field names, if it is not already displayed, and scroll down until you can see the Category field.

4. Drag the Category field to the position in the form where you want to insert the combo box and release the mouse button.

5. Adjust the position and size of the control and its label the same way you have adjusted other controls and their labels. Your screen now should resemble Figure 6-15.

Creating a List for a List or Combo Box

You now need to use the properties dialog box to enter the list that will be displayed in the combo box:

1. Double-click on the drop-down list part of the combo box you just created, or click on the properties button in the toolbar and then click on the drop-down list.

Figure 6-15

The form in Design view with the new Category drop-down list box positioned correctly

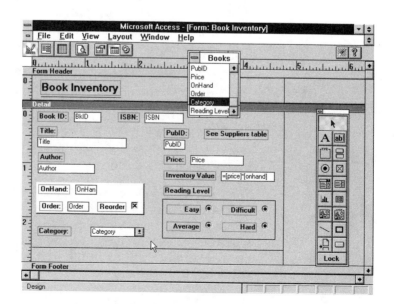

2. Click on the Row Source Type box, and click on the down arrow at the right of the box to display the list of choices. Select Value List.

    Value List specifies that the type of information in each row in the list box will be a value, though not necessarily a number. The values for the form you are building are: Adventure, Biography, Business, etc. These are the values that will be inserted in the database when the form is used.

    The other two choices for the row source type are Table/Query and Field List. Table/Query allows you to attach another table or query to the form. The list or combo box whose row source type is Table/Query will display the leftmost column of the table or query. The Field List choice displays a list of field names for a given table. You can use Field List to identify where in a table to look up something.

3. Click on the Row Source box. Here you will enter the topics or categories that will be listed on the form and from which the user will choose when the combo box list is displayed.

4. Press Shift-F2 to expand the text box. This makes it easier to enter text (see Figure 6-16). Type the list as follows:

    Adventure;Biography;Business;Children;Computer; Cooking;Economics;Explorat.;Flying;Government; Mystery;Science;Sci. Fic.;Social Sci.;Thriller;Travel.

    Type without spaces (except between words) and without pressing Enter at the end of lines. Each category, which is separated by a semicolon (;), will be on a separate line in the combo box on the actual form. Some of the categories are abbreviated so they will fit in the field. Click on OK to leave the Zoom window.

Tip

You can create a list in two or more columns. To do this, click on Column Count in the properties dialog box and type the number of columns you want. Then in the Row Source box, type the values: 1;Adventure;2;Biography;3;Business; and so on. The number will be in the first column and the category name will be in the second.

Figure 6-16

The Zoom window provides a large text entry box for whatever properties text box is currently selected.

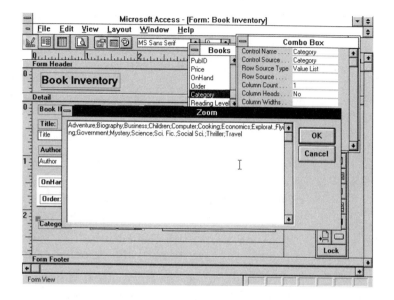

5. Test the combo list by clicking on the form view button. At the first record, click on the down arrow for the Category box. The new list will be displayed as in Figure 6-17. Mystery is the category currently specified for this record. Scroll through the list and move the pointer to a new cate-

Figure 6-17

List and combo boxes are powerful tools on a form for choosing from a fixed list of items.

gory, if you like, to choose it. Then return the category to Mystery.

6.   Click on the design view button to return to Design view.

Using Colors and Other Graphical Attributes

You can easily change the colors or other graphical attributes of various elements on a form to make it easier to read, to call attention to a particular section, or to please your eye. To do this, you simply click on the area that you want to change and then click on the palette button. In the palette you can select whatever options you want to apply to the selected area.

In the Book Inventory form, the text boxes and labels may be easier to read if the background is in a contrasting color. Also, you can emphasize the option group box with a border and a different background color. You must be in Design view to do this. Start by changing the background color for the entire form:

1.   Click anywhere on the background, then click on the palette button in the toolbar. The palette will open as shown here:

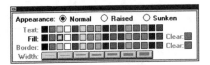

2.   Click on the Fill color you want for the background of the form.

The palette will remain on the screen and you can change any other area or object by clicking on the object and then on a color in the palette. The Clear check box on the far right of the palette, when it is checked, tells you that the object you have selected is transparent and the color behind it will show through. You therefore must turn off the check box before you can apply a color. Depending on the object you select, you can change the color of the text, fill, or border; you can change the line width of a border; and you can make a box look raised or sunken. Experiment with colors and the other graphical attributes to see what you like. For example, change the colors and add a border around the Reading Level option group next:

1.   Click on the option group border. Notice the change in the palette which now reflects the current colors in the selected area.

2.   Click on the check box at the end of the Fill line to clear the × that is displayed. Then click on the color you want for the fill or background of the option group, click on another color for the border, and then click on an appropriate line width for the border. The colors are immediately changed in the design window. Repeat these steps for the label of the option group and for any other object whose colors or other attributes you want to change. See Figure 6-18 for an example.

3.   Double-click on the palette's Control-menu box to close the palette and then double-click on the form's Control-

Figure 6-18

You can customize the color and other graphical attributes of a form in many different ways.

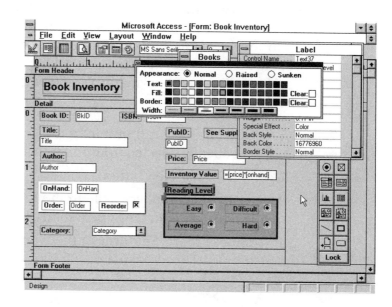

menu box to close the form and return to the Books database. Select Yes to save the changes to the form.

Creating a Main/Subform-Type Form

Frequently, you may want to view data grouped in specific ways. For example, in the Books database you may want to see all of the books in stock that are published by a specific company.

To do this, create a form consisting of a main form and a subform. The main form is based on a table containing a field that is on the "one" side of a one-to-many relationship. The subform is based on a table containing a linking field of the same data type (and possibly the same field name) that is on the "many" side of a one-to-many relationship. Either Access will establish the link automatically when the form is created, or you can establish the link by entering the field names in the properties dialog box for the subform when you are in Design view. When you create this form, you select only the fields that you want to be displayed in both the main and subform sections. The linking fields do not necessarily have to be included in the form, but the tables must contain these fields.

Create a main/subform-type of form that displays the books published by each of the suppliers. Use the Suppliers table for the main form and the Books table for the subform. PubID is the linking field. You will have to establish the link yourself—this will be covered in the following instructions (the Database window should be active):

1. Click on the Form button in the Database window if it is not already selected from your previous work.

2. Click on the New button.

3. Select the Suppliers table from the Select A Table/Query list, and click on the FormWizards button.

4. Choose Main/Subform as the type of form you want in the first FormWizards dialog box and then click on OK.

5. Choose Books as the table for the subform in the second FormWizards dialog box which also shows Suppliers as the table for the main form. Click on Next.

6. Choose the fields from the Suppliers table that you want in the main form and click on the greater-than sign (>) after each. Choose the PubID, Name, and Discount fields. When done, click on Next.

7. Choose the fields from the Books table that you want in the subform and again click on the greater-than sign (>) after each. Choose BkID, Title, Author, and Price. (You do not have to include the linking field, PubID, in the form, but it must be a field in the Books table.) Click on Next.

8. Choose whatever look you want, and then click on Next.

9. In the text box for the title, type **Inventory by Supplier** and click on Open. A dialog box telling you the subform must be saved is then displayed. Click on OK and type **Book subform** as the name. Click on OK.

10. A message is displayed telling you that Access is not able to establish a link automatically; click on OK. (You will establish the link next.) The form will be displayed; however, the data in the subform will not be linked to the data in the main form. If you scroll through the information in the main form using the scroll buttons at the bottom left of the window, you will notice that the data in the subform does not change.

11. To establish the link, click on the design view button on the far left of the toolbar. In Design view, choose Properties from the View menu to display the properties dialog box. Click anywhere on the detail section of the window, then click on the subform window to display the Subform/-Subreport dialog box. The Link Child Fields and Link Master Fields boxes should be blank.

12. Type **PubID** in both the Link Child Fields and Link Master Fields boxes. This will link the main form and the subform using the PubID fields in both tables. Your

Subform/Subreport dialog box should look like the following:

13. Click on the form view button to see the results of the link. Your screen should resemble Figure 6-19.

14. Use the scroll buttons at the bottom left of the window to scroll through the supplier records and see the list of books published by each. Also use the scroll bar on the subform window to scroll through the list of books from each supplier.

15. Choose Save Form As from the File menu, type **Book Suppliers**, and click on OK. Double-click on the form's

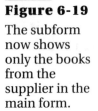

Figure 6-19

The subform now shows only the books from the supplier in the main form.

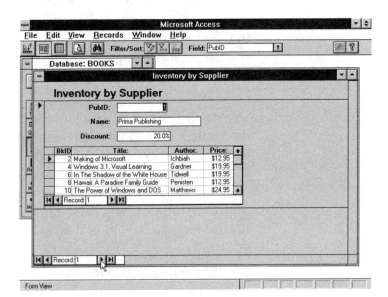

Control-menu box to close the form and return to the Books database.

If you create a subform from a query you will have to establish the link using the properties dialog box. Access will not automatically establish a link when a query is used as the basis of a subform. (Queries are discussed in detail in Chapter 7.)

Using a Form

A form is a convenient way to enter, edit, or view data in a table. You can also use a form to locate specific records, sort data, and group values.

Locating Records

You can scroll through the records in the database using the scroll buttons at the bottom left of the form window. However, it is sometimes quicker to use the Records menu to go to a record, or use the Find command in the Edit menu to go to a record that is based on a specific value.

Using Go To

Use the Go To option in the Records menu to move through the records in the Books table in Form view with these steps:

1. Select the Book Inventory form and click on Open to open the form in Form view.

2. Choose Go To from the Records menu to display the sub-menu shown here:

Your choices are the following:

- **First** to go to the first record in the form
- **Last** to go to the last record in the form
- **Next** to go to the next record following the current one
- **Previous** to go to the record located just before the current one
- **New** to display a blank form for a record that will follow the last record in the form

3. Click on Next to go to the next record in the database.

You can also scroll through the records in the form using the scroll buttons at the bottom left of the form window, as you see here:

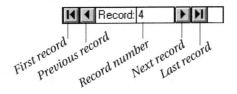

Click on any of the buttons to scroll through the records.

Using the Find Command

If you want to locate a specific record quickly, rather than scroll through the form, use the Find command in the Edit menu. You can select a field, open the Edit menu, choose Find, type the value you want to find, and finally choose Find Next. Or in the Find dialog box, you can choose All Fields, enter a value in the Find What text box, and choose Find First. Access will locate that value in any field. To search for the next occurrence of that value, open the Edit menu again, choose Find, and click on Find Next.

Locate the record in the Books table with 4 as the BkID number. The Book Inventory form in Form view should be displayed on your screen.

1. Click on the BkID field in any record.

2. Select the Edit menu and choose Find, or click on the find button (the binoculars) in the toolbar to display the Find in field dialog box shown below. Click on Current Field if it is not already selected.

3. Type **4** in the Find What text box and click on Find First. The status bar should now show Search succeeded. Click on Close to remove the Find in field dialog box from the window so that you can see the record.

Next, search for a value that is not the value for the entire field and without specifying the field in which it is located:

1. Click on the find button in the toolbar to display the Find in field dialog box. Type **Hawaii** in the Find What box to locate the record containing the word *Hawaii.*

2. Click on the down arrow in the Where box and select Any Part of Field.

3. Click on the All Fields option to turn it on. The name of the dialog box now becomes Find rather than Find in Field.

4. Click on the Find First button to display the record containing *Hawaii.*

Note

When you search for a value in all fields, it takes Access longer to perform the search than if you search through only a specified field.

Other choices in the Find dialog box are the following:

◆ **Where** offers two choices in addition to Any Part of Field. They are Match Whole Field, which is used to locate values that match the complete contents of the field, and Start of Field, which is used to locate values that match the string at the beginning of the field.

◆ **Direction**: Up/Down allows you to click on the button indicating the direction from the current record that you want to search.

◆ **Match Case** is turned on when you want to locate values that match exactly in terms of their upper/lower-case. If this is not turned on, corresponding values will be located regardless of capitalization.

◆ **Search Fields as Formatted** is turned on to find values that are formatted differently in the form than they are in the table. For example, in the table the date format is 3/5/93, but in the form the date format is 5-Mar-93. To locate all dates in March, turn on Search Fields as Formatted, select Any Part of Field in the Where box, and type **Mar** in the Find What box.

◆ **Find Next** is used to locate the next occurrence of the value from the current position.

◆ **Close** is used to leave the Find in field dialog box.

5. Close the Find dialog box.

Using Replace

The Replace command in the Form view's Edit menu is similar to the Find command; however, it is used to replace a value with a different value instead of just finding a value. Try it now:

1. Open the Edit menu and choose Replace to display the Replace dialog box shown here:

The Replace boxes and choices are as follows:

◆ **Find What** is where you type the value to be replaced.

◆ **Replace With** is where you type the value that you want to replace the Find What value.

◆ **Search in: Current Field** is turned on if you only want to search the currently selected field.

◆ **Search in: All Fields** is turned on to locate the value regardless of which field is selected.

◆ **Match Case** is used to locate values that exactly match in capitalization, as well as characters, the value entered in the Find What box.

◆ **Match Whole Field** is used when you want to locate a value that is exactly the same as the value entered in the Find What box. If you turn off this option, then you can enter one word, for example, and Access will locate it regardless of other characters in the field.

◆ **Find Next** takes you to the next occurrence of the value in the Find What box.

◆ **Replace** is chosen when you want to replace the located value with the value entered in the Replace With box.

◆ **Replace All** is used to replace all occurrences of the value in the Find What box with the value in the Replace With box.

◆ **Close** is used to leave the Replace dialog box.

2.   Choose Close to return to Form view.

Adding and Editing Data

One of the advantages of using a form is that it is easier to add or edit data because all fields in one record can be shown in the window at the same time. When you leave a record after adding or editing data in the form, the values are automatically saved in the table. If you want to save the values before leaving the record, open the File menu and choose Save Record.

Adding Records

Try using the Book Inventory form to add records to the Books table. You probably did not enter all the books shown in Figure 4-13 (in Chapter 4). Enter some more of them now with these instructions:

1. Open the Book Inventory form in Form view if it is not already there.

2. Open the Records menu, click on Go To, and then click on New. Your screen should show a record number that is one greater than what you entered, and a blank form.

3. To add a new record, press Tab to move to the ISBN field (and also to move from field to field), and type some more of the data shown in Figure 4-13. The BkID number is entered automatically because the data type is Counter. The field in which the pointer is positioned is displayed in the toolbar.

Note

If you make a mistake in a field, click on the undo button (second from the right in the toolbar) or choose Undo Typing from the Edit menu. If you want to change all characters in the field, choose Undo Current Field from the Edit menu before going to another field. If you want to remove all of the data in a record, choose Undo Current Record from the Edit menu before leaving it.

4. When you have entered all the fields for this record, press Tab. You will go automatically to the next new record, and the record you just entered will be saved.

Tip

You can also open the Records menu and choose Data Entry to add new records. When you use this command, the form for the table is displayed, but you do not see other records. This prevents data in other records from being changed inadvertently.

5. When you have entered the last record you want to enter, press Tab once more to save the last record.

Editing Records

If you find that there are errors in records that are in the table, you can use the form to make the changes by going to the field in a form, selecting the value, and typing a new value.

For example, if the price in the last record you entered was entered as 5.59 instead of 5.95, you can change it to 5.95 with these steps:

1. Open the Book Inventory form if it is not already opened, and choose Go To from the Records menu. Then select Last to go to the last record you entered; or click on the rightmost scroll button to go to the last record.

2. Select (drag across) the value $5.59. Be sure all characters are highlighted.

3. Type **5.95**. As soon as you begin typing, the selection is deleted and the new characters are inserted. When you tab to another record, the change is saved in the table.

4. Make any other revisions you want.

Sorting and Grouping Data

Often you want to sort or group data in a particular order. There are three filter/sort commands that allow you to display data in a form in the order that you want. You start by either clicking on the edit filter/sort button in the toolbar, shown below, or choosing Edit Filter/Sort from the Records menu.

The Filter window is then displayed and you can enter the fields and the specifications for the sort. After specifying the sort, click on the apply filter/sort button shown on the previous page or choose Apply Filter/Sort from the Records menu. When you are done sorting, you can click on the show all records button or choose Show All Records from the Records menu.

Sorting Records

To sort records, you specify the field on which to sort and then choose whether to sort in ascending or descending order. For now, sort the records in the Books table by price in descending order—most expensive to least expensive—with these instructions:

1. Open the Book Inventory form in Form view if it is not already opened.

2. Click on the edit filter/sort button (shown on the previous page), or choose Edit Filter/Sort from the Records menu. The Filter window will open as shown in Figure 6-20.

3. In the grid, click on the down arrow in the Field box to display the list of fields. Select the Price field. It will then appear in the grid.

4. Press ⬇ or click in the Sort box and then click on the down arrow to display the list of sort choices. Choose Descending for the type of sort.

Figure 6-20

The Filter window provides the means of specifying which fields you will sort on and in which order.

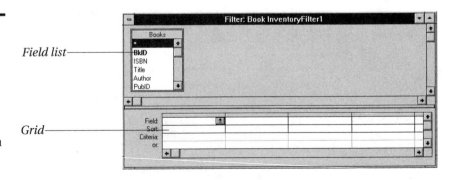

5.   Click on the apply filter/sort button to do the sorting, or choose Apply Filter/Sort from the Records menu.

6.   Scroll through the records to see the new sort order.

7.   Click on the show all records button to restore the original order; or open the Records menu and choose Show All Records.

Grouping Records

Grouping is just another form of sorting. Typically, you group on something that appears in a number of records. The Category field in the Books table is a good example of a field to group on. Group the records in the Book Inventory form by category and then list all the books alphabetically in each category:

1.   Be sure the Book Inventory form is displayed. Click on the edit filter/sort button to show the Filter window.

2.   Click on the Field box in the grid, click on the down arrow, and then choose Category from the list. (The Price field will be replaced.)

3.   Click on the Sort box in the first column. Click on the down arrow to display the choices and select Ascending.

4.   Now click on the Field box in the second column. Then click on the down arrow and choose Title from the list. Set the sort order for Ascending.

5.   To display the records in the new sort order, click on the apply filter/sort button or choose Apply Filter/Sort from the Records menu. Your form window will now show first the books in the Adventure category. As you move from record to record, all records showing Adventure as the category will be displayed, then the records showing the books in the Biography category, followed by Business books. You may also want to switch to Datasheet view to display the records in a table format.

6.   When you are done viewing the records, click on the show all records button, or choose Show All Records from the Records menu to display the records in their original order.

Cleaning Up the Books Table

Before going on to the next chapter, delete the Reading Level field that you added to the Books table. The remaining chapters of this book do not use this field. To do this:

1. Double-click on the form window's Control-menu box to close the form and return to the Books Database window.

2. Click on the Table button, then select the Books table and click on the Design button.

3. Select the row containing the Reading Level name and data type by clicking on the box to the left of the row.

4. Press (Delete) to display the message asking if you want to delete this field. Choose OK to delete the Reading Level field.

5. Double-click on the Table window's Control-menu box to close the window. Choose Yes; you want to save the changes to the table.

▰▰ Summary

Chapter 6 has shown you how to create, modify, and make substantial additions to forms. Among the major points brought out in this chapter are the following:

- ◆ Forms are used to enter and edit data in a layout that is similar to paper forms. You can also display on the screen and print forms containing data from one or several tables.

- ◆ You can create forms using the FormWizards, or you can create them manually using the Blank Form option. When you create a form using a FormWizard, Access leads you through the process by asking you questions. You will be able to select a type of form, specify the fields to be used in the form, enter a title, and select a style for the fields.

- ◆ Controls are used to produce the information that is displayed in a form. Controls consist of field names, labels, text boxes, buttons, check boxes, and groups. The controls are either bound to a field in the table that is the basis for the form, or they are unbound, allowing you to enter whatever information you want.

◆ Each section in the form and each type of control has a set of properties associated with it. The properties dialog box is used to change features related to the section or control that is selected. It can also be used to enter expressions, establish links between main and subform tables, or enter text that is displayed in the status bar of your form.

◆ You can display the data in a form by clicking on the form view button. You can see how the form will look when printed by clicking on the print preview button. The form can be printed from either the print preview, form view, or design view windows.

◆ You can make it easier for a user to enter data by including buttons, check boxes, and lists in the form. The user can select from a list, or enter yes/no values using buttons or check boxes.

◆ Records in a table can be sorted or grouped in a variety of ways using the Edit Filter/Sort option in the Records menu. You can choose the field or fields that will be the basis for the sort and then specify whether to sort in ascending or descending order. In order to group records, you select the field that is to be the basis for the grouping, then choose one or more additional fields that are to be sorted within each group.

In the next chapter you will learn how to create queries that extract information from one or more tables that you can then display in forms or new tables, or print in reports.

Creating and Using Queries

In previous chapters you saw how to design and build a database, how to enter data into tables, and how to create reports and forms that display the data. But you have used only a fraction of the power of Access. In order to tap more of this power, you need to create and use queries. A *query* is a question you ask of the database. Many queries are simple, such as "Who are my Seattle customers?" Others are more complex, such as "Which customers had total orders at least 20 percent higher than the average in the last six months?" With a query you can focus your attention on specific data. Some of the things you can do with queries are:

- Display records matching specified conditions
- Customize the appearance of a table or datasheet
- View data in a different order than it appears in the table
- Use alternate column names
- Display calculated values
- Display data from several related tables at once
- Perform global updates of data meeting specified conditions
- Display unique values

Queries provide one of the most powerful ways to view and manipulate your data.

Types of Queries

You can create several types of queries with Access. Each type serves a different purpose. Later in this chapter you will see how to create and use each type. The types of queries are as follows:

- A *select* query lets you select specific data and produce a new table or datasheet. This is the most common type of query.

- A *crosstab* query lets you create a summary of the detailed values in a table. This is an extremely powerful tool that can help you easily spot trends. For example, you can create a crosstab query to summarize a sales table and display the total purchases by month for each of your customers. You can then graph this summary to see the patterns in the data.

- An *action* query changes your data. For example, you can use an action query to change the prices of all books from one supplier by a fixed percentage. There are four types of action queries:

  a. A *make-table* query creates a new table.

  b. An *update* query changes data.

  c. An *append* query adds data from one table to another.

  d. A *delete* query removes data from a table.

- A *parameter* query lets you run the same query many times using different criteria each time. For example, if you want to display all the purchases made by a specified customer in the last month, create a parameter query. Each time you run the query, Access will prompt you to enter the customer ID number. The query will then display a datasheet showing the sales data for that customer.

A query can be either a single-table query or a multitable query. As the names imply, a single-table query is built from a single data table, and a multitable query is built from several tables. A multitable query is a common way to work with data from several related tables at once. A multitable query makes it easy to compare values between tables.

Creating Additional Tables

In order to perform the exercises in this chapter, you need to create four additional small tables and add some sample data to them. The new tables are:

- Interests, a list of people's interests in books
- Customer Interests, a cross-reference list to show which customers have which interests
- Orders, containing the header information for orders (date, to whom sold, and so forth)
- Order Details, containing the line-item information for orders

Chapter 1 describes the purposes of these tables in detail. The sections that follow explain how to set up the new tables.

Setting Up the Interests Table

The first new table to build is the Interests table. It is the master list of people's interests in books. No matter how many customers have a given interest, the interest description appears only once in this table. The structure of the Interests table is shown in Figure 7-1.

Create the Interests table with the following steps:

1. Start Access and open the Books database.
2. Click on the Table button if it is not currently selected, then click on New. A blank table will appear in Design view.

Figure 7-1

The structure
of the Interests
table

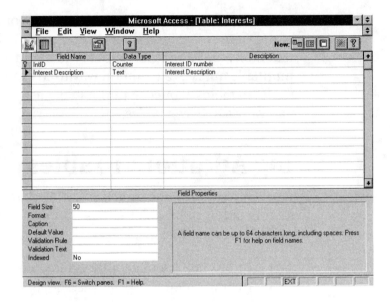

The first field in the Interests table is an interest ID field, IntID,
that serves as the primary key. Follow these instructions to set up
the IntID field:

1. Type **IntID** in the first Field Name text box and press ⌷Enter⌷.

2. Click on the down arrow on the right side of the Data Type
   box, select Counter, and press ⌷Enter⌷.

3. Type **Interest ID number** in the Description field, then
   click the mouse on the primary key button (fourth from
   the left in the toolbar) and press ⌷Enter⌷. You have defined
   the IntID field as the primary key of the Interests table.

4. Type **Interest Description** in the second Field Name box
   and press ⌷Enter⌷.

5. The default data type is Text, with a default field size of 50.
   Press ⌷Enter⌷ to accept these defaults and move to the
   Description field.

6. Type **Interest Description** in the Description field. The
   structure of the Interests table should look like the structure shown in Figure 7-1.

7. Double-click on the table's Control-menu box. A dialog box asks: Save changes to table 'Table1'? Click on Yes. The Save As dialog box opens to allow you to enter the table name.

8. Type **Interests** and press (Enter) to save the changes and return to the Tables list in the Database window.

You must also enter some values into the Interests table. Figure 7-2 shows the values you need for the examples in this chapter.

To enter the interest descriptions, follow these instructions:

1. Highlight the Interests table in the Tables list, then click on the Open button. The Interests table opens in Datasheet view.

2. Press (Enter) to move from the IntID field to the Interest Description field. The word *(Counter)* in the IntID field will change to a number when you move to the next record.

3. Type **Computers** in the first Interest Description field and press (Enter). You move to the IntID field in the next record and the value 1 appears in the IntID field in the first record. You can save one keystroke per record if you press the down arrow once instead of pressing (Enter) twice after typing each interest description.

4. Continue entering the interest descriptions so that your Interests table looks like the table in Figure 7-2.

5. When you have entered all the values, double-click on the Control-menu box to save the values and return to the Database window.

Figure 7-2

Sample data to be entered in the Interests table

	IntID	Interest Description
▶	1	Computers
	2	Wines
	3	Communication
	4	Native American Cultures
	5	Sailing
✳	(Counter)	

Setting Up the Customer Interests Table

The second new table to build is the Customer Interests table, a cross-reference table to show which customers have which interests. As you can see in Figure 7-3, the structure of the Customer Interests table consists of one field to link the table with the Customers table and one field to link the table with the Interests table.

To create the Customer Interests table, follow these instructions (you should be in the Database window):

1. Click on the Table button if it is not currently selected, then click on New. A blank table will appear in Design view.

2. Type **CusID** in the first Field Name box and press (Enter).

3. Click on the down arrow on the right side of the Data Type box and select Number. Although CusID and IntID are the counter data type in the Customers and Interests tables respectively, they are the number data type in this table. This is because you will enter values to cross-reference the Customers and Interests tables. The counter data type would not let you do this.

Figure 7-3

The structure for the Customer Interests table

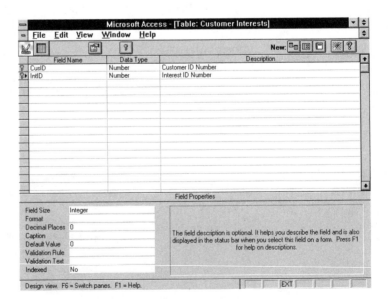

4. Click on right end of the Field Size box in the Field Properties region of the Design view window and select Long Integer. The values generated by the Counter data type for the CusID field in Customers are long integers. To be sure that Access correctly links Customers and Customer Interests, CusID should be a long integer in the Customer Interests table.

5. Click on the Description text box on the CusID line. Type **Customer ID Number** in the Description field and press Enter.

6. Type **IntID** in the second Field Name box and press Enter.

7. Click on the down arrow to the right of the second Data Type box, select Number, and press Enter.

8. Click on the Field Size box in the Field Properties region of the Design view window. Click on the down arrow at the right side of the box and select Long Integer.

9. Click in the Description text box for the IntID line and type **Interest ID Number** and press Enter.

10. Drag across both the CusID and IntID rows to highlight them both. Then click on the primary key button to define the combination of CusID and IntID as the primary key of the Customer Interests table. The CusID field can have duplicate values, as can the IntID field. The combination of CusID and IntID will have unique values.

11. Choose Close from the File menu. A dialog box asks: Save changes to table 'Table1'? Click on Yes, type **Customer Interests** in the Table Name box, and click on OK.

Now you must enter some values into the Customer Interests table. Figure 7-4 shows the values you need for the examples in this chapter.

To enter the customer interests values, follow these instructions:

1. Highlight Customer Interests in the Tables list, then click on the Open button. The Customer Interests table opens in Datasheet view.

CusID	IntID
1	1
1	2
3	2
5	1
5	2
5	3
7	1
7	2
0	0

2. Type 1 in the first CusID field and press Enter to move to the IntID field.

3. Type 1 in the first IntID field and press Enter to move to the next record.

4. Continue entering CusID and IntID values to make your Customer Interests table look like the table shown in Figure 7-4.

5. When you have entered all the values, double-click on the Control-menu box to save the values and return to the Database window.

Setting Up the Orders Table

The third new table to build is the Orders table. It contains the header information for each order placed by a customer. The detail line items for each order are contained in the Order Details table, which you will build after the Orders table. Figure 7-5 shows the Table window in Design view with the structure of the Orders table.

Figure 7-5

The Orders
table contains
the header or
summary
information for
each order that
is placed.

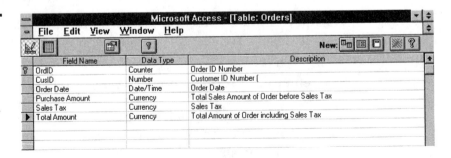

To create the Orders table, follow these instructions:

1. Click on the Table button if it is not currently selected, then click on New. A blank table will appear in Design view.

2. Type **OrdID** in the first Field Name box and press Enter.

3. Click on the down arrow on the right side of the Data Type box, select Counter, and press Enter. Type **Order ID Number** in the Description field, then click the mouse on the primary key button and press Enter. You have defined the OrdID field as the primary key of the Orders table.

4. Open the File menu and choose Save. Type **Orders** in the Table Name box and click on OK.

5. Type **CusID** in the second Field Name box, press Enter, select Number as the data type, click on the Field Size box in the Field Properties area, and select Long Integer. Click on the Description field back on the CusID line. Type **Customer ID Number** in the Description field and press Enter.

6. Type the remaining field names and descriptions and select the data types shown in Figure 7-5. For field properties, select the Short Date format for the Order Date and the Currency format for the three currency fields.

7. Double-click on the Control-menu box. A dialog box asks: `Save changes to table 'Orders'?` Click on Yes to save the changes and return to the Tables list of the Database window.

Now you must enter some values into the Orders table. Figure 7-6 shows the values you need for the examples in this chapter.

To enter the orders values, follow these instructions:

1. Highlight the Orders table, then click on the Open button. The Orders table opens in Datasheet view.

2. Press Enter to move to the CusID field. The word *(Counter)* in the OrdID field will change to a number when you move to the next record.

Figure 7-6

Sample data to
be entered in
the Orders
table

	OrdID	CusID	Order Date	Purchase Amount	Sales Tax	Total Amount
	1	3	3/5/93	$47.29	$3.83	$51.12
	2	7	4/5/93	$43.12	$3.49	$46.61
	3	4	4/8/93	$62.50	$5.06	$67.56
▶	4	3	4/8/93	$29.58	$2.40	$31.98
✱	(Counter)	0		$0.00	$0.00	$0.00

Table: Orders

3. Type **3** in the first CusID field, press (Enter) to move to the
    Order Date field, type **3/5/93**, and press (Enter) to move to
    the Purchase Amount field.

4. Type **47.29** in the Purchase Amount field and press (Enter)
    to move into the Sales Tax field. Note that you do not need
    to type the dollar sign; Access adds this automatically.

5. Type **3.83** in the Sales Tax field, press (Enter), type **51.12** in
    the Total Amount field, and press (Enter). This moves you to
    the OrdID field of the second record and the number 1
    appears as the OrdID value in the first record.

6. Continue entering orders values to make your Orders table
    look like the table in Figure 7-6.

7. When you have entered all the values, double-click on the
    Control-menu box to save the values and return to the
    Database window.

Note

You might be wondering if Access can calculate the values for the purchase amount, sales tax, and total amount from the order details and
from each other. It can, but this requires some programming and is
beyond the scope of this chapter.

Setting Up the Order Details Table

The last new table you need to build is the Order Details table. It
is the companion to the Orders table. Each record in the Order
Details table contains data for one line in an order. By using separate tables for the order headers and order details, you can enter
as many line items as necessary for one order. Figure 7-7 shows
the Table window in Design view with the structure of the Order
Details table.

To create the Order Details table, follow these instructions:

1. Click on the Table button if it is not currently selected, then click on New. A blank Table window will appear in Design view.

2. Type in the field names and descriptions and select the data types shown in Figure 7-7.

> **Note**
>
> **OrdID is a number data type, not a counter data type in the Order Details table, because you will enter values into OrdID to link records in the Order Details table with records in the Orders table.**

3. Set the field size in the Field Properties area to Long Integer for the OrdID, Line Num, and BkID fields. Format the List Price field as Currency and format the Discount field as Percent with no decimal places (the default for a percent is two decimals places). Finally set the field size for the Discount field to Single and for the Quantity field to Integer. (Even though the discount will be displayed as an integer percent value, it must be stored as a decimal value.)

4. Select both the OrdID and the Line Number and click on the primary key button, making this combination the primary key. The OrdID field can have duplicate values, as can the Line Num field. The combination of OrdID and Line Num will have unique values.

5. Double-click on the Control-menu box. A dialog box asks `Save changes to table 'Table1'?` Click on Yes and the Save As dialog box opens. Type **Order Details** in the Table Name box, and click on OK to save the changes and return to the Tables list of the Database window.

Figure 7-7

The Order Details table contains the line items for all orders.

Field Name	Data Type	Description
OrdID	Number	Order ID Number
Line Num	Number	Line-item number in this order
BkID	Number	Book ID Number
List Price	Currency	Publisher's suggested list price
Discount	Number	Percent discount
Quantity	Number	Quantity of this item ordered

Table: Order Details

Figure 7-8

This is the sample data for the Order Details table.

	Table: Order Details					
	OrdID	Line Num	BkID	List Price	Discount	Quantity
	1	1	16	$16.95	10%	1
	1	2	32	$17.95	10%	1
	1	3	2	$12.95	10%	1
	1	4	7	$4.95	15%	1
	2	1	22	$22.95	10%	1
	2	2	10	$24.95	10%	1
	3	1	11	$5.95	20%	2
	3	2	16	$16.95	10%	2
	3	3	10	$24.95	10%	1
	4	1	7	$4.95	10%	2
	4	2	28	$22.95	10%	1
▶	0	0	0	$0.00	0%	

Now you must enter some values into the Order Details table. Figure 7-8 shows the values you need for the examples in this chapter.

To enter the order details values, follow these instructions:

1. Highlight the table Order Details in the Tables list and click on the Open button. The Order Details table opens in Datasheet view.

2. Enter the Order Details records to make your Orders table look like the table in Figure 7-8. You do not have to enter dollar signs in currency fields, but you do have to either enter a percent sign or a decimal for percents. For example, 10 percent must be entered as **10%** or **.1**.

3. When you have entered all the values, double-click on the Control-menu box to save the values and return to the Database window.

Now that you have built the tables needed for the exercises in this chapter, you are ready to create some queries.

Using the Query Window in Design View

In order to create queries, you need to be familiar with the query window in Design view that is shown in Figure 7-9. Think of this as a structured workspace with a set of tools. The tools include the menu bar, the toolbar, and the function keys. The workspace is the query window.

Query Tools

The query tools include a number of sometimes overlapping buttons, menu options, and function keys to help you build and carry out a query. Briefly look at these in the next sections.

Query Toolbar

The query toolbar contains buttons that let you quickly perform tasks you often need. These buttons are shown and described in Table 7-1.

Query Menus

The menus for the query window in Design view provide options for manipulating your queries. These menus and their purpose are described in Table 7-2.

Figure 7-9

The query window in Design view

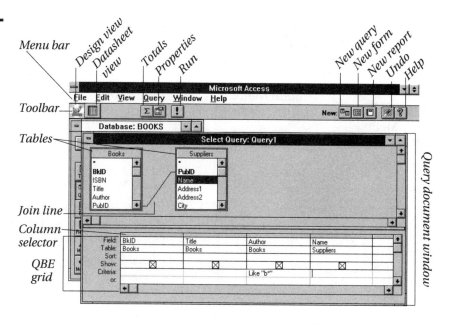

Table 7-1

Query Design
Toolbar
Buttons

Button	Description
	The *design view* button switches to Design view
	The *datasheet view* button switches to Datasheet view
Σ	The *totals* button shows or hides the Total row in the Query-By-Example (QBE) grid
	The *properties* button displays the property list for the query
!	The *run* button runs the query
	The *new query* button creates a new query based on the query currently on the desktop
	The *new form* button creates a new form based on the query currently on the desktop
	The *new report* button creates a new report based on the query currently on the desktop
	The *undo* button undoes your most recent action
?	The *help* button calls up the help system

Table 7-2

Query Menu
Commands

Menu Name	Description
File	Creates new queries and other database objects; closes the query window; saves the active query; exits from Access
Edit	Edits the active query and inserts and deletes rows and columns in the QBE grid
View	Views the active query in various ways; toggles totals and table name rows; sets query properties; sets Access options
Query	Runs the active query; adds and removes tables; specifies the type of query; sets up parameter queries
Window	Arranges, hides, shows, and selects windows
Help	Chooses from various help options

Function Keys

In addition to the global function keys, the function keys described in Table 7-3 are active and useful in the query window in Design view.

Query Window

The query window is divided into two sections. The upper portion contains the tables and their field lists that you have selected to use in the query. *Join lines* between the tables show how the tables are joined together. You can move and size the tables in the upper section by dragging on their title bars or on their borders.

The lower portion of the query window contains the graphical *query-by-example* grid, usually referred to as the *QBE* grid. The QBE grid contains details about the fields, sort specifications, selection criteria, and calculations to use in the query. Most of your work in designing a query takes place in the QBE grid.

Table 7-3

Function Key Assignments in the Query Window in Design View

Function Key	Purpose
F11 or Alt-F1	Makes the Database window the active window.
F2	Toggles between navigation and editing modes. In editing mode you can move the insertion point within the text.
Shift-F2	Opens the Zoom window so you can enter a long expression into the currently selected field. See Figure 7-10 for an example of the Zoom window.
F6	Toggles between the tables in the upper portion and the QBE grid in the lower portion of the query window.
Ctrl-F8	Moves a column in the QBE grid with the keyboard (you can also move a column by dragging it with the mouse). First click on the column selector (the top bar in each column) to select the column, then press Ctrl-F8 and move the column to its new location using the arrow keys. Press Esc to end the move.

Figure 7-10
The Zoom window lets you type long expressions into small input areas.

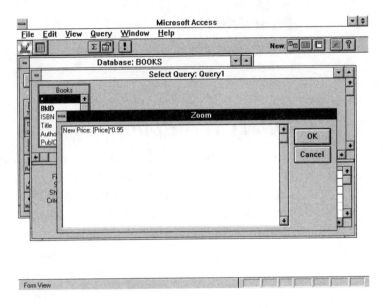

You can drag the line between the upper and lower sections of the query window to change the relative amount of space in the two halves of the window.

With this knowledge of the query window and the tools that you can use in it, you are ready to build your first query—a select query.

Creating Select Queries

Select queries are the most common type of query. In a *select* query you specify criteria that is used to select a subset of the data in one or more tables. For example, you might have 1,000 names in your Customers table, but you want to send a special mailing to only those customers who live in a specific ZIP code. The ZIP code is the criterion used in selecting only those customers whose records have that number in the ZIP code field. With a select query, Access builds a temporary table that contains only customers in the specified ZIP code.

In this section you will build several types of select queries. You will begin with a simple select query and progress to more complex ones. First, though, look at some of the reasons for using a select query.

Reasons for Using a Select Query

A select query lets you view and manipulate data in a variety of ways. You can do the following:

- ◆ View data from one table or from several related tables at the same time
- ◆ Specify selection criteria to work with just a subset of the data in a table
- ◆ Display the data in almost any order
- ◆ Create calculated fields that are automatically updated as you change the values in the regular fields used in the formulas
- ◆ Calculate summary values that span many records

Some typical questions you can answer using the bookstore database and a select query are as follows:

- ◆ Which customers live in Seattle?
- ◆ What are the interests of each customer?
- ◆ What were the total sales in a given time period?
- ◆ What were the total sales of each book in a given time period?
- ◆ What were the total sales of each book in each month in a given time period, arranged in a spreadsheet format?

Notice that the last three questions are progressively more detailed variations of the same theme. In the next several sections you will see how to answer these and other questions with Access queries.

Creating a Select Query with One Table

The simplest query displays information from a single table. You have already created a Customers table and entered data about your customers. When you look at the datasheet for the Customers table, you see all the data in the table, in the order it was entered. Suppose you want to see the names of only the customers who live in Seattle. You can do this by creating a select query that specifies a criterion limiting which customers you see.

Opening the Design View Window and Choosing a Table

The first step is to open the query window in Design view and choose a table which the query will use to make the selection:

1. Click on the Database window if it is not active and click on the Table button if necessary.

2. Select the Customers table and click on the new query button in the toolbar (fifth from the right). This opens the query window in Design view with the Customers table already selected for use in the query, as shown in Figure 7-11.

Choosing Fields

The second step is to choose the fields or columns that will appear in the resulting temporary table. Since in this exercise you are using only the Customers table, all the fields will come from that table. Choose the fields with these steps:

Figure 7-11

When you start a new query design with a table already selected or open, Access adds the table to the query.

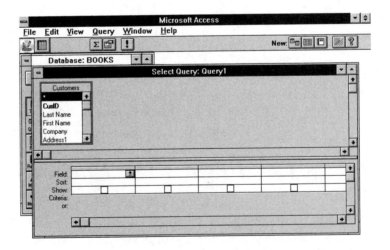

1. In the Customers field list, double-click on CusID, Last Name, First Name, and City, in that order. Each field becomes a column in the query-by-example (QBE) grid in the bottom portion of the query window, as shown here:

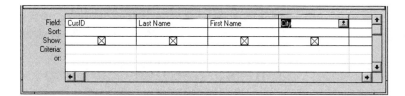

You can also add a field to the QBE grid by dragging the field name from the field list to the desired column in the QBE grid. If you drag a field onto an existing field in the QBE grid, Access inserts the new field at that location and moves the remaining fields to the right. Any fields to the left of the insertion point stay in place.

2. Click on the datasheet view button (second from the left) to see the query results at this point. Your results will be similar to those shown in Figure 7-12. The resulting temporary table or datasheet for a query is called a *dynaset* (a

Figure 7-12

The query datasheet shows data only for the fields included in the query.

"dynamic set of data"). Each time you activate the query, Access analyzes the query specifications and displays the current data that matches those specifications. This assures that you see the most current data whenever you use the query.

3. Click on the design view button on the far left of the toolbar to return to the query window in Design view.

Entering a Search Condition

To see only the customers who live in Seattle, you must tell Access to select only those records that have the word *Seattle* in the City field. In other words, you must enter a selection criterion of *Seattle* in the City field. To do this, follow these instructions:

1. Click in the Criteria row in the City column and type the word **Seattle** as shown here:

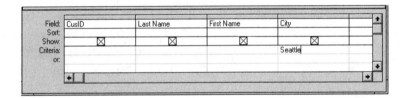

You do not have to capitalize the word. Access ignores capitalization in this case. If you enter more than one word—for example, San Francisco—you must enclose the words in quotation marks.

2. Click on the datasheet view button to see the results, which look like this:

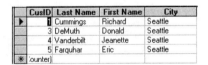

3. When you are through looking at the results, click on the design view button to return to the query window in Design

view. Notice that Access has automatically enclosed the word *Seattle* in quotation marks.

Specifying a Sort Order

If the select query produces more than a few rows of data, you will probably want to sort the rows to make it easier to find a particular entry:

1.   To sort the results of the current query by last name, click in the Sort row in the Last Name column. Click on the down arrow on the right side of the Sort box and then click on Ascending from the drop-down list:

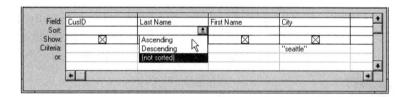

     This choice tells Access that you want to sort the results by Last Name in ascending order—with *A* first and *Z* last.

2.   Click on the datasheet view button to see the results. The rows in the datasheet appear in alphabetical order by last name, as shown here:

3.   Click on the design view button when you are through looking at the results.

If there are several customers with the same last name, you can further sort the data by first name with this instruction:

◆   In the query window in Design view click on the Sort box in the First Name column. Click on the down arrow on the right side of the Sort box and choose Ascending from the drop-down list.

Since the current data has no duplicate last names, this additional sort has no effect. If you add data with duplicate last names, the query will sort it by last name and then by first name within each duplicate last name.

Hiding a Column in the Datasheet

Since the current query shows only customers from Seattle, there is no need to display the City column. It was included for the previous example to verify that the records selected matched the search criteria. To omit the City column from the dynaset:

1. Click on the Show check box in the City field of the QBE grid. The × disappears from the check box, indicating the City field will not appear in the dynaset.

2. Click on the datasheet view button. The results are shown here:

CusID	Last Name	First Name
1	Cummings	Richard
3	DeMuth	Donald
5	Farquhar	Eric
4	Vanderbilt	Jeanette
(Counter)		

3. Click on the design view button to return to that view.

To save the query, follow these instructions:

1. Double-click on the design window's Control-menu box.

2. Click on the Yes button in the save changes dialog box.

3. Type **Seattle Customers** for the name of the query.

4. Click on the OK button.

5. Once the query is saved, click on the Query button in the Database window and you will see the Seattle Customers query listed.

6. To view the Seattle Customers dynaset again, highlight Seattle Customers in the Queries list, then click on the Open button (or double-click on the name of the query).

7. To close the dynaset, double-click on the Control-menu box of the dynaset.

To revise the Seattle Customers query, do either of the following:

♦   Highlight Seattle Customers in the Queries list, then click on the design view button

♦   If you are still looking at the dynaset for the query, click on the design view button

After you make any changes, double-click on the design window's Control-menu box and click on Yes if you want to save the changes.

Adding Parameters to the Query

The query you just created is useful for looking up the names of your Seattle customers. You could make similar queries to see customers in other cities, but if you have customers in many cities, you will wind up with many queries. A far better approach is to create a query that asks you for the name of a city, then displays the names of the customers in that city. Such a query is known as a *parameter* query.

Making a Parameter Query

To make a parameter query, you first make a select query and then change the item you are searching for to a parameter. Rather than make a new select query from scratch, make a copy of the Seattle Customers query as follows:

1. In the Database window click on the Query button if it is not already selected.

2. Highlight the name Seattle Customers and press Ctrl-C. This copies the Seattle Customers query to the Clipboard.

3. Press Ctrl-V. In the Paste As dialog box that appears, type **Customers for a Specified City** and click on OK.

To modify this new query so it becomes a parameter query that lets you specify a city each time you use it, use these instructions:

1. Highlight the name Customers for a Specified City and click on the design view button.

2. Click on Seattle in the first Criteria row of the City column to place the insertion point there.

3. Press F2 to highlight the entire contents of the Criteria box.

4. Type [**Customers for what city?**] to replace the word *Seattle*. The square brackets are required; they tell Access that this is the title of a parameter, rather than literal text to use in a search.

5. To test the query, click on the datasheet view button. Access displays a dialog box asking for the name of a city, as shown here:

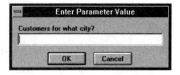

6. Type **Seattle** and click on OK. Access displays the same list of names you saw for the earlier query.

7. To save the query, double-click on the Datasheet view window's Control-menu box and click on Yes in the save changes dialog box that appears.

To test the parameter query further, do the following:

1. Highlight the name Customers for a Specified City and click on the Open button (or double-click on the name Customers for a Specified City).

2. In the Enter Parameter Value dialog box, type **Bellevue** and click on OK. Access shows you the names of the customers from Bellevue.

3. To close the datasheet, double-click on the Datasheet view window's Control-menu box.

Using Pattern Matching in a Parameter Query

You can make the parameter query even more flexible by telling Access to match patterns rather than exact values. Try pattern matching next:

1. In the Database window click on the Query button if it is not already selected.

2. Highlight the name Customers for a Specified City and click on the design view button.

3. Click on the expression [Customers for what city?] in the Criteria row of the City column.

4. If the entire expression is highlighted, first press F2 to remove the highlight, then press Home to move the insertion point to the beginning of the expression.

5. Type the word **Like** to the left of the left square bracket. A space following the word *Like* is optional.

Note

Like is an operator that looks in the current field for similar, though not necessarily exact, occurrences of the text that follows it.

6. Click on the Show check box in the City field of the QBE grid. An × appears in the check box, indicating that the City field will appear in the dynaset. Since you will be using a pattern instead of an exact city name, you want to see the names of the cities that match the pattern you enter.

7. To save the changes, choose Save from the File menu. Then click on the datasheet view button to test this revision.

Table 7-4

Wildcard
Characters

Character	Used to Indicate
*	Any number of characters in place of the *
?	Any single character (letter or number) in place of the ?
#	Any single number in place of the #
[ ]	A range of letters or numbers in place of the [ ]
!	Not; any character or range but the one following the !

8. In the Enter Parameter Value dialog box, type **B*** and click on OK. Access shows you the names of the customers from all the cities whose names begin with the letter *B*.

9. Double-click on the datasheet's Control-menu box to close it and return to the Database window.

The asterisk (*) in Step 8 tells Access to accept zero or more characters where it appears. It is one of several *wildcard* characters that you can use in pattern matching. This and other wildcard characters are described in Table 7-4.

For example, [2-7] indicates that a single digit in the range 2 through 7 is acceptable, and [m-r] indicates that a single character in the range *m* through *r* is acceptable. Use ! inside square brackets to indicate unacceptable values. For example specifying [!b]* for the city matching pattern tells Access to show the names of customers in all cities whose names do not begin with *B*. Patterns with wildcards can be very useful. Play with them until you are comfortable with them.

Creating a Select Query with Two Tables

You can create a select query to view data from several related tables at once. Recall that two related tables in a normalized database have a one-to-many (1:M) relationship. In the bookstore database, the Suppliers table has a 1:M relationship with the Books table (one supplier supplies many books, but any given book has only one publisher who is the supplier in this case). The Books table identifies each supplier by publisher ID number (field PubID). To show both the name of a book and the name of the book's supplier, you need to display data from the Books table and Suppliers table at the same time.

Selecting Multiple Tables for the Query

To start a new query with fields from both the Books and Suppliers tables, follow these instructions:

1. In the Database window click on the Query button if it is not already selected.

2. Click on the New button. The query window appears in Design view, along with the Add Table dialog box, which lets you choose tables and existing queries to use in the current query as you can see here:

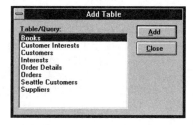

3. Double-click on Books and on Suppliers and then click on the Close button.

The upper portion of the design window now shows two lists containing the names of the fields from each of the tables you selected. If you need to add another table to the query, open the Query menu and choose Add Table. To delete a table from the query, click anywhere in the field list for the table and press Delete. Access does not ask you to confirm the deletion, so use caution.

Linking Tables in a Query

If you had previously defined a relationship between the Books and Suppliers tables, Access would automatically link them in the query. In this case, no relationship has been defined, so follow these steps to link the tables manually:

1. Point on the PubID field in the Books field list, press and hold hold down the mouse button, drag the pointer to the PubID field in the Suppliers field list, and release the button. Access draws a *join line* indicating that the two tables are linked through the PubID fields, as shown here:

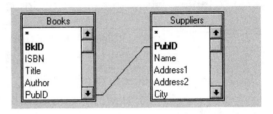

Caution

Be sure to use the correct fields to join the tables. Access does not warn you if the fields are not correct at the time you join the tables. If you get an error message such as `Type Mismatch` **when you try to view the datasheet, or if the datasheet seems to contain strange results, verify that you used the correct fields to join the tables.**

2. You can select fields from multiple tables to be included in a query just as you did from a single table. Double-click on the Title field in the Books field list and the Name field in the Suppliers field list. Both field names appear in the QBE grid in the lower portion of the design window, as seen here:

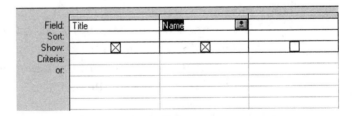

3. Click on the datasheet view button to see the dynaset for the query. It should look similar to the one shown in Figure 7-13.

Figure 7-13

The dynaset for a multitable query can show data from all the tables included in the query.

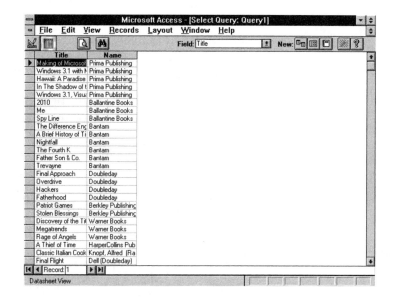

4.   Click on the design view button to return to the query window in Design view.

Displaying Table Names in the QBE Grid

When you work with a multitable query, you will find it convenient to show the name of the source table for each field included in the query. To display the table names, open the View menu and click on Table Names. A new row appears in the QBE grid, showing the name of the source table for each field, as shown here:

Field:	Title	Name	
Table:	Books	Suppliers	
Sort:			
Show:	☒	☒	☐
Criteria:			
or:			

If you want the Table line to automatically appear in all the queries you make, follow these instructions:

1.   Open the View menu and choose Options. Access displays the Options dialog box.

2. Click on Query Design in the category list. Options pertaining to query design appear in the lower portion of the options dialog box.

3. Click on the Show Table Names box.

4. Click on the down arrow on the right side of the box, then click on Yes. The dialog box should appear as below:

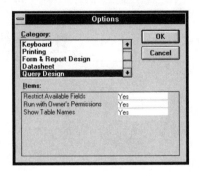

5. Finally, click on OK to close the Options dialog box and save the new settings. Every new query you create from now on will show the Table line unless you open the View menu and turn off the Show Table Names option.

Sorting across Tables

When you include multiple tables in a query, you can perform operations that include multiple tables. For example, you can sort on fields from both tables. To perform such a sort in the query you are currently building, follow these steps:

1. Click in the Sort row in each column and choose Ascending.

2. Click on the datasheet view button to look at the dynaset. You will see that the results are sorted by title. Since each title is unique, you do not see any effect of sorting by supplier name.

3. Click on the design view button to return to the Design view.

Access sorts in the order it encounters the columns in the QBE grid from left to right. To sort first by supplier name, you need to rearrange the columns, as follows:

1. Click on the column selector for the Name column.

2. Point on the column selector a second time and press and hold down the mouse button as you move the mouse pointer to the Title column. As you move the mouse pointer, notice that the tail of the pointer has a small rectangle attached to it. Also notice that the left edge of the column with the pointer becomes highlighted. This indicates where Access will insert the column you are moving.

3. With the pointer in the Title column, release the button. The Name column moves to the left of the Title column, as seen here:

Field:	Name	Title	
Table:	Suppliers	Books	
Sort:	Ascending	Ascending	
Show:	☒	☒	☐
Criteria:			
or:			

4. Click on the datasheet view button and display the dynaset again. You will see that the data is now sorted first by supplier name, then by book title within each supplier, as shown here:

Name	Title
Ballantine Books	2010
Ballantine Books	Me
Ballantine Books	Spy Line
Bantam	A Brief History of Ti
Bantam	Father Son & Co.
Bantam	Nightfall
Bantam	The Difference Eng
Bantam	The Fourth K
Bantam	Trevayne
Berkley Publishing	Patriot Games
Berkley Publishing	Stolen Blessings
Dell (Doubleday)	Final Flight
Doubleday	Fatherhood
Doubleday	Final Approach
Doubleday	Hackers
Doubleday	Overdrive
HarperCollins Pub	A Thief of Time

5. To save the query, double-click on the datasheet's Control-menu box, click on Yes, and name the query **Books and Publishers**.

Modifying the Query

Suppose you want to have quick access to a list of books from your best supplier. You can modify the Books and Publishers query to show only the books for that supplier:

1. Click on the Books and Publishers query in the Database window and then click on the design view button.

2. Click on the Criteria box in the Name column and type **"Prima Publishing"** there. Be sure to enclose the name in quotation marks because it contains a space—you will get a syntax error otherwise. The dynaset, as shown below, now shows only the books from Prima:

Name	Title
Prima Publishing	Hawaii: A Paradise
Prima Publishing	In The Shadow of t
Prima Publishing	Making of Microsof
Prima Publishing	Windows 3.1 with N
Prima Publishing	Windows 3.1, Visua

3. To save the query under a new name, open the File menu, choose Save Query As, and name the query **Books from Prima**. Then double-click on the Control-menu box and return to the Database window.

Creating a Select Query with Three Tables

The Customer Interests table exists to cross-reference the Customers table and the Interests table. In order to see the names of your customers along with the names of their interests, you need to link together all three tables in one query.

1. In the Database window click on the Query button if it is not already selected.

2. Click on the New button to start a new query.

3. In the Add Table dialog box, double-click on Customers, Customer Interests, and Interests, in that order. (The order

is important only because it places the tables that are going to be linked next to one another.) Click on Close.

4. Drag the CusID field from the Customers field list to the CusID field in the Customer Interests field list. Then drag the IntID field from the Customer Interests field list to the IntID field in the Interests field list. The query design should look similar to the layout shown in the upper portion of Figure 7-14. The three tables are now linked.

5. Double-click on Interest Description from the Interests field list, then double-click on Last Name and First Name from the Customers field list. You do not have to pick any fields from the Customer Interests field list. The Customer Interests table acts only as a bridge between the other two tables. The selected fields appear as columns in the QBE grid in the order selected. Notice that the Table row shows you the name of the source table for each field.

6. Click on the right end of the Sort box in each column and choose Ascending from the drop-down list. After you do this, the QBE grid should look similar to the one shown in Figure 7-14.

7. Click on the datasheet view button to see the dynaset for the query. The dynaset shows the data as if it were in a single table. The data is grouped by Interest Description, with customer names arranged alphabetically within each Interest Description group.

8. Close the query and save it as **Customer-Interest Cross-Reference**.

Creating a Select Query with Calculated Fields

In addition to displaying data that comes directly from a table, a query can also display data generated by calculations in the in this chapter, you created fields for the list price of a book, the discount given for the book, and the quantity purchased. You did not create fields for the price after the discount, or for the

Figure 7-14

A query can sort and display data from tables that are linked through an intermediate cross-reference table.

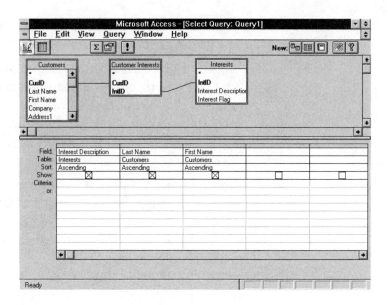

extended amount (price times quantity) for a given line item. There is no reason to store those two values, because they can both be calculated from other values entered into the table.

In this example, you will create a query that contains all the fields from the Order Details table plus calculations for the discounted price and extended amount. When you change a list price, discount, or quantity, Access will generate new values for the calculated fields in the same record and immediately display the results.

Creating the Query

Create the new query with these instructions:

1. Click on the Table button if it is not already selected.

2. Click on the Order Details table and click on the new query button in the toolbar. This opens the query window in Design view with the Order Details table already selected for use in the query.

    You are going to include all the Order Details fields in the query. Normally you would just double-click on the asterisk to include all the fields, but if you did that, you wouldn't be able to control the placement of the fields in the query or work with the individual fields, since they all appear in a single column in the QBE grid.

3. Double-click on the list title. This highlights all the field names and removes the highlight from the asterisk.

4. Click in the highlighted area of the field list and drag the pointer to the QBE grid. When you move the pointer into the QBE grid, the pointer appears as a set of overlapping rectangles.

5. Release the mouse button with the pointer in the QBE grid. Access enters the names of all the Order Details fields into the grid in the order they appear in the field list.

6. Use the horizontal scroll bar so you can see the Quantity field and then click on its column selector.

7. Press ⟮Insert⟯. Access inserts a blank column, as shown below (the column widths have been adjusted to better illustrate what happens):

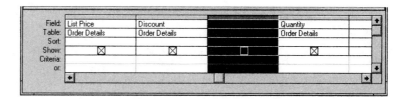

8. Click on the Field box in the new column and type

    Selling Price: CCur([list price]*(1-[discount]))

    in the box. Be sure to enclose *list price* and *discount* in square brackets to tell Access they are field names. This formula tells Access to create a calculated field named Selling Price. The value is calculated by multiplying (*) the value in the List Price field by one minus the value in the Discount field. Recall that the Discount field actually contains a decimal value, even though the display shows a percent value. CCur is an Access function that treats the resulting value as currency.

9. Click on the Field box in the blank column to the right of the Quantity field to create another calculated field.

10. Press [Shift]-[F2] to open the Zoom window and then type

    Ext Amt: CCur((CInt(100*[selling price])*[quantity])/100)

    in this window. This expression creates a calculated field named Ext Amt. (The name Extended Amount would make the field too wide in the datasheet.) CInt is an Access function that rounds a value to a whole number. The calculation is somewhat complex to eliminate rounding errors due to the binary arithmetic performed by the computer. If you just use **CCur([selling price]*[quantity])** some of the results will be off by a penny. Granted, this is not a lot of money, but it makes the results look strange and someone is going to notice that. It takes less time to enter this complex expression than to explain over and over again why some of the numbers are off by a penny. You only have to type the expression once for Access to use it for every record entered into the Order Details table.

11. Click on OK and then save the query by double-clicking on the Control-menu box, clicking on Yes in the save changes dialog box, typing **Order Details with Calculated Fields** in the Save As dialog box, and clicking on OK.

Testing the Query

Now see how powerful and convenient the calculated fields are. Test the query with these steps:

1. In the Database window click on the Query button if it is not already selected.

2. Highlight Order Details with Calculated Fields and click on the Open button (or double-click on the name of the query). The dynaset will open as shown in Figure 7-15 (the column width has been reduced in this figure to display all the columns).

Figure 7-15

A query with
calculated
fields not only
saves file space
but also
shortens data
entry time and
reduces errors.

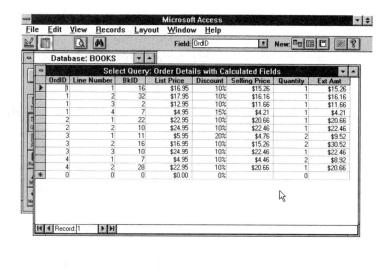

3. Hand-check a couple of rows and you will see that the
   Selling Price and Ext Amt columns show the correct calculations.

4. In the first row, change the value for Discount from 10 to
   15 percent. To do this, type either **15%** or **.15** and press
   [Enter]. You will see the values change in both the Selling
   Price and Ext Amt columns.

5. Still in the first row, change the value for Quantity from 1
   to 2 and press [Enter]. You will see the value change in the
   Ext Amt column.

6. Double-click on the Control-menu box to close the query
   and answer No to not save the changes you just made.

From now on, use this query to enter order details, rather than
enter data directly into the Order Details table.

Creating a Select Query with Summary Values

In addition to performing calculations within a record, a query
can perform summary (*aggregate*) calculations involving many

records. An overall summary calculation involves all the records in the table. A group summary calculation involves a set of records having something in common, such as the same order number. Table 7-5 describes the summary operators available in Access. In each case the value returned is either for the entire table or for each group, depending on how you set up the query. You will see examples of both overall and group summaries later in this section.

Creating a Query with an Overall Summary Calculation

Suppose you want to see the total amount of all orders made in April 1993. The Orders table shows the date and amount of each order. You can use those values to calculate the total order amount for any given time period. To create a query that shows the overall summary value, follow these instructions:

1. Click on the Table button of the Database window if it is not already selected.

2. Click on the Orders table and click on the new query button in the toolbar. This opens the query window in Design view with the Orders table already selected for use in the query.

3. In the Orders field list, double-click on Order Date and Purchase Amount. Access adds these two fields to the QBE grid.

4. Click on the Criteria row in the Order Date column and type **4/*/93**.

5. Click on the datasheet view button to verify that the records selected are in the specified range.

6. Click on the design view button to return to the query window in Design view and notice that the expression 4/*/93 has been changed to `Like "4/*/93"` by Access.

7. Click on the totals button (third from the left in the toolbar). This opens a Total row in the QBE grid containing default values of Group By.

8. Click on the Total row in the Order Date column.

9. Click on the down arrow on the right side of the box, then click on Where in the drop-down list. This tells Access that it should do its totaling based on the criteria in this field.

10. Click on the Total row in the Purchase Amount column.

Table 7-5

Summary Operators Available in Access

Summary Operator	Description
Sum	Returns the sum of the nonblank (non-null) values in the field. The data type can be number, currency, counter, date/time, or yes/no.
Avg	Returns the average of the non-null values in the field. The data type can be number, currency, counter, date/time, or yes/no.
Count	Returns the number of records that do not have a null value in this field. Works with any data type.
Count(*)	Returns the number of records, including those with a null value in this field. Works with any data type.
Min	Returns the smallest non-null value in this field. Works with any data type.
Max	Returns the largest non-null value in this field. Works with any data type.
First	Returns the first value in this field, even a null value. Works with any data type.
Last	Returns the last value found in this field, even a null value. Works with any data type.
Stdev	Returns the standard deviation of the values in this field. The data type must be number or currency, and must contain at least two records with non-null values.
Var	Returns the variance of the values in this field. The data type must be number or currency, and must contain at least two records with non-null values.

11. Click on the down arrow on the right side of the box, then click on Sum in the drop-down list. Your QBE grid should now look like this:

Field:	Order Date	Purchase Amount	
Total:	Where	Sum	
Sort:			
Show:	☐	☒	☐
Criteria:	Like "4/*/93"		
or:			

12. Click on the datasheet view button and you will see a single item labeled SumOfPurchase Amount as shown here (depending on the width of your column, the word *Amount* may or may not be showing):

SumOfPurchase Amount
$85.60

13. Close the query and name it **Total Sales - April 1993**.

In addition to calculating a single overall total, a query can create groups having common values and calculate subtotals for those groups. You will create such a query shortly, but first you need to define the relationships between the tables used in the query.

Defining Relationships between Tables

In the next example you will build a query that uses three tables plus an existing query. You have already seen that you can link two tables in a query by clicking and dragging the connecting field from one table to the other. If you use the same tables in other queries, you must link them again in each new query.

Instead of manually linking the tables in each new query, you can have Access automatically create the links if you define the relationship in advance. Once you define it, Access will use the relationship every time you build a query involving those tables.

The tables between which you will define a relationship are Suppliers and Books. The tables are linked by PubID.

Before you can define a relationship between two tables, you must be sure the data types of the linking fields will let you define the relationship. In the Suppliers table, PubID is a counter data type. Access stores counter values as long integers. To define the relationship, you must first be sure the data type of the PubID field in Books is number and the field size is Long Integer. To check this and make any necessary changes, use the following steps:

1. Click on the Table button in the Database window if it is not already selected.

2. Click on the Books table and then on the design view button.

3. Click in the Data Type box on the PubID line.

4. If the data type is not Number, click on the down arrow at the right side of the box and select Number from the drop-down list.

5. Click in the Field Size box in the Field Properties section of the Design view window.

6. If the field size is not Long Integer, click on the down arrow at the right side of the box and select Long Integer from the drop-down list.

7. To save your changes, double-click on the design window's Control-menu box and answer Yes to save the changes.

To define a relationship between Suppliers and Books, continue on with these steps:

1. Click on the Suppliers table.

2. Open the Edit menu and choose Relationships. Access opens the Relationships dialog box, with Suppliers already selected as the primary table.

3. Click on Many in the Type box if it is not already selected.

4. Click on the down arrow at the right end of the Related Table box and choose Books from the drop-down list.

5. Click on the down arrow at the right end of the Select Matching Fields box and choose PubID from the drop-down list.

6. Click on Enforce Referential Integrity. This tells Access to do the following:

   ◆ Allow a record in Books only if it has a PubID value that matches a PubID value in Suppliers

   ◆ Allow a record to be deleted from Suppliers only if there are no records in Books that have a corresponding PubID value

At this point your Relationships dialog box should look like this:

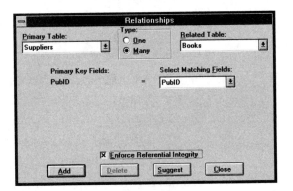

7. Click on Add to store the relationship.

8. Click on Close to close the dialog box.

Now when you use Suppliers and Books together in a query, Access will automatically link the tables by PubID.

You could also define relationships between Orders and Order Details, and between Books and Order Details. But you will usually use the query entitled Order Details with Calculated Fields rather than the Order Details table itself. You cannot establish a permanent relationship between a query and a table, or between two queries. You can, however, manually link a query to a table or a query to another query.

Creating a Select Query with Groups and Subtotals

Suppose that in addition to the overall sales in a given time period, you want to list the total book sales by supplier name for that same time period. This is more complicated than the last query in several ways. First, the query must show subtotals instead of a single grand total. Second, the analysis requires data from three tables and an existing query:

♦ The Orders table contains the order date, so you can determine which orders occurred in the time period.

♦ The Order Details with Calculated Fields query contains the sales total for each book in an order.

♦ The Books table identifies the supplier of each book.

♦ The Suppliers table contains the name of each supplier.

Creating the Query   To create this query, follow these steps:

1. Click on the Orders table and then click on the new query button in the toolbar. This opens the query window in Design view with the Orders table already selected for use in the query.

2. Open the Query menu and choose Add Table. The Add Table dialog box appears.

3. In the Table/Query list, double-click on Order Details with Calculated Fields, Books, and Suppliers, in that order. Then click on Close.

4. If you have already defined the relationship described in the previous section, "Defining Relationships between Tables," Access automatically links the Suppliers and Books tables. If you have not done this, you must link the tables now. Do this by dragging the PubID field in the Books field list to the PubID field in the Suppliers field list.

5. Drag the OrdID field in the Orders field list to the OrdID field in the Order Details with Calculated Fields field list.

6. Drag the BkID field in the Order Details with Calculated Fields field list and to the BkID field in the Books field list. At this point the tables should be linked as shown here:

7. Double-click on the following tables and fields in the order shown: Suppliers/Name, Orders/Order Date, Order Details with Calculated Fields/Ext Amt.

8. Click on the totals button in the toolbar. The Total line appears in the QBE grid with Group By in each field.

9. Click on the right end of the Total box in the Order Date field, opening the drop-down list.

10. Click on Where. Access removes the × from the Show box, because you cannot display a field if the Total box contains *Where.*

11. Click on the Criteria row in the Order Date field and type **4/*/93**. This tells Access to show you all the orders placed in April 1993. As soon as you move from this box the expression will be changed to `Like "4/*/93"` by Access.

12. Click on the right end of the Total box in the Ext Amt field and select Sum. At this point the QBE grid should look like this:

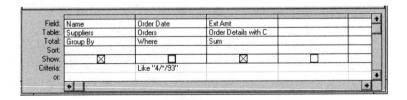

13. Click on the datasheet view button and you will see a list of supplier names and the total sales of books from each supplier for April 1993 like that shown here:

Name	SumOfExt Amt
▶ Bantam	$30.52
Berkley Publishing	$8.92
Morrow, William &	$20.66
Prima Publishing	$44.92
Simon and Schus!	$9.52
Wiley, John & Sor	$20.66

14. Click on the design view button to return to the query window in the Design view window.

You can make the query more flexible by letting the user enter a range of dates for which to see the summary values. To do this follow these steps:

1. Drag across the Criteria box in the Order Date field to highlight the contents.

2. Type **Between [Start Date] And [End Date]** and press ⸢Enter⸥. [Start Date] and [End Date] specify parameters for which Access will ask you to enter values when you run the query.

Ensuring Valid Date Entries   To be sure the user enters valid dates, you can tell Access what data type to expect for each of the parameters. To do this, follow these steps:

1. Open the Query menu and select Parameters.

2. The insertion point should be in the first box in the Parameter column; type **Start Date**.

3. Press ⸢Tab⸥ to move to the first box in the Data Type column.

4. Click on the down arrow at the right of the box and click on Date/Time in the drop-down list.

5. Click on the second box in the Parameter column, type **End Date**, and press ⸢Tab⸥.

6. Click on the down arrow at the right of the box and click on Date/Time in the drop-down list.

7. Click on OK to save the values.

8. Click on the datasheet view button.

9. Access asks you for the start date. Type **4/1/93** and press Enter.

10. Access asks you for the end date. Type **4/30/93** and press Enter. Access shows you the same values as when the Order Date was specified as 4/*/93. But with this revised query you can see the totals for any range of dates.

11. Double-click on the datasheet's Control-menu box.

12. Click on Yes to save the query, type **Sales Volume by Supplier** when requested, and click on OK.

Creating a Crosstab Query

Sometimes the datasheet of a query has a format that is awkward to interpret. A typical example occurs when you subtotal a series of values on a monthly basis, as seen here:

Month	Title	Book Amount
March	Making of Microsof	$11.66
March	Patriot Games	$4.21
March	A Brief History of Ti	$15.26
March	Hackers	$16.16
April	Windows 3.1 with M	$44.92
April	Dragon	$4.76
April	A Brief History of Ti	$30.52
April	Hard Drive	$20.66

A spreadsheet layout such as that shown below is easier to interpret and to use in graphs:

Title	March	April
History of Time	15.26	30.52
Dragon		4.76
Hackers	16.16	
Hard Drive		20.66
Making of Microsof	11.66	
Patriot Games	4.21	
Windows 3.1 with M		44.92

This spreadsheet layout is called a *crosstab*. Next, create a crosstab query that provides a spreadsheet layout showing the total sales of each book in each month for a specified time period, similar to the above illustration. Follow these steps:

1.   Click on the Table button if it is not already selected.

2.   Click on the Orders table and then click on the new query button. This opens the query window in Design view with the Orders table already selected for use in the query.

3.   Open the Query menu and choose Add Table. The Add Table dialog box appears.

4.   In the Table/Query list double-click on both Order Details with Calculated Fields and Books and then click on the Close button.

5.   Drag the OrdID field in the Orders field list to the OrdID field in the Order Details with Calculated Fields field list.

6.   Drag the BkID field in the Books field list to the BkID field in the Order Details with Calculated Fields field list. The three lists are now linked.

7.   Click on the Field box in the first column in the QBE grid. Type the following expression to show the name of each month:

   Month: Format([order date],"mmmm")

   Format is an Access function that lets you specify a display format. The notation "mmmm" produces the full name of the month. Use "mmm" if you want to see the three-letter abbreviation for each month. For detailed information about the Format function, search on Format in the Access help system.

8.   Double-click on Title in the Books field list, Ext Amt in the Order Details with Calculated Fields field list, and Order Date in the Orders field list—in that order—to move them to the Field boxes in the QBE grid.

9.   Click on the Show box of the Order Date field to hide the field.

10. Click on the Criteria row of the Order Date field and type */*/93 to select all the data from 1993. The QBE grid should now look similar to this:

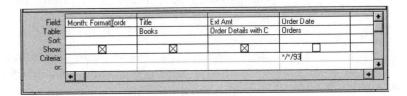

Field:	Month: Format([orde	Title	Ext Amt	Order Date	
Table:		Books	Order Details with C	Orders	
Sort:					
Show:	☒	☒	☒	☐	
Criteria:				*/*/93	
or:					

11. Click on the datasheet view button. The dynaset at this point shows one record for each order detail record in the time period.

12. Click on the design view button to return to the design window.

13. Click on the totals button in the toolbar to display the Total row in the QBE grid.

14. Click on the right end of the Total box for the Month field (first column) and select Group By from the drop-down list.

15. If Group By is not already entered in the Total box of the Title column, select it.

16. Click on the right end of the Total box of the Ext Amt column and select Sum from the drop-down list.

17. Click on the right end of the Total box of the Order Date column and select Where from the drop-down list. The QBE grid should now look like this:

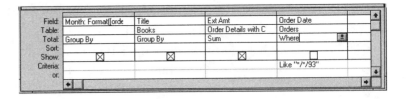

Field:	Month: Format([orde	Title	Ext Amt	Order Date	
Table:		Books	Order Details with C	Orders	
Total:	Group By	Group By	Sum	Where	☝
Sort:					
Show:	☒	☒	☒	☐	
Criteria:				Like "*/*/93"	
or:					

18. Click on the datasheet view button. The datasheet shows that the results are now grouped by month and title, as shown in the next illustration:

Month	Title	SumOfExt Amt
April	A Brief History of Ti	$30.52
April	Dragon	$9.52
April	Hard Drive	$20.66
April	Patriot Games	$8.92
April	Whirlwind	$20.66
April	Windows 3.1 with M	$44.92
March	A Brief History of Ti	$15.26
March	Hackers	$16.16
March	Making of Microsof	$11.66
March	Patriot Games	$4.21

Tip

The months are arranged alphabetically, not chronologically. You can insert a column to the left of the others and define it as:

```
Month Num: DatePart("m",[Order Date])
```

This would force the months to group by month number, which would put them in the correct order. This step is not required for the crosstab, so you can skip it.

19. Click on the design view button to return to the query window in Design view.

20. Open the File menu and choose Save. Type **Sales by Book per Month - 1993**. You are not through yet, but you have already put a lot of work into building this query. You should save it now to safeguard your work. You can always delete the query later if you decide you do not need it.

21. To convert this query to a crosstab query, open the Query menu and choose Crosstab. In the QBE grid, a Crosstab row appears, and the Show row disappears.

To create the crosstab you need to specify three parameters: the row headings, the column headings, and the values to place in the intersections. Follow these steps:

1. Specify the Month (first) column as providing the column headings by clicking on the right end of Crosstab box in the Month column and selecting Column Heading from the pull-down list.

2. Use the same procedure to specify the Title column as providing the Row Headings and the Ext Amt column as providing the Values.

3. If you added a Month Num column, delete it by clicking on the column selector and pressing the ⌊Delete⌋ key. The QBE grid should now look similar to this:

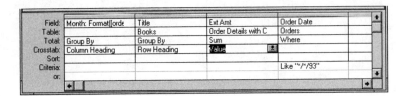

4. Click on the datasheet view button to see the crosstab query, which looks like a spreadsheet:

Title	April	March
A Brief History of Ti	$30.52	$15.26
Dragon	$9.52	
Hackers		$16.16
Hard Drive	$20.66	
Making of Microsof		$11.66
Patriot Games	$8.92	$4.21
Whirlwind	$20.66	
Windows 3.1 with M	$44.92	

Notice that the month names are again arranged alphabetically, rather than chronologically. You will fix that next.

Specifying Fixed-Column Headings

Access has an option that lets you arrange the column headings exactly as you want. To do this, follow these steps:

1. Click on the design view button to return to the query window in Design view.

2. Click on the properties button in the toolbar and then click on Fixed Column Headings. In the text box type the full month names in the same order you want to see them appear in the fixed column locations, like this (you do not have to type the quotation marks; Access will add them automatically):

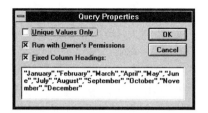

The values you enter must match exactly the values that Access will generate for the column headings. If the formula for the Month column generates three-letter month abbreviations, you must enter the same abbreviations here.

3.   Click on the datasheet view button to see the final result. The fixed column headings force the crosstab columns to appear in the desired order as shown here:

Title	January	February	March	April	May
A Brief History of Ti			$15.26	$30.52	
Dragon				$9.52	
Hackers			$16.16		
Hard Drive				$20.66	
Making of Microsof			$11.66		
Patriot Games			$4.21	$8.92	
Whirlwind				$20.66	
Windows 3.1 with M				$44.92	

Crosstab Query: Sales by Book per Month - 1993

Note   **Unlike a spreadsheet, you cannot calculate grand totals down the columns or across the rows. However, you could create a report based on the crosstab and create those totals in the report.**

4.   Double-click on the datasheet's Control-menu box and click on Yes to save the changes.

Displaying Unique Values

A table often has some redundant data. This is especially true of cities, states, and ZIP codes in address lists. Access will let you isolate the unique values in the redundant data. For example, suppose you want to see the names of the cities where you have customers. If you have several customers in one city, a plain select query will show the city name once for each customer. Instead you can tell Access to display unique values in the query's dynaset.

To display a list of unique city names from the Customer list, follow these steps:

1. Click on the Table button if it is not already selected.

2. Highlight the Customers table.

3. Click on the new query button. This opens the query window in Design view with the Customers table already selected for use in the query.

4. Double-click on City in the Customers field list to place it in the first column in the QBE grid.

5. Click on the datasheet view button to make a quick check of the datasheet, which shows that Seattle appears a number of times.

6. Click on the design view button, click on the properties button (fourth from the left), and then click on Unique Values Only, as shown here:

Be sure Restrict Available Fields is also selected, or you will get an error when you run the query. Access cannot have both unique values and unrestricted fields.

7. Click on OK to save the query properties and then click on the datasheet view button to display the datasheet and see a list of unique city names. Note that they are also sorted, as you can see in the following illustration:

City
▶ Bellevue
Bellingham
Black Diamond
Bow
Clinton
Edmonds
Kent
Lake City
Langley
Redmond
Renton
Seattle

8.   Double-click on the query's Control-menu box and save it as **Unique Cities**.

Displaying Records with No Match (Outer Joins)

When you create a query with two linked tables, Access normally shows results only for records that have matching values in the linking fields in both tables. But sometimes you want to see all the records from one of the tables, even if there is no matching value in the other table.

For example, if you create the query shown in Figure 7-16, the dynaset will look like this:

Last Name	LastOfOrder Date
▶ DeMuth	3/5/93
Rondell	4/5/93
Vanderbilt	4/8/93

These results show only customers who have placed an order, as well as the date of each customer's last order.

Suppose you want to see all the names in your Customers table, even if they have no orders on record. In addition, you want to see the last order date for each customer who has placed an order. To accomplish this, follow these steps:

Figure 7-16

This query design will show only customers who have placed an order.

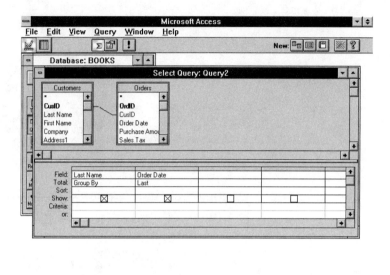

1. Click on the Table button if it is not already selected and click on the Customers table.

2. Click on the new query button to open the query window in Design view with the Customers table already selected.

3. Open the Query menu and choose Add Table. The Add Table dialog box appears.

4. In the Table/Query list double-click on Orders and then click on Close.

5. Drag the CusID field in the Customers field list to CusID in the Orders field list. This links the tables.

6. Double-click on Last Name in the Customers field list and on Order Date in the Orders field list. The query at this stage will display the names and all the order dates of customers who have placed orders.

7. Click on the totals button. This opens the Total line in the QBE grid.

8. If the Total box in the Last Name column does not contain Group By, click on the right of the Total box and select Group By from the drop-down list.

9. Click on the right of the Total box in the Order Date field and select Last from the drop-down list. The query at this stage will display the names and the last order date of customers who have placed orders.

10. To display all the customers, double-click on the line joining the two table lists in the upper portion of the design window. This opens the Join Properties dialog box.

11. Click on the second choice to tell Access to include all the Customers records, as shown here:

12. Click on OK to close the Join Properties dialog box. Notice that the line joining the tables has become an arrow pointing from the Customers table to the Orders table.

13. Click on the datasheet view button. The dynaset now shows all the customers, as well as the date of the last order for customers who have placed orders, as shown here:

Last Name	LastOfOrder Dat
Anderson	
Barton	
Cummings	
Dailey	
DeMuth	3/5/93
Devereaux	
Eskenazi	
Fakkema	
Farquhar	
Gallagher	
Martinez	
Potter	
Rondell	4/5/93
Sato	
Stevens	
Vanderbilt	4/8/93

14. Close the query and name it **Last Order Date of Each Customer**.

Using a Select Query as the Basis of a Form or Report

If your purpose for creating a select query is to provide data for a form or a report, you can make all the fields from the tables used in the query available to the form or report, even if the fields do not appear in the QBE grid. For example, suppose you want to send letters to all of your customers who have an outstanding balance. Follow these steps to create a query that will extract the correct data for that report:

1. Click on the Table button and on the Customers table if they are not already selected.

2. Click on the new query button to open the query window in Design view with the Customers table already selected.

3. Double-click on the BalDue field to add it to the QBE grid.

4. Click on the Criteria box of the BalDue column in the QBE grid and type **>0**. This criterion will extract all the customers with a positive balance due.

5. To make data available from all the fields, click on the properties button to open the Query Properties dialog box and click on Restrict Available Fields to turn off the option. The Query Properties dialog should look like this:

6. Click on OK to close the Query Properties dialog box, then look at the results by clicking on the datasheet view button. All the fields appear in the result. Notice that BalDue is the first field in the datasheet.

Tip

If you click on the Show box of the BalDue column in the design window, you will hide this instance of BalDue, but it will still appear in its normal position in the datasheet.

7. Double-click on the Control-menu box. Save the query as **Balances Due.**

Creating Action Queries

All of the queries you have seen so far create dynasets that display data directly from tables and from calculations. None of the queries changed any data. There are times, however, when you need to make bulk (*global*) changes to your data. For example, you might need to increase the list prices of all books from one supplier by ten percent. If the change involves more than a few books, this can be tedious to do manually. With an action query, you can have Access automatically change the prices.

There are four types of action queries:

- ♦ A *make-table* query creates a new, permanent, data table.
- ♦ A *delete* query removes records from a table.
- ♦ An *append* query adds data from one table to another.
- ♦ An *update* query changes the values in a table based on formulas you enter in the query.

In each case, you can limit the action to just the records matching criteria you specify.

Caution

Action queries are powerful tools and can be dangerous if not used correctly. If you use the wrong criteria or calculations, you may lose valuable data. The first safeguard is to make sure you have a current valid backup of your database before you run an action query. You should back up your data regularly anyway, but especially before you run action queries. The second safeguard is to first set up an action query as a select query, to see what data appears in the dynaset. This is the data that will be affected by the action query. Once you are satisfied that the query is selecting the proper data, you can convert it to an action query and run it.

Creating a Make-Table Query

Although you should usually avoid having redundant data in your database, there are times when it is useful to create duplicate data sets. For example, you might want to create a sample table to test an update query that will change your data. By testing it on the sample table, you can avoid problems if the update goes awry. Or you might want to create an archive table to move seldom-used data from an active table so processing on the active table goes faster.

Suppose you want to create a reference table that combines data from the Books and Suppliers tables. You want the data combined into one table so you can export it for use in a spreadsheet (Access exports data only from tables, not from queries). Follow these instructions to create the reference table ready for export:

1. Click on the Table button and on the Books table if they are not already selected.

2. Click on the new query button to open the query window in Design view with the Books table field list displayed.

3. Choose Add Table from the Query menu, double-click on Suppliers, and click on the Close button.

4. Access should automatically link the tables. If not, drag PubID from the Books field list to PubID in the Suppliers field list.

5. In the Books field list double-click on Title, Author, and Price.

6. In the Suppliers field list double-click on Name.

7. Click on the right end of the Sort box in the Title column and select Ascending from the drop-down list.

8. Click on the left edge (to the left of the word *Price*) in the Field box for the Price column and type **List Price:**. The colon is required. This designates List Price as the title of the field.

9. Click on the left edge (to the left of the word *Name*) in the Field box for the Name column and type **Publisher:**. Again

the colon is required to designate Publisher as the title of the field. At this point your QBE grid should look like this:

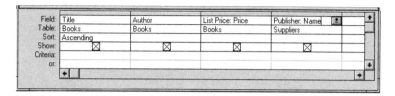

10. Click on the datasheet view button to display the data that will be copied to the new table. It should look like Figure 7-17.

11. Click on the design view button to return to the query window in Design view. If the datasheet did not show the results you expected, correct the problem before continuing.

12. Once you are satisfied that the query produces the data you want, open the Query menu and choose Make Table. A Query Properties dialog box appears. Type **Books plus Publishers** for the table name. Leave the other options as they are. The dialog box should look like this:

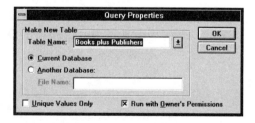

13. Click on OK to close the dialog box.

14. Click on the run button (the exclamation point in the toolbar) to create the new table. Access tells you how many rows it will copy and waits for your permission to create the new table, as shown here (your number of rows may be different):

15. Click on OK to create the new table.

16. Double-click on the Control-menu box of the design window, click on Yes to save the query, type **Make Books plus Publishers Table,** and click on OK.

17. Click on the Query button in the Database window and notice in the Queries list that the icon for the new query includes an exclamation point:

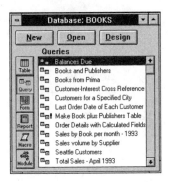

This warns you that this is an action query, so you do not unknowingly change your database. Running the query will update the new table with the latest entries in the Books and Publishers tables. You may or may not want this to happen.

18. Click on the Table button, then double-click on Books plus Publishers. The contents of the table are identical to the datasheet from the earlier select query shown in Figure 7-17.

19. Open the File menu and choose Save to save the new table.

Note
Be sure you understand the difference between a table produced by a make-table query and a dynaset produced by a select query. The table is a snapshot of the data as it exists when the query was run. It contains its own set of data that can be manipulated without affecting, or being affected by, the data in the original tables. A dynaset does not actually contain any data. It simply displays data as it currently exists in tables and as the result of calculations.

Figure 7-17

Look at an action query first as a select query to make sure the query produces the data you expect.

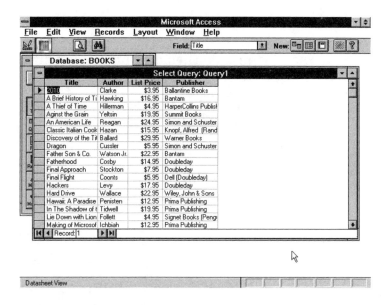

Creating a Delete Query

Suppose you need to delete all of one publisher's books from the new table you just created. You can do this easily with a delete query, as follows (the new Books plus Publishers table should be open):

1. Click on the new query button. This opens the query window in Design view with the Books plus Publishers table already selected for use in the query.

2. Double-click on the Publisher field to add it to the QBE grid.

3. Click on the Criteria box in the Publisher column and type **"Prima Publishing"** (the quotation marks are required because of the space between the words). Your Design view should look like this:

4. Click on the datasheet view button to check the datasheet and verify that only Prima Publishing shows up in the results. Then click on the design view button to return to the Design view.

5. Open the Query menu and choose Delete to make this a Delete query.

6. Click on the run button. Access warns you that it is about to delete a certain number of rows and waits for your permission to continue, as shown here (your number of rows may be different):

7. Click on OK to actually do the deletion.

8. Double-click on the Control-menu box of the design window. Click on Yes to save the query, type **Delete Prima from Books plus Publishers Table**, and click on OK.

Access indicates deleted rows in the open Books plus Publishers table by using the notation #Deleted, as you can see in Figure 7-18.

9. Double-click on the Control-menu box for the Books plus Publishers table to close it. Then click on the Open button in the Database window to reopen the same table. Notice that the marked rows are gone.

10. Double-click on the Control-menu box for the Books plus Publishers table to close it again.

Creating an Append Query

Whoops! You just realized that you deleted the wrong records from the Books plus Publishers table. Fortunately that table is not the master source of the data, so you can add the missing data back into the table using an append query. Use the following steps:

Figure 7-18

A table that is
open during a
delete query on
the table will
have the
deleted records
marked with
"#Deleted."

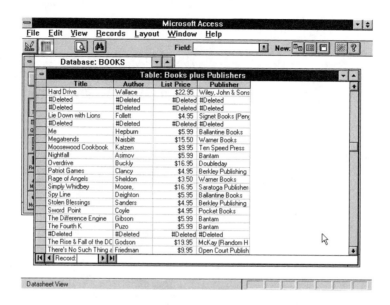

1.   Click on the Query button and on the query named Make
     Books plus Publishers Table. This already has the struc-
     ture required to append data into all the columns of the
     table called Make Books plus Publishers.

2.   Click on the design view button to open the query win-
     dow in Design view.

3.   To avoid destroying the original make-table query, first
     save the query under a new name. Open the Files menu,
     choose Save As, name the query **Append Prima to Books
     plus Publishers Table**, and click on OK.

4.   To convert the query into an append query, open the Query
     menu and choose Append. A Query Properties dialog box
     opens up with Books plus Publishers in the Table Name
     list box like this:

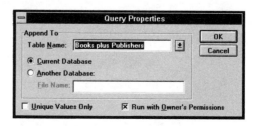

5. Click on OK to accept the default values in the dialog box. A new row appears in the QBE grid. The Append To row lets you specify the destination for the data from each of the source fields. Notice that the Append To row has no entries for the List Price or Publisher columns:

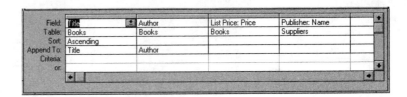

Field:	Title	±	Author		List Price: Price	Publisher: Name		±
Table:	Books		Books		Books	Suppliers		
Sort:	Ascending							
Append To:	Title		Author					
Criteria:								±
or:								

This is because the Books plus Publishers table uses different field names than the Books and Suppliers tables for the same data. You need to tell Access which columns to use as destinations for the data from the Price and Name fields.

6. Click on the right end of the Append To box of the List Price column and select List Price from the drop-down list.

7. Click on the right end of the Append To box of the Publisher column and select Publisher from the drop-down list.

8. To limit the append action to books from Prima, click on the Criteria box in the Publisher column and type **"Prima Publishing"** (the quotation marks are required). The QBE grid should now look like this:

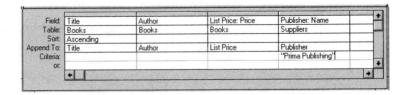

Field:	Title	Author		List Price: Price	Publisher: Name		±
Table:	Books	Books		Books	Suppliers		
Sort:	Ascending						
Append To:	Title	Author		List Price	Publisher		
Criteria:					"Prima Publishing"		±
or:							

9. Double-click on the Control-menu box and click on Yes to save the changes.

10. Double-click on the Append Prima to Books plus Publishers query to append the records. Access displays a dialog box to warn you it is about to modify data:

11. Click on OK. Access displays another dialog box to tell you how many rows it will append:

12. Again click on OK. Access adds the records to the end of the Books plus Publishers table.

13. When the action is finished, click on Table in the Database window, double-click on the Books plus Publishers table, and scroll to the bottom of the datasheet where you will see the books from Prima Publishing, as shown in Figure 7-19.

14. Double-click on the Control-menu box of the Books plus Publishers table window to close it. Click on Yes to save the changes.

Caution

When you append data from one table to another, be sure the receiving field sizes are large enough to accept the data. If a receiving field is too small, Access will truncate the data without warning.

Figure 7-19

Appended
records are
always added at
the end of a
table.

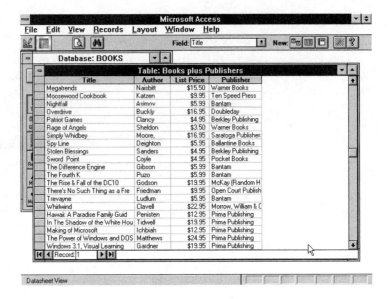

Creating an Update Query

The action queries you have seen so far (make-table, delete, append) have added or removed rows of data, but have not changed the values in existing rows. An update query changes the data in tables without adding or deleting rows. A typical example of an update query would be to change a group of prices according to a formula.

For example, suppose Prima announces a general price decrease of five percent. You can create an update query to calculate the new prices and replace the old values in the books table with the new values. As with any action query, you should start by making a select query to be sure that the proper data will be changed. Do that with these instructions:

1. Click on the Table button and on Books if they are not already selected.

2. Click on the new query button to open the query window in Design view with the Books table selected.

3. Open the Query menu and choose Add Table. The Add Table dialog box appears.

4. In the Table/Query list double-click on Suppliers and then click on the Close button.

5. Access should automatically link the tables. If not, drag PubID in the Books field list to PubID in the Suppliers field list.

6. In the Books field list double-click on both Title and Price.

7. In the Suppliers field list double-click on Name.

8. Click on the Criteria box in the Name column and type **"Prima Publishing"** (the quotation marks are required). At this point the QBE grid should look like this:

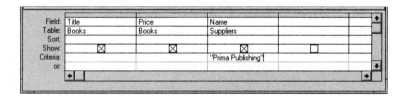

9. Click on the datasheet view button to display the data that will be affected by the query. It should looks like this:

Title	Price	Name
Making of Microsof	$12.95	Prima Publishing
The Power of Winc	$24.95	Prima Publishing
Hawaii: A Paradise	$12.95	Prima Publishing
In The Shadow of t	$19.95	Prima Publishing
Windows 3.1, Visua	$19.95	Prima Publishing

10. Click on the design view button to return to the query window in Design view.

11. If the datasheet did not show the results you expected, review the steps above before continuing.

12. In the design window, open the Query menu and choose Update. An Update To row appears in the QBE grid.

13. Click on the Update To box in the Price column and type **[price]*0.95**. The QBE grid should look like the following illustration:

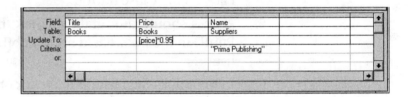

14. Click on the run button and then on OK to tell Access to proceed with the update.

15. When the update is finished, open the Query menu and choose Select.

16. Click on the datasheet view button and you will see that the prices are five percent lower than they were before you ran the query, as shown here:

Title	Price	Name
▶ Making of Microsof	$12.30	Prima Publishing
The Power of Winc	$23.70	Prima Publishing
Hawaii: A Paradise	$12.30	Prima Publishing
In The Shadow of t	$18.95	Prima Publishing
Windows 3.1, Visua	$18.95	Prima Publishing

17. Click on the design view button, open the Query menu, and select Update. This leaves the query the way you built it for the next time you run it.

18. Double-click on the Control-menu box of the design window, click on Yes to save the query, type **Reduce Prima Prices**, and click on OK.

About Queries and SQL

All the queries in this chapter were built using the Access query window in Design view. This style of query design is known as *Query-by-example* (QBE). It is one of two major methods of querying a database. The other major query method is known as

Structured Query Language or SQL (pronounced either *s q l* or *sequel*).

Access generates an SQL statement for each query you design. At any time while you are designing a query, if you want to see the SQL statement that is equivalent to your design, open the View menu and choose SQL. A dialog box containing the SQL statement will appear, as shown here for the last query you did:

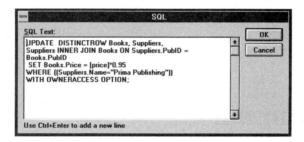

If you are familiar with SQL, you can modify the statement and observe the effects of the change on the QBE design. SQL statements can be copied to the Clipboard and pasted into record selection statements for macros, forms, and reports. The use of SQL statements is beyond the scope of this book.

Common Problems with Action Queries

Access identifies three types of errors when you run an action query:

- ◆ **Key Violations**. Recall that a primary key must have unique values. If an append or update query would result in duplicate key values in a table, Access will issue an error message. You will have to change one of the values before you can add the new data. The easiest way to avoid key violations is to use the counter data type for primary keys and let Access generate the key values for the records that are appended or updated.

◆ **Conversion Errors.** If an append or update query tries to place data in a field with an incompatible data type, Access will give an error message. For example, if you try to append Text data to a Number field, you will cause a conversion error.

◆ **Locked Records.** If you are making global changes to one or more tables on a network and Access encounters records that are locked by other users, it will warn you that it cannot perform the action on those records. In such a situation, you usually should cancel the query and try it again later. If you complete the query in spite of the warning message, some records might be left unchanged.

Summary

Queries give you a very powerful tool with which to manipulate your data. In this chapter you have seen how to do the following operations:

◆ Build a select query to display data meeting specified conditions from one or more tables

◆ Build a make-table query to create new tables from existing tables

◆ Build an update query to perform global changes to data in tables

◆ Build a delete query to delete records from a table

◆ Build an append query to add records from one table to another

◆ Specify conditions to limit the records affected by a query

◆ Define computed columns in a query

◆ Perform summary calculations in a query

◆ Create groups in a query

◆ Modify a query

The next chapter shows you how to bring data into Access from other database and spreadsheet applications and how to transfer data out of Access to those and other applications.

Transferring Data

There are many database management applications like Access and almost as many different formats as there are applications. If you have been using another database application or have an associate who has, and you now want to utilize that information in Access, you can do so by either attaching the existing information or by importing it. By *attaching* a table, Access can work with some database files in their original format, without creating a new table. By *importing* a table, Access makes a copy of an existing non-Access table in the Access format. Both Attach Table and Import are options in the File menu and require that a new or existing database be open.

You can use the Attach Table option to work with database files in the following application formats:

- Btrieve
- dBASE III and IV
- Paradox 3.x
- Microsoft SQL Server

Alternatively, you can use the Import option to copy and change the formats of files from other applications into Access tables. These applications include all those listed above plus the following:

- Excel
- FoxPro 2.0
- Lotus (WKS, WK1, and WK3)
- Text (delimited)
- Text (fixed-width)

Possibly by the time you read this, Paradox 4.x, FoxPro 2.5, Oracle, DB2, and Rdb will have been added to the list of application formats that Access can attach. These are to be added during 1993.

Guidelines for Transferring Data

The first question you have to ask yourself is, "How do I want to use this data: should the original format remain intact or should it be changed to the Access format?" Your answer will determine how you proceed.

The important considerations as you decide between the Import and Attach Table options are as follows:

- With the Import option the files are copied and changed into the Access table format and there is no remaining link to the original file. You can use the new table like any table created in Access, doing such things as working in the design window to add or delete controls. Use this option when you have no further need to work with the data in its original format.
- The Attach Table option is useful if there is more than one database program in use within your work group or company. When you use Attach Table, the table remains in its original format. The data in the attached table is not transferred; instead there is a link formed between Access and the attached table. In addition, an icon is placed in the Database window to indicate that the table is linked. You can open the table and edit it like any other in Access, but you are actually editing in the original table. Any changes you make to the table will be observable in the other application. If you delete the icon you are only removing the link between Access and the original table.

Analyzing the Database Structure

When you transfer data within Access and between applications you usually need to know the structure of the incoming tables. Often when data is transferred, the properties of the fields are changed and you need to use the design view window to restore them. Included with Access is a program called Database Analyzer that analyzes the structure of the original table and places it in a new table that can be viewed or printed. There are several steps that must be taken to install and run the program.

First, the MSACCESS.INI file, which is in the directory in which you have placed Windows—usually C:\WINDOWS—needs to be changed by adding a line with ANALYZER.MDA in it. If you are in Access, save any open files and exit to the Windows Program Manager. In any case you should be in the Windows Program Manager.

1. Start the Windows Notepad application by double-clicking on its icon. Click on Open in the File menu and select MSACCESS.INI from the directory in which you placed Windows.

2. Scroll to just beneath the [Libraries] section header in MSACCESS.INI, press [Enter] to create a new line, and then type **analyzer.mda=** on that new line.

3. From the File menu choose Save to save MSACCESS.INI and then close Notepad by double-clicking on its Control-menu box.

4. Start Access by double-clicking on its icon.

Next, make a macro to run Analyzer. Macros are covered in detail in Chapter 9, but for now you need this simple macro. Make it using these steps:

1. Open the BOOKS.MDB database or any one you want to analyze. Click on the Macro button and on New in the Database window. The Macro window will appear where you can construct the macro.

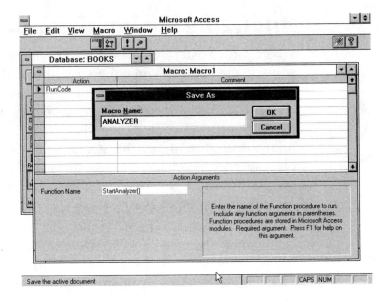

2. In the first line in the Action column, click on the arrow
    on the right side, then scroll down to RunCode and click
    on it. RunCode now appears on the first line in the Action
    column.

3. Click in the Function Name box in the Action Arguments
    section and type **StartAnalyzer()**. There is no space in the
    function name and parentheses are required.

4. Choose Save in the File menu. The Save As dialog box appears.
    Type the name **ANALYZER**, as you see in Figure 8-1.

5. Click on OK. Close the Macro window by double-clicking
    on its Control-menu box. The macro name will appear in
    the Books Database window each time the Macro button
    is clicked.

Access is now ready to run the Database Analyzer in the Books
database. If you want to run the Analyzer macro in another database, you need to copy the macro you created into that database.
Use the macro to run Database Analyzer by following these steps:

1. Click on the Macro button in the Books Database window
    and then click on the run button. The Database Analyzer
    dialog box appears.

2.   Click on the Table button in the dialog box and all the Books database tables appear in the Items Available list. Select the Books table or any other table you want to analyze and click on the right arrow to move it to the Items Selected list as you see here:

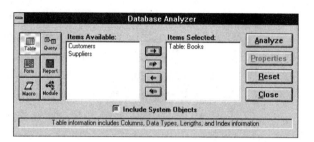

You can select as many tables as you wish and move them to Items Selected, then click on Analyze.

3.   The Select an Output Database dialog box appears and you select the database in which to store the analysis. This can be the Books database or an empty database set up for this purpose. Click on OK and the Process Completed information box appears, where you read the message and again click on OK. Then click on Close in the Database Analyzer dialog box.

4.   A new table appears in the Database window, named "@TableDetails." When you open this table the structure for all the tables you selected is shown. This table can be printed like any other. The @TableDetails table for the Books table looks like this:

TableName	Name	Type	Length	IndexName
Books	BkID	Long	4	PrimaryKey
Books	ISBN	Text	10	ISBN
Books	Title	Text	30	Title
Books	Author	Text	20	Author
Books	PubID	Integer	2	
Books	Price	Currency	8	
Books	OnHand	Integer	2	
Books	Order	Integer	2	
Books	Category	Text	10	

Record: 1

You can analyze the structure of any of the objects in the Database window including tables, queries, forms, reports, macros, and modules.

Preparing to Transfer Data

Before you can transfer data, whether it is from another Access table or another database format, you must prepare Access to perform the transfer. To do this, you must first open the database which is going to receive the imported or attached table or which contains the table to be exported. The File menu will change to include the Import, Export, and Attach Table options, as you see here:

You can only perform these transfer operations if you have an existing database open in Access. This means that you may have to create a new database into which you import or to which you attach an external table.

Transferring between Two Access Databases

You can work with tables from other Access databases while working in the Database window. When you open the Database window, you notice there is no way to open an additional database. However, Access has provided a way to work with tables from several databases without actually having them open.

Attaching Access Tables

You can attach as many tables as you wish to your Database window and use them as though they are part of that database. The only indication that they are attached is that Access has placed an arrow on the table icon in the Database window.

Suppose you need to look at a table named Employees, located in another database, while you still have the Books database open. Employees is located in the database named C:\ACCESS\NWIND.MDB (if C:\ACCESS\ is the path to your Access files). This is a sample database that was copied to the Access directory when you did the initial setup and installation. To see how to attach tables from another Access database, follow these steps:

1. Open the database BOOKS.MDB, if it is not already open, by choosing Open Database in the File menu, selecting the C:\BOOKSTOR directory, choosing the file BOOKS.MDB, and clicking on OK.

> **Tip**

> **When you open the File menu, you see at the bottom of the menu a list of the last four databases that have been opened. If the database you want is in the list, click on it or type its number to open it. This saves time by skipping the steps with the Open Database dialog box.**

2. Open the File menu again and click on Attach Table. The Attach dialog box opens with Microsoft Access selected as you see here:

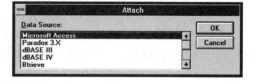

    Since the table you are planning to attach was created using Access, click on OK.

3. The Select Microsoft Access Database dialog box appears. Make certain the Directories list box has C:\ACCESS. Then

click on NWIND.MDB in the File Name list box, as shown
in Figure 8-2, and click on OK.

4.   The Attach Tables dialog box appears. Select the Employees
     table as you see here:

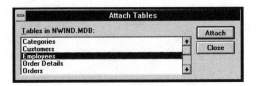

5.   Click on Attach and an information box will appear telling
     you that Employees is successfully attached. Click on OK
     and then on Close.

When the Database window reappears, you see that Employees
has been added to the list of tables in the Books database. You
can tell it is attached because there is an arrow over the Employees icon, as shown here:

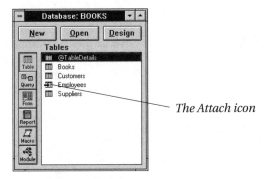

The Attach icon

The attached table can be used much like other tables in the window. You can edit the information in the fields but you cannot
make changes to the table structure. If you attempt to open the
table in Design view, you get a question box explaining that most
properties cannot be modified and asking if you want to open
anyway. The field properties that can be changed are these:

   ◆   Caption
   ◆   Decimal Places

Figure 8-2

The Select
Microsoft
Access
Database
dialog box
allows you to
select an Access
database
containing the
table to be
attached.

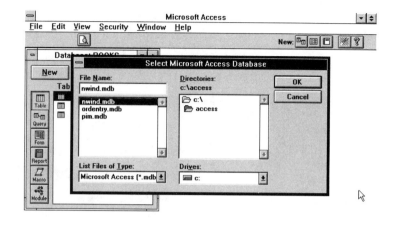

- ◆ Default Value
- ◆ Format
- ◆ Validation Rule
- ◆ Validation Text

Remember that any changes you make to the attached table will
appear in the original table as a permanent change.

Importing Access Tables

Importing tables differs from attaching them in one very important way. The Import command makes a copy of the table to be
imported and does not form a link between the original table and
the Access table it creates. The database where you are working
receives a new table, to which you can make any changes you
like. The original table, though, will not be affected. Try these
steps to import an Access table (use the same table as before in
order to demonstrate the difference between importing and
attaching):

1. From the File menu choose Import and a dialog box will
    appear in which you can choose the database source.

Make certain Microsoft Access is highlighted and click on OK. The same Select Microsoft Access Database dialog box that you saw in Figure 8-2 will appear.

2. Make certain the Directories list box is displaying C:\ACCESS. Click on NWIND.MDB in the File Name list box, then click on OK.

3. The Import Objects dialog box appears as you see here:

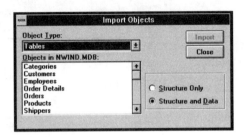

The Object Type drop-down list box gives you the opportunity to select what you want to import: tables, forms, reports, etc. Tables is highlighted and you can use that, but there are other choices if you click on the drop-down list arrow to the right of the Object Type list box.

4. Click on Employees in the list box below to select it. You are going to import the Employees table.

5. Another choice in this dialog box is whether you want to import the table with its contents, or just import its structure. The Structure Only option is valuable if you want to use another table's format and then put in your own data. For this exercise, choose Structure and Data.

6. Click on Import and an information box appears to tell you Employees1 is successfully imported. The number 1 was added to the name because there is already a table called Employees. Click on OK and then on Close.

You can see there is no arrow on the icon for Employees1. This indicates that it is an Access table in this database and is not linked to any other database.

To see the difference in the way two tables can be used, use the following steps:

1. Select the attached table, Employees, and then click on Design. A question box appears to tell you Employees is an attached table and to ask if you want to open it anyway. In this case choose Cancel.

2. Select Employees1 and click on Design. You can see that this table does not have any restrictions and can be changed as you see fit. Close this table by double-clicking on the Control-menu box in the title bar.

3. Delete the two Employees tables by selecting each of them in turn and pressing (Delete) or choosing the Delete option in the Edit menu. For the Employees1 table that you imported, you are actually deleting the table in the Books database. For the Employees table that you attached, all you are doing is deleting the link. The original table in the NWIND database is not affected by either operation.

Exporting to Access

There is very little difference between exporting and importing an object when you are working with two Access databases. What you are doing is copying a report, table, form, or other object from the open database in which you are working to another existing Access database.

Creating an Empty Database

In order to try the Export option, you will need an Access database to receive the exported object. Use these steps to create an empty database:

1. Choose the New Database command in the File menu. The New Database dialog box appears.

2. Select C:\BOOKSTOR in the Directory list box. This will be the directory to receive the new database that you create.

Figure 8-3

The New
Database
dialog box
allows you to
name a new
database.

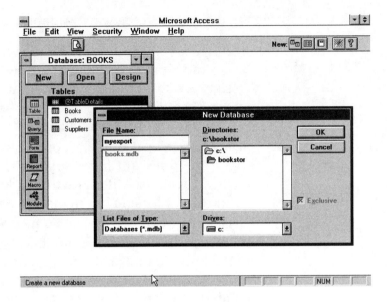

3.   Give the new database a name by clicking in the File
     Name text box and typing some name such as **myexport**,
     as you see in Figure 8-3. Click on OK.

4.   You should have a blank Database window with the title
     bar containing `Database: MYEXPORT`. Close the window,
     because the database you export to does not have to be
     open. Do this by choosing Close Database in the File
     menu or double-clicking on the Database window Control-
     menu box.

When you are ready to delete this database file, you must use
Windows File Manager or the DOS DELETE command because
Access does not have an internal command for deleting databases.

Exporting to an Access Database

When you export, you do not move the original table but rather
copy it to a new database. Suppose you need the Customers table
from the Books database in the new database, but you want to
enter a different group of customer names.

Use these steps to export a table structure:

1. Open the database where the object you want to export is located. In this case open the Books database. Select the Customers table by clicking on it, to indicate it is to be exported.

2. Choose Export in the File menu. The Export dialog box appears as you see here:

3. Choose Microsoft Access as the data destination to use and click on OK. The Select Microsoft Access Object dialog box will appear. This allows you to select the object—in this case a table—that is to be exported. You can also make the choice of whether to export only the structure of the table or to include the data in the table.

4. Make sure the Object Type is Tables and the Objects in BOOKS list box has Customers selected. Choose Structure Only and your dialog box should appear as you see here:

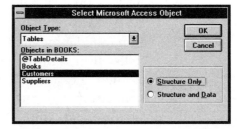

This dialog box is similar to the one you saw earlier in the attaching instructions, except this one shows the table to be exported.

5. Click on OK. The Export to File dialog box appears. This is where you select the file to receive the copy of the table; in this case the file will be MYEXPORT.MDB. Double-click on MYEXPORT.MDB.

6. The Export dialog box appears with the name of the table that you selected earlier in the Database window, displayed and highlighted. You can type a new name to distinguish it from the original. Type any name you like; for instance, type **Customer Prospects.** The screen will appear as you see here:

7. Click on OK and the file structure is exported to the new database.

What these steps accomplish is to put an empty table structure named Customer Prospects into the Myexport database. The new table is ready to receive the information you want to put in it. This table has no connection or link to the original table named Customers in the Books database.

To see the new table, ready to receive information, use these steps:

1. Close the Books database by double-clicking on its Control-menu box.

2. Open the File menu and you should see MYEXPORT.MDB in the list at the bottom of the File menu. If you see it in the list, then click on it. If MYEXPORT.MDB is not in the list, then open it in the usual way by clicking on Open Database and double-clicking on MYEXPORT.MDB in the Open Database dialog box. The Myexport database opens with Customer Prospects selected.

3. Click on Open and the table, Customer Prospects, opens ready to receive new data.

   The table can also be opened in Design view if there are changes to be made to the structure.

4.   After taking a look at the new table, you have no more use for it, so close it by double-clicking on its Control-menu box and then delete it by pressing ⌈Delete⌋. Close the Myexport database window by double-clicking on its Control-menu box.

Transferring between Access and Other Formats

As mentioned earlier in the chapter, Access has the ability to interact with many other application formats. This is a real asset if you have been working with another database program and now want to transfer your work to Access. Perhaps your company is going to use Access in addition to your old database program. In any case, you will appreciate the ease with which you can attach and work with a file in its native format, or import a file into the Access format.

Importing dBASE IV Files

Suppose you have been using dBASE IV as your database application and now want to transfer your tables and other objects into your Access databases. You can use the Import command for this since you want to copy the dBASE files into an Access format without forming a link between the two applications.

To demonstrate the import option, Microsoft has provided a sample dBASE IV file that you can use as the database to import. This file is located in the Access directory and is named NEW-CUST.DBF.

Import this dBASE IV file with the following steps:

1.   Open the Books Database window. This will be the database you use to receive the imported dBASE file.

2.   Choose Import in the File menu. The Import dialog box will appear. Scroll the Data Source list box so you can see

dBASE IV. Click on dBASE IV and the Import dialog box will appear as you see here:

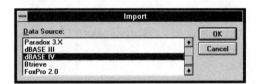

3. Click on OK and the Select File dialog box appears with the List Files of Type drop-down list box displaying dBASE IV (*.dbf). In this dialog box you select the directory and the file to import. When you select the Access directory you see the file NEWCUST.DBF, as shown in Figure 8-4.

4. Double-click on NEWCUST.DBF to import the dBASE file. An information box appears that tells you the file is successfully imported. Click on OK and then on Close in the Select File dialog box.

The dBASE IV file you imported has now been copied to an Access table named NEWCUST, located in the Books

Figure 8-4

With dBASE IV shown as the file type in the Select File dialog box, you can import dBASE files.

database. There is no link formed from the Access table to the dBASE file.

The imported table will have the same name as the original dBASE file and will be shown in capital letters until it is renamed.

5. Change the name of the imported table to make it more descriptive, using up to 64 characters. Select NEWCUST in the Database window, then choose Rename in the File menu.

6. A dialog box appears that allows you to insert a name. Type a name such as **New Customer List from dBASE.** Your dialog box should appear as you see here:

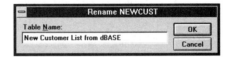

Click on OK and the name in the Database window is changed.

In order to make the new table better fit your purpose, you can change the fields and their properties, as well as set a primary key field.

When dBASE files are imported, Access converts the dBASE data types to the Access equivalents. These types are shown in Table 8-1.

Table 8-1

Access Equivalents to dBASE Data Types

dBASE Data Type	Access Data Type
Character	Text
Date	Date/Time
Logical	Yes/No
Memo	Memo
Numeric	Numeric

Attaching a dBASE IV File

You can attach a file that was created in dBASE IV format and has the .DBF extension. An attached file is not copied to Access but a link is formed that allows you to work with the file in its original database and in the dBASE IV format. You can use the table just like any other Access table except that you cannot alter much of its design, and you can still use the dBASE IV file in the dBASE program.

Once again use the sample NEWCUST.DBF dBASE IV file located in the Access directory and attach it to the Books database using the following steps. The Books database should still be open; it is the Access database to which you want to attach the dBASE file.

1.   Choose Attach Table in the File menu. The Attach dialog box appears.

2.   Choose dBASE IV in the Data Source list box and click on OK. The Select File dialog box appears.

3.   Select the dBASE (.DBF) file to be attached by clicking on NEWCUST.DBF in the C:\ACCESS directory and then clicking on Attach.

      The next dialog box, Select Index, gives you the opportunity to select the index (.NDX) files normally associated with the dBASE file. In this case there are none associated with NEWCUST, as you can see in Figure 8-5. If there were index files, you could select as many as needed by choosing one file at a time and clicking on Select. An information message box called Added Index would then appear in which you would click on OK.

4.   Click on Close in the Select Index Files dialog box and an information message box appears to tell you the file is successfully attached as you see here:

Figure 8-5

Select the index
files associated
with the
database files
you are
attaching,
using the Select
Index Files
dialog box.

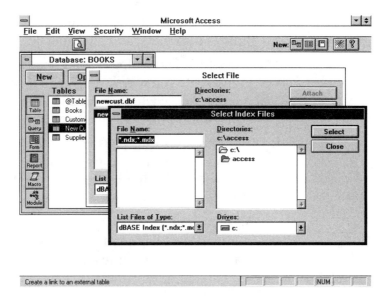

5. Click on OK in the information box and then click on Close
    in the Select File dialog box. The Database window now
    has a new table called NEWCUST and you can see the
    arrow in the icon indicating that it is attached.

Once the table is attached it can be renamed, using up to 64
characters as you did with the imported table. This can give a
better description of its contents and does not affect the link to
the dBASE file.

Importing Paradox Tables

If Paradox is the database application you have been using and
you need to move some of the files into an Access database, you
can do it if the Paradox password is available. This is not the
Access password, which might also be needed. Importing copies
the Paradox files into Access format without affecting the original
table.

These are the steps to import Paradox files:

1. Open the Access database which is to receive the imported
    Paradox file, then choose the Import command in the File
    menu. The Import dialog box appears.

2. Choose Paradox 3.X in the Data Source list box of the Import dialog box and click on OK.

3. The Select File dialog box appears and you can select the Paradox file you want to import. When you click on Import, Access checks whether the file uses a password, if it does, you are prompted for the Paradox password.

4. When the correct password is entered the Successfully Imported information box appears. Click on OK, then on Close. A new table appears in the Access database with the same name as the Paradox file.

5. You can rename the file by choosing the Rename command in the File menu. This can be a descriptive name of up to 64 characters and spaces.

Access changes the Paradox data types into the closest match of the Access data types. After importing any table, you need to open it in Design view and check the data types and the field sizes. Paradox data types and their Access equivalents are shown in Table 8-2.

Attaching Paradox Tables

You can attach a Paradox file to an open Access database and then use the file as you would any other Access table—except you cannot change the design. Like the other file formats, attaching a Paradox file does not copy it, but forms a link to the original application.

Table 8-2

Access Equivalents to Paradox Data Types

Paradox Data Types	Access Data Types
Alphanumeric	Text
Currency	Number
Date	Date/Time
Number	Number
Short number	Number

Use these instructions to attach Paradox files:

1. Open the Access database to which you want to attach the Paradox tables.

2. Choose Attach Table in the File menu. The Attach dialog box appears.

3. Choose Paradox 3.X and then click on OK. The Select File dialog box appears.

4. Choose the Paradox file (.DB) you want to attach and click on Attach.

5. If a password is needed to open the Paradox table in the Paradox application, then you must enter that password before attaching the table. A dialog box will appear so you can type the password and then click on OK.

6. If the Paradox file has an index file (.PX), the Select Index Files dialog box appears and you can select the index file associated with the table you are attaching.

   Access cannot open a Paradox data file unless these .PX files are available.

7. Close the Select Index dialog box and the Successfully Attached information box appears. Click on OK, click on Close, and the table is attached to the Access database, using the same name as the Paradox file. This name can be changed to be more descriptive without affecting the Paradox file.

Transferring Text Files

Access can transfer text files in a delimited format or in a fixed-field-width format. The delimited-text format has fields separated by a special character such as a comma, tab, or space. A fixed-width text file has the same number of spaces in each record and the same number of spaces in corresponding fields in each record. If the text does not fill the field, then spaces are used to fill it out. When Access handles fixed-width files, it must be told where each field begins in the record.

Exporting to Delimited-Text Files

Delimited-text database files are often used to supply the names and addresses to a word-processing program for mail merging. When Access exports an Access table to a delimited-text file, it places all the fields in one record into single lines of text, with the delimiters you choose between each record.

Suppose you want to export the Books table to another application that uses delimited-text files. Use the C:\BOOKSTOR directory to receive the new file. Produce the export file with these steps:

1. Open the Books database and select the Books table if it is not already selected.

2. In the File menu choose Export and the Export dialog box appears.

3. Select Text (Delimited) as the Data Destination and click on OK. The Select Microsoft Access Object dialog box appears.

4. Select the object that you want to export—for example the Books table—and click on OK. The Export to File dialog box appears.

    You can give the new text file a name and destination directory. BOOKS.TXT is in the File Name list box as the default name but you can type in a name such as **Inventry.** With this name and the directory C:\BOOKSTOR, your screen should look like Figure 8-6.

    Access will add the extension .TXT to Inventry. Remember, this is a DOS file so you can have no more than eight letters before the extension. Click on OK and the Export Text Options will appear.

5. In the Export Text Options dialog box (see Figure 8-7), make these changes:

    a. If there is no × in the Store Field Names in First Row check box, click on it to cause the column names to appear in the first line of the text file.

    b. Click on the Options button to open the lower part of the dialog box. Select the text delimiters, usually a

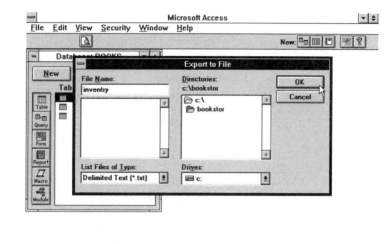

double quote mark ("), and for the field separator,
either a comma or a tab.

c. The Specification Name list box is blank, and since
    you do not have a saved specification for the delim-
    iters, leave it blank. Without a specification, the

delimiters are set with the default characters and you can use those in this exercise.

d.   If you change these options you should click on Save As and save them for other similar files you might want to export in the future.

6.   Click on OK and Access will create a DOS file named INVENTRY.TXT and place it in the C:\BOOKSTOR directory. If you view this text file with the DOS Editor or a word processor, you will see that the table has been copied to a delimited format like the one you see in Figure 8-8.

Notice that the first line in Figure 8-8 contains the column headings. In all the lines the fields are separated by commas and any text data is enclosed in quotation marks. Each record is separated by a carriage return.

Importing Delimited-Text Files

In order to import a delimited-text file, it must have been set up beforehand with a consistent number of delimiters separating each field. If a field is blank, simply use a pair of delimiters with no space between them. You can import the file you just created,

Figure 8-8

You can read a delimited- or fixed-width-text file with a word-processing program or a text editor.

```
Microsoft Word - INVEVTRY.TXT
File  Edit  View  Insert  Format  Tools  Table  Window  Help

Normal        Courier New        12     B I U

"BkID","ISBN","Title","Author","PubID","Price","OnHand","Order","Category"¶
1,"042511872X","Stolen·Blessings","Sanders",6,4.9500,5,2,"Mystery"¶
2,"1559582251","Making·of·Microsoft","Ichbiah",1,12.9500,3,1,"Business"¶
3,"0446360074","Rage·of·Angels","Sheldon",7,3.5000,4,1,"Mystery"¶
4,"1559581824","Windows·3.1,·Visual·Learning","Gardner",1,19.9500,6,2,"Computer"¶
5,"0553281798","Trevayne","Ludlum",4,5.9500,4,1,"Mystery"¶
6,"1559581085","In·The·Shadow·of·the·White·Hou","Tidwell",1,19.9500,3,1,"Government"¶
7,"0425109720","Patriot·Games","Clancy",6,4.9500,6,2,"Thriller"¶
8,"1559582332","Hawaii:·A·Paradise·Family·Guid","Penisten",1,12.9500,2,1,"Travel"¶
9,"0451146425","Lie·Down·with·Lions","Follett",11,4.9500,2,1,"Mystery"¶
10,"1559581832","The·Power·of·Windows·and·DOS","Matthews",1,24.9500,2,1,"Computer"¶
11,"0671742760","Dragon","Cussler",14,5.9500,3,1,"Mystery"¶
12,"044020447X","Final·Flight","Coonts",10,5.9500,2,1,"Thriller"¶
13,"0345370066","Spy·Line","Deighton",3,5.9500,1,1,"Thriller"¶
14,"0962876607","Simply·Whidbey","Moore",,20,16.9500,5,2,"Cooking"¶
15,"0671691988","An·American·Life","Reagan",14,24.9500,3,1,"Biography"¶
16,"055305340X","A·Brief·History·of·Time","Hawking",4,16.9500,1,1,"Science"¶
17,"0671665545","Sword··Point","Coyle",13,4.9500,0,1,"Thriller"¶
18,"0061000043","A·Thief·of·Time","Hillerman",8,4.9500,1,1,"Mystery"¶
19,"0553070118","Father·Son·&·Co.","Watson·Jr.",4,22.9500,1,1,"Biography"¶
20,"0345377702","Me","Hepburn",3,5.9900,3,1,"Biography"¶
21,"0553290991","Nightfall","Asimov",4,5.9900,0,1,"Sci.·Fic."¶
22,"0471568864","Hard·Drive","Wallace",12,22.9500,3,1,"Biography"¶
23,"0671700553","Against·the·Grain","Yeltsin",15,19.9500,0,1,"Biography"¶

Pg 1   Sec 1   1/1   At 1"   Ln 1   Col 1   75%
```

INVENTRY.TXT, as an example of the way Access imports delimited text. Use these steps to do that:

1. With the Books database still open, choose the Import option in the File menu. The Import dialog box appears.

2. Select Text (Delimited) and click on OK. The Select File dialog box appears.

3. Select INVENTRY.TXT in the File Name list box as the delimited-text file to be changed to an Access table. Click on Import. The Import Text dialog box appears.

4. Click on Options to open the dialog box fully. You will see that this dialog box is very similar to the Export Text Options dialog box. Some of your options are as follows:

    ◆ The First Row Contains Field Names check box tells Access how to handle the first row in the text file. Click on it to turn it on if the column names are in the first row. If it is not turned on, Access treats the first row as data.

    ◆ An area in this box that did not appear in the Export Text dialog box is Table Options. This tells Access whether to append the text to an existing table or to create a new table. If the data is to be appended it must have the same field structure and data types, as well as the same column names.

    ◆ The Specification Name list box allows you to use a delimiter specification you saved from previously imported text files of the same type. If a specification is not entered, Access uses the default delimiters unless you change them. Be sure these match the text file to be imported.

5. Click on the First Row Contains Field Names check box to select it.

6. Make sure the Create New Table control button is selected.

7. You can use the default delimiters since these were used to export to text. These are double quotation marks for text-type data and a comma to separate fields.

8. When the Import Text Option dialog box is set up the way you want it, click on OK. The Import Results information box appears as you see here:

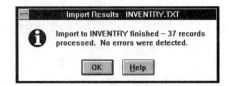

If there are errors in the imported table, the Import Results box will inform you. Access will go ahead and create as much of the table as possible and also create a table named Import Errors, which you will see in the Database window. The Import Errors table name includes the name of the registered Access user, as you see here:

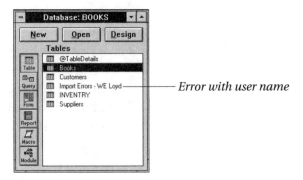

Error with user name

In a network environment, this keeps your Import Errors table separated from errors tables created by other users.

The name of the imported table appears in the Tables list box in capital letters to distinguish it from the original list of tables. It will remain in capital letters until it is renamed, using the Rename option in the File menu.

If you open the INVENTRY table to look at it and then open the Books table, you see there is very little or no difference between the two. In this case nothing was lost going from Access to text and then from text back to Access.

Transferring Fixed-Width Text Files

The fixed-width text file format is often used by main-frame computers and older PC programs to transfer data. Importing and exporting fixed-width text is similar in most ways to working with delimited text with one major exception: before importing or exporting, you must tell Access where each field begins and how many spaces it includes by supplying an import/export specification.

The import/export specification is created by choosing Imp/Exp Setup in the File menu. The Import/Export Setup dialog box appears in which you can enter all the information pertaining to each field in the table to be transferred. If you were to create a specification for the Suppliers table in the Books database, it would look similar to Figure 8-9. After all the field information is entered, you click on Save As and give the specification a name. The specification shown in Figure 8-9 was given the name Sample.

Using this specification you could export the Suppliers table to a fixed-width text file. You could also use it to import or attach a text file that matched those specifications.

Figure 8-9

Use the Import/Export Setup dialog box to specify the field properties for a fixed-width text file.

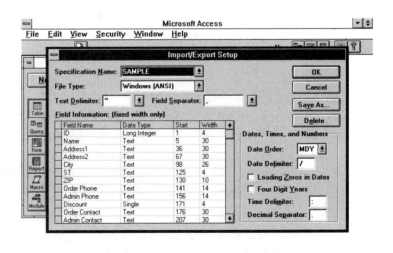

Transferring Data to and from Spreadsheets

Access can export data to and import data from spreadsheet applications such as Microsoft Excel and Lotus 1-2-3. The Lotus files can have extensions of WKS, WK1, and WK3. Spreadsheets can be brought into Access in their entirety or with only the data in designated cells. The only limiting factors are whether the data is set up in the spreadsheet so it will fit in a table and whether each column has the same data types throughout. The steps to import from any of the spreadsheets are similar and so only Excel is demonstrated here. To show this option, first create an Excel (.XLS) file by exporting the Books table.

Exporting an Access Table to Excel

Use the Export option to copy an Access table to Excel with these steps:

1. Open the Access database containing the table to be exported, in this case use BOOKS.MDB. Then choose Export in the File menu. The Export dialog box appears.

2. Select Microsoft Excel in the Data Destination list box. Click on OK and the Select Microsoft Access Object dialog box appears.

3. Select the table you want to export from the Tables list box; as an example, use the Books table. When it is selected, click on OK. The Export to File dialog box appears.

4. Type a name for the .XLS file. Select the directory C:\BOOKSTOR as the one to contain the file and type a name such as **Inventry** in the File Name list box. When you click on OK, Access copies the Books table to an Excel file named INVENTRY.XLS.

The file is ready for use in an Excel application. You can also use it in the next section as an Excel spreadsheet to be imported or attached to an Access table.

Importing Excel Spreadsheets to Access Tables

As shown earlier in this chapter, the Import option copies the imported information to an Access table. You can import data from Excel spreadsheets with these steps:

1. With the Books Database window still open, choose Import in the File menu. The Import dialog box appears.

2. Select Excel in the Data Source list box and then click on OK. The Select File dialog box appears.

3. Select the directory and the Excel (.XLS) file to be imported. Here, select the .XLS file you created, C:\BOOKSTOR\ INVENTRY.XLS. Click on Import.

   The Import Spreadsheet Options dialog box appears. This box tells Access whether the first row contains the field names, whether you want a new table or merely want the data appended to an existing table, and what is the range of cells to be imported.

4. Make the following entries in the Import Spreadsheet Options dialog box:

   a. Click on the check box for First Row Contains Field Names; this box should now contain an ×.

   b. Choose Create New Table, if it is not already selected.

   c. Click in the Spreadsheet Range text box to place the text insertion point there. Assume you want only the first ten rows of information from the spreadsheet. You type the cell range in the normal spreadsheet format with the column letter followed by the row number. Since you want the column names in the new table, use the first eleven rows and columns A through I. Type the range in the form, **A1..I11,** as you see in the next illustration:

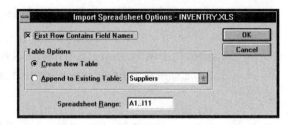

5.   Click on OK and the Import Results information box appears. Again click on OK and then on Close.

This completes the import process. You now have a new table named Inventry containing the first ten records from INVEN-TRY.XLS. You should open the new table in Design view and adjust the field properties. You will find that one of the changes from the original Books table is the width of the text fields, which are now 255 spaces. This tends to make the file larger than necessary and to take extra disk space.

Since you have no further need for the Inventory table, delete it by selecting it and pressing ⌑Delete⌑ on the keyboard. Close the Books Database window.

◗ Summary

Chapter 8 has shown you how to transfer information between Access and other applications including databases, spreadsheets, and even word processors. Among the major points made in the chapter are the following:

◆   Use Attach to work with files in their original application format.

◆   Use Import to copy other Access objects and files from other applications. Import creates a new Access table in the open database.

◆   When transferring data, you need to know the database's structure and properties. Use the Database Analyzer to create a new table containing the structure of the database.

- ◆ Attach other Access tables to an open database so you can work with more than one database at a time.

- ◆ Access can export a table and change it to the format of a different application. Export does not change the original table, however.

- ◆ A database must be open in order to import into it. An empty database can be created to receive an imported table by choosing New Database in the File menu.

- ◆ Text files are transferred in delimited or fixed-width formats. To export you must select the delimiters or use the default.

- ◆ To transfer fixed-width text, you must supply the starting point for each field and its width in an import/export specification.

- ◆ Access can transfer data to and from spreadsheets that are set up in a form that fits a table and have the same types of data in a column.

The next chapter will introduce you to macros—how to create them and how to use them.

Putting It Together with Macros

All your work so far has been interactive. If you wanted to print a report, you manually told Access to print it; if you wanted to run a query, you manually activated the query. Some queries, forms, and reports have decision-making capabilities, but you still have to activate them manually. In this chapter you will see how to automate some tasks or let other users work with your database without their having to learn how to use Access. Macros give you a way to control your database without writing programs.

What Are Macros and What Can You Do with Them?

A *macro* is a set of standard actions that Access performs when you run it. Macros are an easy way to automate operations that you perform again and again. Once you develop a macro, you can run the operation repeatedly and be confident that it will run the same way each time.

Access provides a menu of standard actions that you can use in a macro. Here are examples of ways you can use macros:

- Open a secondary form while you are looking at data on a primary form

- Look up a value in a table and automatically place the value in a control on a form

- Create a form that acts as a menu to let users pick which database operations to perform

- Associate macros with form and report properties to control what happens under different circumstances

- Automatically transfer data to a spreadsheet using the export feature of Access

These are just a few examples. Once you get familiar with the macro actions, you will be able to automate many of your database operations.

Note — **If you want to perform tasks that macro actions do not support, look into the Access Basic programming language. This is a full-featured language with roots in Microsoft Visual Basic. In addition, you can use the RunCode action to call Access Basic functions from within your macros. Using Access Basic is beyond the scope of this book.**

The Macro Window

You create macros in the Macro window. A typical Macro window is shown in Figure 9-1. You add actions, comments, macro names, and conditions in the upper portion of the window. You select the actions from a list of standard actions, as you will see later in this chapter. A comment is optional and serves as a reminder about the purpose of the action. A macro name is required only if you create macro groups. You will also learn about macro groups later in this chapter. A condition is optional and lets Access determine whether or not to perform an action based on the results of the test given in the condition.

You specify *arguments* in the lower portion of the window. An argument is a value that Access needs in order to carry out an action. Each action requires different arguments. The arguments shown in Figure 9-1 are for the OpenForm action.

Figure 9-1

The Macro window provides a unique workspace and set of tools.

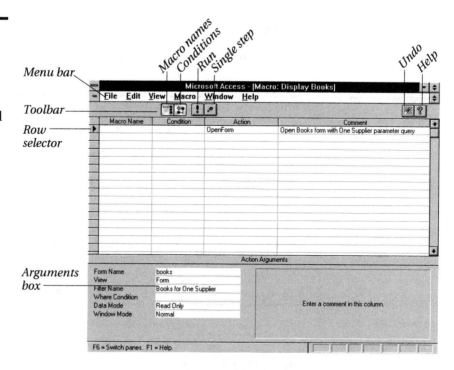

Toolbar

The Macro window toolbar contains buttons that let you quickly perform common tasks. The toolbar buttons are shown in Table 9-1.

Table 9-1

Macro Window Toolbar Buttons

Button	Purpose
	The *macro names* button shows or hides the macro names column
	The *conditions* button shows or hides the conditions column
	The *run* button runs the macro
	The *single step* button moves through a macro one action at a time and is used for debugging a macro
	The *undo* button undoes your most recent action
	The *help* button calls up the help system

Menus

The macro menu bar contains the menus shown in Table 9-2.

Table 9-2

Macro Window Menu Commands

Menu Name	Purpose
File	Creates new database objects; closes the Macro window; saves the active macro; runs a macro; exits from Access
Edit	Edits the specifications of the active macro
View	Toggles the Macro Names and Conditions columns; sets Access options
Macro	Runs or single-steps through the active macro
Window	Arranges, hides, shows, and selects windows
Help	Chooses from various help options

Function Keys

In addition to the global function keys, the function keys shown in Table 9-3 are useful in the Macro window.

Table 9-3

Function Key Assignments in the Macro Window

Function Key	Purpose
F11 or Alt-F1	Makes the Database window the active window.
F2	Toggles between navigation and editing modes. In editing mode you can move the insertion point within a block of text.
Shift-F2	Opens the Zoom box so you can enter long expressions into small input boxes.
F6	Toggles between the upper and lower portions of the Macro window.
Ctrl-F8	Moves an action and its related columns with the keyboard. First click on the row selector to select a row, then press Ctrl-F8 and use the arrow keys to move the row to its new location. Press Enter to end the move.

Standard Macro Actions

As was mentioned earlier, you select macro actions from a list of standard actions. Although you will use only some of the available actions in this chapter, it is useful for you to see the range of macro actions available. Table 9-4 lists and describes the macro actions available in Access. For detailed information about how to use a specific action, see the Actions Reference section in the Access help system.

Table 9-4

Actions
Available for
Macros

Macro Action	Purpose
AddMenu	Places a new drop-down menu in a form's custom menu bar
ApplyFilter	Applies a filter to a form or report
Beep	Makes the computer beep
CancelEvent	Cancels the event that started this macro
Close	Closes an Access window
CopyObject	Copies a database object
DoMenuItem	Activates an Access menu command
Echo	Tells Access whether to display screen changes while a macro runs
FindNext	Locates the next record meeting specified criteria
FindRecord	Locates the first record meeting specified criteria
GoToControl	Moves the focus to the specified control
GoToPage	Moves the focus in the current form to a specified page
GoToRecord	Moves the focus to the specified record
Hourglass	Displays an hourglass image while a macro is running
Maximize	Maximizes the active window
Minimize	Minimizes the active window
MoveSize	Moves/resizes the active window

Table 9-4 (continued)

Actions Available for Macros

Macro Action	Purpose
MsgBox	Displays a message box
OpenForm	Opens a form
OpenQuery	Opens a select or crosstab query, or runs an action query
OpenReport	Opens a report
OpenTable	Opens a table
Print	Prints the active datasheet, report, or form
Quit	Exits Access
Rename	Renames a database objectRepaintObject Updates a database object
Requery	Updates a control in the active object
Restore	Restores a maximized or minimized window to its former size
RunApp	Runs an external application
RunCode	Runs an Access Basic Function procedure
RunMacro	Runs a macro
RunSQL	Runs the SQL statement of an Access action query
SelectObject	Selects a specified database object
SendKeys	Types keystrokes directly into an application
SetValue	Sets the value of a field, control, or property
SetWarnings	Activates/deactivates system messages
ShowAllRecords	Displays all records in a form's underlying table or query
StopAllMacros	Halts all currently running macros
StopMacro	Halts the macro that is currently running
TransferDatabase	Transfers data between two databases
TransferSpreadsheet	Transfers data between a database and a spreadsheet
TransferText	Transfers text between a database and a text file

Macros and Events

Although you can sometimes run a macro directly from the list of macros in the Database window, you will usually attach a macro to an event. If the event occurs, Access runs the macro. An event occurs when the property associated with the following objects or actions is realized:

- Forms
- Controls on forms
- Records on forms
- Reports
- Report sections
- Saving data

Table 9-5 describes the events that can occur in Access. You will learn how to associate macros with events later in this chapter.

Using Expressions and Functions in Macros

You have already created some expressions in Access. In Chapter 7 you used them to create calculated fields and establish criteria for filtering records. You can also use expressions with macros. Expressions can result in values that you store in a table (such as a calculated amount), or they can simply provide a true or false answer to choose between two alternative paths in a macro.

Expressions are made up of the following elements:

- An *operator* specifies the operation to perform on elements of the expression. Typical operators are +, -, /, *, &, and Like. For example, [**Selling Price**]*[**Quantity**] multiplies two values; the Like operator finds similar text.

- An *identifier* specifies the value of a field, control, or property. For example, **Forms![Order]![OrdID]** identifies the OrdID control on the Order form.

Event	Occurs
After Update	After updating the data entered in a control
Before Update	Before updating the data entered in a control
On Close	Upon closing a form or report
On Current	When a record becomes the current record, but before it is displayed
On Dbl Click	When you double-click on a control
On Delete	Before deleting a record
On Enter	Upon entering a control
On Exit	Upon leaving a control
On Format	When the data for the report section has been selected but not yet formatted for printing
On Insert	Before inserting a new record
On Menu	Designates a menu bar macro containing a custom menu for the form; not time-dependent
On Open	Upon opening a form or report, but before the contents are displayed
On Print	After the data for a report section has been formatted for printing, but before it is printed
On Push	Upon choosing a command button

◆ A *function* is a calculation built into Access. For example, **Weekday([Order Date])** calculates the number of the day of the week for the date in the Order Date field of the current record. To see an alphabetized list of the functions available in Access, open the Help menu, choose Contents, then click on Functions in the reference section. You can also create your own functions using Access Basic. Creating functions is beyond the scope of this book.

◆ A *literal value* is a value that is used exactly as you type it in the expression. For example, **[Our Cost]*1.5** could be used to calculate the list price of an item, if the list price is always 1.5 times Our Cost. Use literal values sparingly in expressions, because they can be difficult to track down and change.

♦ A *constant* is the name of a value that never changes. This differs from a literal value in that the value of the constant does not appear in the expression. For example, **True** always has a value of -1. Although you could use the literal value -1, an expression will usually be more readable if you use True.

You can build an expression from any valid combination of the elements listed above. If an expression is not valid, Access will display an error message when you try to use it. It is advisable to test an expression with simple values so that you can verify the results. You will see several examples of expressions in this chapter.

Using Macros with Forms

A common way to use macros in Access is with forms. Most end-users will work with forms rather than directly with tables. You will see later how to set up a system that guides users through a set of forms by using a menu you set up on a master form. First, look at how to use macros with forms themselves.

Using a Macro to Show Related Items on a Second Form

A common use of a macro is to open one form from another. For example, you might be looking at a form containing supplier information and decide you want to see a list of the books from that supplier. To accomplish this goal you will build a macro that displays a list of books from the supplier shown on the current form. You will then associate the macro with the On Push property of a command button you place on the form. When you use the form and push (click on) the button, Access will run the macro and display the related books. Begin by creating forms for suppliers and books.

Creating Forms for Suppliers and Books

If the Books database is not open, use the File menu to open it now. All the examples in this chapter use the Books database and start with the assumption that you are in the Books database window.

Quickly make a Suppliers form with the FormWizards and then modify it, as you have done in Chapter 6. Use the following steps:

1. Click on the Form button and then on New.

2. Select the Suppliers table as the basis of the form and click on FormWizards.

3. Select Single-column and click on OK.

4. Select all fields by clicking on >> and then click on Next.

5. Select Embossed and again click on Next.

6. Accept Suppliers as the form title and click on Design.

7. Drag the toolbox over to the right side and then drag the right edge of the form right to 4¼ inches.

8. Drag the State and ZIP fields up on the line with the City field, delete the State label, and type **,St** in the City label, as shown in Figure 9-2.

9. Drag the Admin Phone field up on the line with Order Phone and then drag the bottom three fields (Discount, Order Contact, and Admin Contact) up to fill in the space.

10. Close and save the form by double-clicking on its Control-menu box, answering Yes to save the form, typing **Suppliers** as the name, and clicking on OK.

Next, and even more quickly, build a Books form with these steps:

1. With the Form button still depressed in the Database window, again click on New.

2. Select Books as the table and click on FormWizards.

3. Select Single-column and click on OK.

4. Select all the fields by clicking on >> and then click on Next.

5. Select Embossed and again click on Next.

Figure 9-2

The Suppliers
form for which
you will build
macros

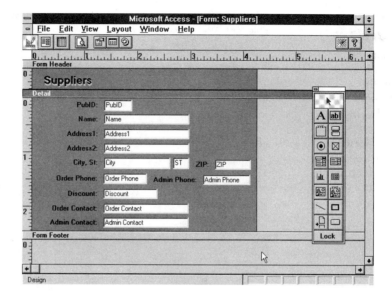

6. Accept Books as the title and click on Design.

7. Double-click on the Control-menu box, answer Yes to save
    the form, type **Books** as the name, and click on OK.

Now you are ready to create macros that use these two forms.

Creating the Macro to Open a Second Form

The first macro you create will open the Books form from the
Suppliers form. The finished macro is shown in Figure 9-3. In the
next section, you will attach this macro to a command button
that you will add to the Suppliers form.

The macro first will test the PubID field of the current supplier in
the Supplier form to make sure it contains a value. If it is empty
(null), the macro will stop. If PubID contains a value, the macro
will open the Books form in Datasheet view, set the PubID value
for the Books form equal to the current PubID value on the
Suppliers form, and display the Books data having that PubID
value.

Create this macro with these steps:

1. Click on the Macro button in the Database window and
    click on New to start a new macro.

Figure 9-3

This macro, which is called from the Suppliers form, will display the books in the Books form that are related to a selected supplier.

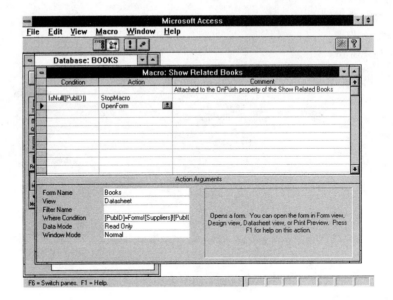

2. In the comment column of the first row of the new macro, type **Attached to the On Push property of the Show Related Books command button on the form**. It is a good practice to use the first line of the macro for a comment describing the macro.

3. Click on the conditions button in the toolbar. This displays the Condition column.

4. Click on the Condition box in the second line of the macro. Type **IsNull([PubID])**. This condition checks to see if the PubID field is null (empty). If it is, Access performs the action on the current line of the macro (which you are about to enter); otherwise, it skips to the next line.

5. Click on the right end of the Action box in the second line of the macro and select StopMacro from the drop-down list. If the PubID field is null, this action stops the macro.

6. Click on the right end of the Action box in the third line of the macro and select OpenForm from the drop-down list. Fill in the action arguments in the lower portion of the Macro window as shown in Table 9-6.

7. Double-click on the Control-menu box. In the dialog box that appears, click on Yes to save the changes, type **Show Related Books** as the name, and click on OK.

Adding the Macro to a Command Button on a Form

Next, you will attach the macro you just created to a command button on the Suppliers form. You could type the specifications for the macro in the properties dialog box of the command button, but Access provides a drag-and-drop shortcut. To attach the macro to the command button, use the following steps:

1. Click on Suppliers in the Database window.

2. Click on the Design button to open the Suppliers form in Design view.

3. Open the Window menu on the menu bar and choose Tile. Access rearranges the screen so the Suppliers form and the Database window are both visible on the screen, as shown in Figure 9-4.

4. Use the horizontal scroll bar to scroll the Suppliers form so you can see the blank area in the upper-right corner of the form.

5. Click on the Macro button in the Database window to display the list of Macros.

Table 9-6

Arguments for OpenForm Action

Argument	Value
Form Name	Books
View	Datasheet
Filter Name	(leave blank)
Where Condition	[PubID]=Forms![Suppliers]![PubID]
Data Mode	Read Only
Window Mode	Normal

Figure 9-4

Tiled windows allow you to see some part of all the open windows.

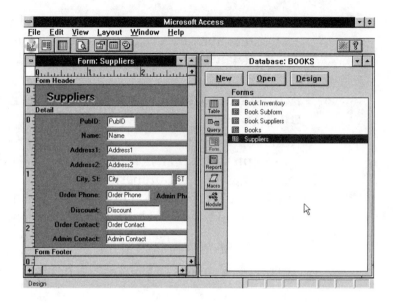

6. Drag the macro named Show Related Books from the Macros list to the blank area in the upper right of the Suppliers form. When you release the mouse button and drop the macro on the form, Access places a command button there. Access sets the button's Caption and On Push properties both to Show Related Books.

7. If necessary, adjust the size of the Form in Design view so you can position the command button more easily.

8. Adjust the size of the command button so the full name appears and move the command button to a suitable location, as shown in Figure 9-5.

9. Click on the properties button in the toolbar (fifth from the left). This opens up the properties dialog box for the command button. If the properties dialog box is blank, move it so the command button is visible, then click on the command button so the properties dialog box reflects its properties. Your properties dialog box should look similar to that shown in Figure 9-6 except for Control Name.

10. Rename the button by typing **Show Related Books** in the Control Name box.

Figure 9-5

By dragging a macro to a form in Design view, a button that calls the macro is automatically added to the form.

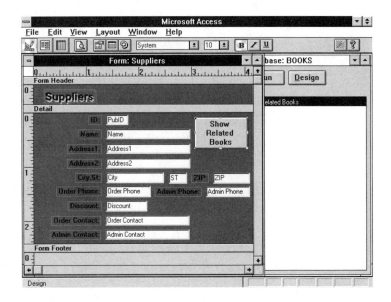

11.   Double-click on the Control-menu box to close the properties dialog box.

12.   Click on the form view button in the toolbar. You will see data appear in the form.

Figure 9-6

Command Button properties dialog box

Command Button	
Control Name	Button33
Caption	Show Related Books
Picture	[none]
Transparent	No
Auto Repeat	No
Status Bar Text . .	
On Push	Show Related Books
On Enter	
On Exit	
On Dbl Click	
Default	No
Cancel	No
Visible	Yes
Display When . . .	Always
Enabled	Yes
Left	3.27 in
Top	0.08 in
Width	1 in
Height	0.64 in
Fore Color	0
Font Name	System
Font Size	10
Font Weight	Bold
Font Italic	No
Font Underline . . .	No
Help Context Id . .	0

13. Click on the Show Related Books command button. If the Books list contains books from the currently selected supplier, a book list will appear, as shown Figure 9-7.

14. Once you are satisfied that the button works, double-click on the Control-menu box of the Books list to close it.

15. Double-click on the Control-menu box of the Suppliers form to close it. Click on Yes to save the changes to the form.

You can now use the Suppliers form anytime you want to see information about a supplier, including a list of the books from that supplier.

Using a Macro to Find a Record

If you want to see information about a particular supplier, you can use a combo box with a macro to pick a supplier from an alphabetized list. This technique uses a query, a macro, and a form together. It demonstrates one way you can synchronize various parts of your database. Figure 9-8 shows the Suppliers form modified to let you look up a specific supplier.

Figure 9-7

A list of books related to the currently selected supplier is displayed when you click on the new command button.

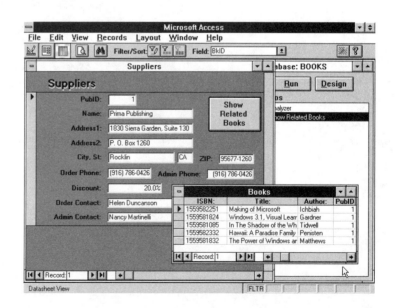

Figure 9-8

The combot box
on this
Suppliers form
lets you search
for a specific
supplier.

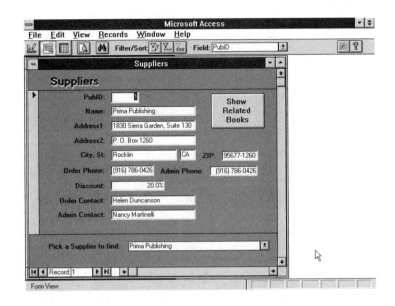

Creating a Query to Display a Look-up List

First create a query that displays an alphabetized list of supplier
names. This query will provide the values for the combo box that
you place on the form. It is a simple query with only one field.
Create the query as follows:

1. Click on Table in the Database window and then click on
   Suppliers.

2. Click on the new query button in the toolbar to open the
   Query window in Design view with the Suppliers table
   already selected for use in the query.

3. Double-click on the Name field. This places a copy of the
   Name field in the first column of the QBE grid.

4. Click on the right end of the Sort box in the Name column
   and choose Ascending from the drop-down list to sort the
   results of the query by name. At this point the QBE grid
   should look like the illustration that appears at the top of
   the following page.

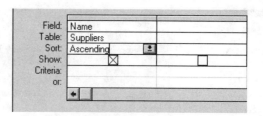

5.   Test the query by clicking on the datasheet view button. You will see an alphabetized list of supplier names.

6.   To save the query double-click on the Control-menu box, click on Yes in the save changes dialog box, type **Suppliers Name List** for the name of the query, and click on OK.

Creating a Macro to Find a Record

Selecting a supplier name from the look-up list is only the first step. Next you must create a macro that finds the first suppliers record containing the supplier name you select. Create this macro with the following steps:

1.   Click on the Macro button in the Database window and click on New to start a new macro.

2.   Click on the Comment box in the first row of the new macro and type **Attached to the After Update property of the Supplier Names combo box on the Suppliers form.**

3.   Click on the right end of the Action box in the second line of the macro and select GoToControl from the drop-down list. Click on the Control Name box in the arguments section and type **Name**. When the macro is activated from the Suppliers form, this action will cause the Supplier Name field to be the active field.

4.   Click on the Comment box in the GoToControl line and type **Causes the Name field to become active**.

5.   Click on the right end of the Action box in the third line of the macro and select FindRecord from the drop-down list.

6.   Fill in the action arguments in the lower portion of the Macro window as shown in Table 9-7. You must type

Argument	Value
Find What	=[Supplier List]
Where	Match Whole Field
Match Case	No
Direction	Down
Search As Formatted	No
Search In	Current Field
Find First	Yes

Table 9-7

Arguments for
FindRecord
Action

=[**Supplier List**]. The other values are the defaults which you can choose from drop-down lists.

With the argument values shown here, FindRecord will search for the first record in the Suppliers table that has a value in the Name field matching the name you choose from the control named Supplier List. You will create this control in the next section.

7. Click on the Comment box in the FindRecord line and type **Find Supplier record with name matching name chosen from combo box**. Your Macro window should look like that shown in Figure 9-9.

8. To save the macro, double-click on the Control-menu box. In the dialog box that appears, click on Yes to save the changes, type **Find Supplier Record**, and click on OK.

Linking the Query, Macro, and Form

You have now created the query and the macro required to look up a supplier while you work with the Suppliers form. The next step is to link together the query, the macro, and the form. You will do this by placing a combo box control on the Suppliers form using these instructions:

1. Click on Form in the Database window and then click on Suppliers.

Figure 9-9

This macro will find the first Supplier record containing the supplier name you select.

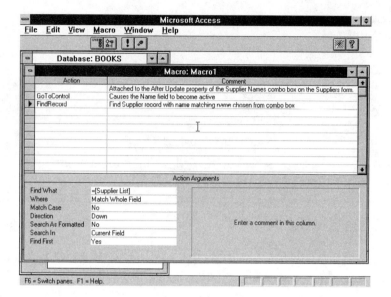

2. Click on the design button.

3. Maximize the design window to give yourself some working room.

4. If the toolbox is not visible, open the View menu and choose Toolbox.

5. Click on the combo box control icon in the toolbox. Move the mouse pointer to the Form Footer area and click the left mouse button to place the control. You will adjust the position and size of the control in the next steps.

6. Click on the label control that Access placed with the combo box, then click on the properties button in the toolbar. This opens the properties dialog box for the label control.

7. Drag across the contents of the Caption box and type **Pick a Supplier to find:**.

8. Drag across the number in the Width box and type **1.39**. This is just wide enough to accommodate the new caption.

9. To save the new caption, double-click on the Control-menu box of the properties dialog box.

10. Use the mouse and the handles on the label control to move the label to a position that will display the entire caption without obscuring any of the combo box control.

11. Click on the combo box control and then click on the properties button in the toolbar to open the properties dialog box for the combo box control.

12. Change the values in the properties dialog box so they match the values shown in Table 9-8. For properties not listed, use the default values. Notice how these properties bring together the Find Supplier Record macro, the Suppliers Name List query, the Supplier List control, and the Suppliers form.

13. To save the new property values, double-click on the Control-menu box of the properties dialog box.

14. Use the mouse and the handles on the combo box control to make the control wider. Nothing else will go on this line, so make it large enough to accommodate the largest supplier name you expect to appear in the list.

15. To test the look-up feature, click on the form view button, then click on the down-arrow to the right of the combo box. Your Suppliers window should look like that shown in Figure 9-10.

16. Select a name from the list. If everything works right, Access will update the form to display the data for the supplier whose name you selected. You can then click on the Show Related Books button to see the books from that supplier. If the look-up does not work right, check the values you entered in the properties of the combo box control

Table 9-8

Values for Combo Box Properties

Property	Value
Control Name	Supplier List
Row Source Type	Table/Query
Row Source	Suppliers Name List
After Update	Find Supplier Record

Figure 9-10
The combo box will list all of the suppliers alphabetically, using the Suppliers Name List query.

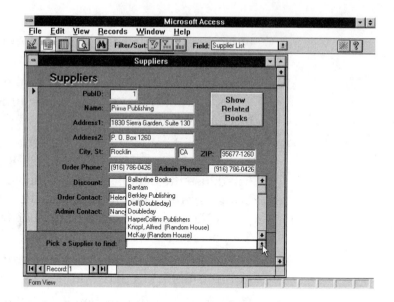

and the values you used for the arguments of the Find Supplier Record macro.

17. Double-click on the Control-menu box of the Suppliers form to close the form. Click on Yes to save the form.

You can now use the Suppliers form as a convenient point-and-click tool to look up information about a supplier and the books from that supplier.

Creating a Custom Set of Menus for a Form

You can use macros to create custom menus for a form. The custom menu options can activate choices on regular Access menus, or they can perform actions that you create with other macros. The AddMenu macro action lets you name a menu and specify another macro that contains options for the menu's associated drop-down list. This second macro is a macro group that contains one or more named macros. Each name becomes an option on the drop-down list for the custom menu, and the actions associated with the name are carried out when you choose the menu option.

In this section you will create a custom menu bar for the Suppliers form. The menu bar will have two menus, Exit and GoTo.

To create the custom menu bar, you will need to create three macros. The first two macros contain the menu options for the drop-down lists. The third macro names the menus that appear on the menu bar and associates the first two macros with those names. You will then associate the third macro with the On Menu property of the Suppliers form.

Creating the Menu Macros

The custom Exit menu has only one option, to let the user exit from the form. The macro that defines the custom Exit menu looks like this:

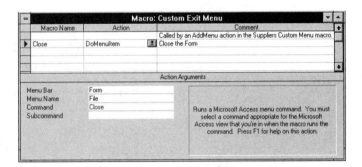

Create this macro with these steps:

1. Click on the Macro button in the Database window if it is not already selected.

2. Click on New to start a new macro.

3. Click on the Comment box in the first row of the new macro and type **Called by an AddMenu action in the Suppliers Custom Menu macro.**

4. Click on the macro names button (on the left in the toolbar) to open the Macro Name column.

5. Click on the Macro Name box in the second line and type **Close**.

Table 9-9

Arguments for DoMenuItem Action

Argument	Value
Menu Bar	Form
Menu Name	File
Command	Close
Subcommand	(none)

6. Click on the right end of the Action box in line two and select DoMenuItem from the drop-down list. Fill in the action arguments in the lower portion of the Macro window as shown in Table 9-9. All three of the values shown come from drop-down lists.

7. Click on the Comment box in line two and type **Close the Form**.

8. Double-click on the Control-menu box. In the dialog box that appears, click on Yes to save the changes, type **Custom Exit Menu** for the name, and click on OK.

The macro for the custom GoTo menu contains two names, each of which is a menu option; it is a *macro group*. All the options in one menu must appear in one macro. The name of each option will appear in the drop-down list for the menu. The macro that defines the custom GoTo menu looks like the following illustration:

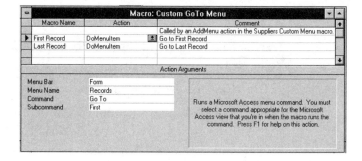

Create this macro with these steps:

1. Click on the Macro button in the Database window if it is not already selected.

2. Click on New to start a new macro.

Table 9-10

Arguments for
DoMenuItem
Action for First
Record Macro

Argument	Value
Menu Bar	Form
Menu Name	Records
Command	Go To
Subcommand	First

3. Click on the Comment box in the first row of the new macro and type **Called by an AddMenu action in the Suppliers Custom Menu macro**.

4. Click on the macro names button to open the Macro Name column.

5. Click on the Macro Name box in line two and type **First Record**.

6. Click on the right side of the Action box in line two and select DoMenuItem from the drop-down list. Fill in the action arguments in the lower portion of the Macro window as shown in Table 9-10. All four of the values come from drop-down lists.

7. Click on the Comment box in line two and type **Go to First Record**.

8. Click on the Macro Name box in line three and type **Last Record**.

9. Click on the right end of the Action box in line three and select DoMenuItem from the drop-down list. Fill in the action arguments in the lower portion of the Macro window as shown in Table 9-11.

Table 9-11

Arguments for
DoMenuItem
Action for Last
Record Macro

Argument	Value
Menu Bar	Form
Menu Name	Records
Command	Go To
Subcommand	Last

10. Click on the Comment box in line three and type **Go to Last Record.**

11. Double-click on the Control-menu box. In the dialog box that appears, click on Yes to save the changes. Save the macro as **Custom GoTo Menu**.

Creating the Menu Bar

The next macro creates the custom menu bar with two AddMenu actions. Each action adds one menu to the menu bar and names the macro to be run when the user opens that menu. It references each of the two custom menu macros you just created. The macro that defines the menu bar looks like this:

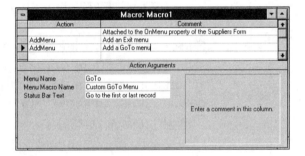

Create this macro with these steps:

1. With the Macro button selected in the Database window, click on New to start a new macro.

2. Click on the Comment box in the first row of the new macro and type **Attached to the OnMenu property of the Suppliers Form**.

3. Click on the right side of the Action box in line two and select AddMenu from the drop-down list. Fill in the action arguments in the lower portion of the Macro window as shown in Table 9-12. The value for Menu Macro Name comes from a drop-down list. The other two values must be typed.

Table 9-12

Arguments for
AddMenu
Action for the
Exit Menu

Argument	Value
Menu Name	Exit
Menu Macro Name	Custom Exit menu
Status Bar Text	Exit from the form

4. Click on the comment box in line two and type **Add an Exit Menu**.

5. Click on the right end of the Action box in line three and select AddMenu from the drop-down list. Fill in the action arguments in the lower portion of the Macro window as shown in Table 9-13. The value for Menu Macro Name comes from a drop-down list. The other two values must be typed.

6. Click on the Comment box in line two and type **Add a GoTo menu**.

7. Double-click on the Control-menu box. In the dialog box that appears, click on Yes to save the changes. Save the macro as **Suppliers Custom Menu**.

Assigning the Custom Menu Macro to a Form

Now that you have created the macros for the custom menu, you must tell Access to use this menu, instead of the regular menu, with the Suppliers form. You will do this by associating the Suppliers Custom Menu macro with the On Menu property of the Suppliers form.

Table 9-13

Arguments for
AddMenu
Action for the
GoTo Menu

Argument	Value
Menu Name	GoTo
Menu Macro Name	Custom GoTo Menu
Status Bar Text	Go to the first or last record

To associate the macro with the form, follow these steps:

1. Click on Form in the Database window and then click on Suppliers.

2. Click on the design button.

3. Click on the properties button in the toolbar. This will open the properties dialog box for the form.

4. Click on the On Menu property box. Click on the down-arrow at the right side of the box and select Suppliers Custom Menu from the drop-down list. The properties dialog box should look similar to this illustration:

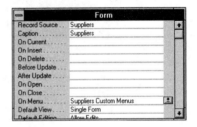

5. Double-click on the Control-menu box of the properties dialog box to close it and save the new value.

6. Double-click on the Control-menu box of the Suppliers form to close the form. Answer Yes to save the changes to the form. Now when you use the Suppliers form, you will see a menu with the choices Exit and GoTo, as shown in Figure 9-11.

7. With Form and Suppliers still selected in the Database window, click on Open to see the new menu bar.

8. Click on the GoTo menu to open it. You will see the two options: First Record and Last Record.

9. Click on Last Record. You will go to the last record in the Suppliers table.

10. Click on the Exit menu and then click on Close. The Suppliers form will close and you will return to the Database window.

Figure 9-11

Custom menus allow you to lead a novice through a database.

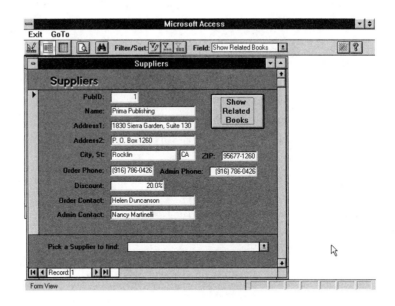

Creating Menus to Control Your Database

In addition to creating custom menu bars, you can create custom menus to control your entire database. You create one or more forms with command buttons and associate macros with the command buttons. For example, the following illustration shows a form being used as a control menu for viewing tables in the Books database:

Creating a Macro Group for a Control Menu

You will find it easier to organize the macros for a control menu if you create a macro group for each form containing command buttons. Each macro in the group is associated with one button on the form. The macros for the Table View Menu form are shown in Figure 9-12.

Use the following steps to create this macro group:

1. Click on the Macro button in the Database window and click on New.

2. Click on the Comment box in the first row of the new macro and type **Attached to the buttons on the Table View Menu form**.

3. Click on the macro names button to open the Macro Name column.

4. Click on the Macro Name box in line two and type **Books**.

5. Click on the right end of the Action box in line two and select OpenTable from the drop-down list.

Figure 9-12

The macros in the Table View Menu macro group

6. Click on the right end of the Action box in line three and select MoveSize from the drop-down list. Fill in the action arguments in the lower portion of the Macro window for both lines two and three as shown in Table 9-14.

7. Click on the Comment box in line two and type **Open the Books table.**

8. Click on the Comment box in line three and type **Adjust the position and size of the datasheet.**

9. By copying, repeat Steps 4 through 8 for the macros named Customers (line 5), Orders (line 8), and Suppliers (line 11). Select lines 2 and 3, press Ctrl-C to copy them to the Clipboard, then select lines 5, 8, and 11 in succession and press Ctrl-V at each. The only changes from one macro to the next are the macro name, the value of the Table Name argument, and the reference to the table name in the Comment box. In each case, the table name is the same as the macro name (Customers, Orders, and Suppliers). Use Figure 9-12 as a guide. The MoveSize arguments are the same for all four macros.

10. Double-click on the Control-menu box to close the macro. Click on Yes to save the macro, name it **Table View Menu Buttons,** and click on OK.

Table 9-14

Settings for Books Macro Actions

Action	Argument	Value
Open Table	Table Name	Books
	View	Datasheet
	Data Mode	Read Only
MoveSize	Right	1 in.
	Down	1 in.
	Width	4 in.
	Height	2 in.

Creating a Form to Act as a Control Menu

Now that you have the macros ready, you will prepare a form that serves as a menu. This is a simple form, containing only text and command buttons. Each command button is associated with one of the macros you created in the previous section. Create the form as follows:

1. Click on the Form button in the Database window.

2. Click on the New button. The New Form dialog box appears.

3. Click on Blank Form. A blank form appears.

4. Drag the lower edge of the Detail section down so you can add four command buttons and a title. If necessary, you can adjust the size further as your work progresses.

5. If the toolbox is not visible, open the View menu and choose Toolbox to make it visible and drag it to the right side.

6. Use the command button tool in the lower right of the toolbox to place four command buttons on the new form, as shown in Figure 9-13.

7. Click on the first command button, then click on the properties button in the toolbar. This opens the properties dialog box for the command button, as shown here:

8. Click on the Control Name box and type **Books**.

9.   Click on the Caption box and type **Books** again.

10.   Click on the right end of the On Push box and select Table View Menu Buttons from the drop-down list. Press (F2) and type **.Books** at the end of the macro name to tell Access to run the Books macro in the macro group. Table View Menu Buttons.Books is how the contents of the On Push box should look when you are done.

11.   Click on each of the other buttons and repeat Steps 8 through 10 for each. Assign the Customers, Orders, and Suppliers macros to the end of the On Push property. When you are done, double-click on the Control-menu box for the properties dialog box.

12.   Click on the label tool in the toolbox (the *A* in the upper left). Position the pointer above the buttons, click the left mouse button and type **Press a button to view a table**. If necessary, use the mouse to position the label.

13.   Double-click on the Control-menu box. In the dialog box that appears, click on Yes to save the changes. Save the form as **Table View Menu**.

Figure 9-13

Command buttons on a form can serve as a custom menu.

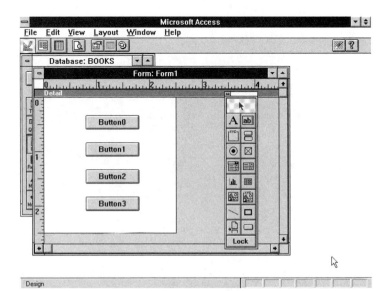

14. In the Database window, open the Table View Menu form. Click on each of the buttons to view the named table. After you have tested the form, close it and close the database.

Summary

In this chapter you saw how to create and use macros. This has included:

◆ Using a Macro window to add actions, arguments, and comments

◆ Assigning a macro to an event

◆ Using macros to link forms together

◆ Using macros to create custom menu bars

◆ Using macros to create a custom menu form

This chapter has just scratched the surface of using macros. Short of writing programs with Access Basic, macros give you the most powerful tools for controlling your database.

Index

Notes

Austin   Autum
stephen   Maria

David   meridith
hailey   ccmner
lorenzoie   miney, to

ONE KISS

Notes

Dear Mrs Com

thank you for

coming to school

every day.

I love you

And I miss you

Computer Books Available from Prima Publishing

DESQview: Everything You Need to Know

Jonathan Kamin

Kamin is the best at explaining technical information to nontechnical people. This outstanding guide to getting the most out of Quarterdeck's popular multitasking system also provides valuable information on the top-selling memory management software QEMM. Kamin shows you how to set up your system for maximum efficiency. He also provides information on running Windows applications under DESQview.

Jonathan Kamin is the author of *DOS 5: Everything You Need to Know* (Prima, 1991). He runs a computer consulting firm in Lake Oswego, Oregon.

400 pages	$22.95
7 3/8" x 9 1/4"	paperback
1-55958-238-3	Available now

Word for Windows 2: The Visual Learning Guide

David C. Gardner & Grace Joely Beatty

The Fastest, Easiest Way to Learn How to Use Word for Windows 2

The authors of the best-selling *Windows 3.1: The Visual Learning Guide* apply their unique teaching style to the top-rated word-processing program from Microsoft. The Visual Learning Guides are a unique new series of computer books created by learning experts, based on their years of experience as university researchers and training consultants for Fortune 500 companies. Beware of imitations! Hundreds of FULL-COLOR graphics combined with friendly, straightforward text and innovative layouts that stimulate whole-brain learning make it possible for you to dive right into Word for Windows 2 and make it work for you immediately. You can master your goals quickly and painlessly with this book. In simple lessons, the you'll learn quickly how to:

- Set up and style a letter
- Use special features like cut, copy, paste, and "drag and drop" moving
- Apply special visual effects such as borders and background shading

"You can't find better end-user documentation writers anywhere in the world!"
— Douglas T. Williams, Senior Vice President, Chase Manhattan Bank

272 pages	$19.95
7 3/8" x 9 1/4"	paperback
1-55958-240-5	Available now

Harvard Graphics for Windows: The Art of Presentation

Gerald E. Jones

Learn the Secrets of Effective Communication!

 *Full Color Insert!*

Harvard Graphics for Windows is one of the most powerful and widely used software tools for creating presentation graphics. Now you can learn the secrets the experts know about communicating clearly and effectively. Graphics expert Gerald Jones teaches you the fundamentals of good layout and design, including how to:

- Choose the right kind of chart or graph to convey information
- Learn how to make intangible ideas visible
- Arrange graphics and text for maximum impact.

Once you have mastered the concepts of good design, Jones takes you through a tutorial on Harvard Graphics for Windows. You'll learn everything you need to know to use the program easily and effectively. The book closes with a section on gaining the professional edge by understanding the best procedures for putting together presentations and shows, technical aspects of computer graphics and graphic arts production, and the use of color as a design tool.

A full-color insert with 16 plates showcases the variety of dramatic images you can create with Harvard Graphics for Windows.

Gerald E. Jones is a writer and producer who lives in Santa Monica, California. He supervised the development of the ARTIS business graphics service system and is a former contributing editor to Computer Graphics World magazine.

672 pages	$27.95
7 3/8" x 9 1/4"	paperback
1-55958-210-3	Available now

LotusWorks 3: Everything You Need to Know

Sandra E. Eddy

Illustrated, Step-by-Step Tutorials Teach You Everything You Need to Know to Master This Popular Suite of Software Programs

Lotus Development Corporation has shipped more than one million copies of this all-in-one software program that includes a spreadsheet, dBASE-compatible database, word processor, and telecommunications module. Focusing on the latest version of LotusWorks 3, which has even more powerful features, veteran author Sandra Eddy takes you from the basics to more advanced features in easy-to-follow, step-by-step tutorials. The clear, goal-oriented text is liberally sprinkled with screen shots, special tips, and shortcuts. Once you have mastered the essentials, you'll learn to print customized spreadsheets with graphics, automatically dial a telephone number from the program, cut and paste text and graphics among all services, and much more.

Sandra E. Eddy is the author of *Encyclopedia for Windows* (Prima, 1993). A resident of Medford Lakes, New Jersey, Eddy has seven years of experience as a technical writer on diverse subjects ranging from artificial intelligence to commercial software.

496 pages	$24.95
7 3/8" x 9 1/4"	paperback
1-55958-184-0	Available now

Windows 3.1: The Visual Learning Guide

David C. Gardner & Grace Joely Beatty

The Fastest Way to Get Started in Windows 3.1!

If you've hesitated to move to Windows or to upgrade to version 3.1, wait no longer! Gardner and Beatty are here to smooth out the learning curve with their beautiful, full-color learning guides. Hands-on examples guide you through specific tasks that lead to general principles. Master a task, and the text asks you what you want to do next. Accomplish your goals immediately. The graphical approach, with screen shots on every page, lends itself perfectly to the graphical Windows environment. The Visual Learning Guides set a new standard in computer book publishing.

"The Gardner Beatty Group's documentation expertise is unparalleled. Their combination of learning psychology, computer training experience, and popular writing skills always produces a superior product."
> — Michael Torre, First Vice President, Dean Witter Reynolds, New York

Drs. Gardner and **Beatty** are licensed psychologists who specialize in computer software training and documentation design. They live near San Diego, California.

288 pages	$19.95
7 3/8" x 9 1/4"	paperback
1-55958-182-4	Available now

Encyclopedia for Windows

Sandra E. Eddy

The Hands-on Reference You'll Use Every Day!

This one-of-a-kind resource is a Windows dictionary and complete command reference rolled into one. Whatever your needs—whether you're a beginner, the office guru, or even a software developer—*Encyclopedia for Windows* is the one tool you cannot afford to be without. Hundreds of illustrations show you every screen and dialog box. Every important Windows feature and capability is listed from *A* to *Z*. Key terms and concepts are defined briefly and lucidly. Complete how-to explanations are given for every task you need to accomplish. Can't remember how to select a printer port? . . . remove a Calendar appointment? . . . select and insert text? . . . comprehend your WIN.INI file? It's all here in this handy, profusely illustrated alphabetical reference. This work-a-day tool will help you get the job done fast and easily by telling you exactly what you need to know, when you need to know it. Fully cross-referenced, immediately accessible, and up-to-date, this invaluable resource is based on Windows 3.1.

Sandra E. Eddy lives in Medford Lakes, New Jersey, and is the author of *LotusWorks 3: Everything You Need to Know* (Prima, 1992).

928 pages	$29.95
7 3/8" x 9 1/4"	paperback
1-55958-213-8	Available in March

Excel 4 for Windows: The Visual Learning Guide

Grace Joely Beatty & David C. Gardner

The Fastest Way to Learn Excel 4 for Windows!

Learning experts Grace Joely Beatty and David C. Gardner apply their tested teaching techniques to the latest Excel 4 for Windows. The unique graphical approach of Prima's Visual Learning Guides takes you through the basics of spreadsheet design and creation in a way that makes it virtually impossible for you to get lost or confused. Compressed text and goal-oriented tasks, combined with hundreds of screen shots and graphics, allow you to move from beginning concepts to importing graphics and using dynamic data exchange (DDE) features in the shortest time possible. Full-color screen shots let you see the screens just as you see them on your monitor.

Drs. Beatty and **Gardner** have served as consultants to major corporations that have undergone system-wide computer conversions.

272 pages $19.95
7 3/8" x 9 1/4" paperback
1-55958-211-1 Available now

Excel 4 for Windows: Everything You Need to Know

Christopher Van Buren

From the Basics to Advanced Features and Functions — a Complete Tutorial!

Noted author Christopher Van Buren introduces you to Excel 4 for Windows with clear, straightforward tutorials that teach you everything you need to know to accomplish your goals. You'll learn the best uses for a spreadsheet, examine the special strengths and features of Excel, review different techniques for working with Excel under Windows, and master every important feature of the program. From the essentials of running Excel to tips on setting up your printer to working with drawing tools and graphics, this is your complete guide. You will learn how to create and manipulate 3-D charts and graphs, databases, and macros. A special section filled with examples will show you how to develop templates, financial worksheets, and statistical models; use what-if tables and the Solver; convert and parse imported text; and create time-billing worksheets. If you've never used Excel before or want to enhance your skills with the latest version, *Excel 4 for Windows: Everything You Need to Know* is the only book you will need.

Christopher Van Buren is the author of *Spreadsheet Publishing with Excel for Windows* (Ventana Press, 1991). He lives in San Mateo, California.

592 pages $24.95
73/8" x 91/4" paperback
1-55958-212-X Available now

Quattro Pro 4: Everything You Need to Know
Michael R. Hyde

A Beginner's Guide to Basic Spreadsheet Concepts and the Powers of Quattro Pro 4

Quattro Pro 4: Everything You Need to Know introduces you to the basics of designing and building a spreadsheet, then teaches you the fundamentals of creating and importing graphs, manipulating blocks of data, working with databases, and more. The book's clear descriptions and interactive tutorials get you started quickly and easily. Author Michael Hyde explains the latest features, including the SpeedBar and custom style sheets. Detailed coverage is given to the sometimes tricky tasks of setting up printers and printing spreadsheets and graphs in landscape and portrait modes.

Michael R. Hyde is uniquely qualified to know the problems faced by new and upgrade users of Quattro Pro because of his years with Borland's technical support staff. Hyde lives in San Jose, California.

240 pages	$19.95
7 3/8" x 9 1/4"	paperback
1-55958-208-1	Available now

Novell NetWare Lite: Simplified Network Solutions
Thom Duncan

A Practical Guide to Installing and Running a Peer-to-Peer Local Area Network

Novell NetWare is by far the leading local-area network (LAN) software in the world today. With NetWare Lite, Novell now turns its attention to the relatively low-cost, peer-to-peer networking market. This affordable approach to computer networking, which does not require a client server, provides a clear upgrade path to and compatibility with higher versions of NetWare. In informal, non-technical language, *Novell NetWare Lite: Simplified Network Solutions* provides hands-on tutorials for setting up, running, and troubleshooting a NetWare Lite local-area network. You will find tips for optimal installation, walk-throughs for potential problems, and advice that can't be found in the manuals. Discussions of various network alternatives for groups, departments, and small-to-medium-sized businesses are included as well.

Thom Duncan, a resident of San Mateo, California, was formerly a technical editor for Novell, Inc., and is currently reviews editor for *LAN Times* magazine. He has been writing on technical subjects since 1976.

272 pages	$24.95
7 3/8" x 9 1/4"	paperback
1-55958-186-7	Available now

NetWare 3.x: A Do-It-Yourself Guide
Charles Koontz

A Straightforward, Practical Guide to Setting Up and Maintaining a Local-Area Network with Novell NetWare 3.X

For anyone who is suddenly faced with the challenging task of setting up and running a network, *LAN Times* editor Charles Koontz provides a plain-English guide to the realities. *NetWare 3.x: A Do-It-Yourself Guide* will help you avoid time-consuming and costly mistakes. Koontz discusses each part of the network: workstations, cabling, servers, interface cards, backup systems, software, and—the most often overlooked component—people. After installing NetWare 3.x to match your file server, you will learn how to test the new installation, knowing what is likely to go wrong and how to fix it. You will also learn how to:

- Set up users, groups, and managers
- Define directories, access control, and login scripts
- Install application software, printers, and backup systems
- Add Macintosh computers to your PC network

Even if you have never had formal training as a network administrator, this book will guide you through the pitfalls to success.

Charles Koontz, a certified NetWare engineer, is managing/senior reviews editor for *LAN Times* magazine. He lives in Provo, Utah.

352 pages	$24.95
7 3/8" x 9 1/4"	paperback
1-55958-207-3	Available now

WINDOWS Magazine presents
The Power of Windows and DOS Together
Martin S. Matthews & Bruce Dobson

This Essential Reference Will Help You Customize Windows and DOS 5 for Maximum Efficiency

Microsoft's Windows 3 and DOS 5 have been enormous, instant successes—with millions of copies of each sold in a very short time. Now Windows 3.1 brings needed improvements that will make Windows a more capable file manager and an even more appealing graphical environment. *The Power of Windows and DOS Together* is the ultimate guide to working efficiently with the two systems. This major supplement to the reference manuals and training materials that come with the two programs is an information-filled guide to using Windows and DOS with greater depth and creativity. It will give you vital information that is missing in almost every other book and manual.

Martin S. Matthews has coauthored 17 books. A resident of the Seattle, Washington area, Matthews has more than 25 years of computing experience and was a beta tester for both Windows 3.1 and DOS 5. **Bruce Dobson** has a Computer Science degree from the University of Washington.

512 pages	$24.95
7 3/8" x 9 1/4"	paperback
1-55958-183-2	Available now

Smalltalk Programming for Windows
Dan Shafer with Scott Herndon & Laurence Rozier

Veteran programming author Dan Shafer introduces you to the power of pure object-oriented programming with Smalltalk/V for Windows. Step-by-step procedures show you how to build practical applications. All applications described in the book are included on the disk. This book was written with the full support and cooperation of Digitalk.

Dan Shafer has authored and coauthored more than 30 computer books for programmers, as well as designed and developed several products. He founded and runs Graphic User Interfaces, Inc., a software design and consulting firm in Redwood City, California. **Scott Herndon** has extensive experience with computer networks, operating systems, and databases and specializes in object-oriented design and Smalltalk programming. **Laurence Rozier** has coauthored and worked as a technical assistant for several books and articles on object-oriented databases and creating virtual reality.

400 pages $39.95
7 3/8" x 9 1/4"   paperback
1-55958-237-5   Available now
Includes 3½" double-density disk

QuickTime: Making Movies with Your Macintosh
Robert Hone

Unleash Your Visual Creativity by Making Movies with Your Macintosh!

Documentary filmmaker (PBS' "The Machine That Changed the World") Robert Hone introduces QuickTime users to effective presentation techniques. Hone focuses on the use of Adobe Premiere and other products in conjunction with QuickTime to edit and produce exciting QuickTime movies. This filmmaker's view of QuickTime is the most unique book yet produced on the revolutionary new software from Apple.

Robert Hone has many years of experience as a documentary film producer, director, and writer for corporate clients and PBS. He also designs multimedia products for museums.

600 pages $24.95
7 3/8" x 9 1/4"   paperback
1-55958-242-1   Available in March

Other Prima Computer Books

To order by phone with Visa or MasterCard, call (916) 786-0426, Mon.–Fri., 9–4 Pacific Standard Time.

To order by mail fill out the information below and send with your remittance to: Prima Publishing, P.O. Box 1260, Rocklin, CA 95677-1260

Quantity	Title	Unit Price	Total
_____	_____	_____	_____
_____	_____	_____	_____
_____	_____	_____	_____
_____	_____	_____	_____
_____	_____	_____	_____

Subtotal: _____

7.25% Sales Tax (CA only): _____

Shipping:* _____

Total: _____

Name _____

Street Address _____

City _____ State _____ Zip _____

Visa/MC# _____ Exp. _____

Signature _____

---

* $4.00 shipping charge for the first book and $0.50 for each additional book.